2352 05128048 2

 W9-ANM-122

628.86
RANDIER, JEAN
NAUTICAL ANTIQUES FOR THE
COLLECTOR   ($9.98)

WAYNE PUBLIC LIBRARY

MAIN LIBRARY
475 Valley Road
Wayne, N. J. 07470

Books may be returned at any
branch of the library.

SEP 28 1979

Nautical Antiques
for the Collector

Jean Randier

Doubleday & Company, Inc., Garden City, New York 1977

Overleaf: Royal Navy helmsman.
Victorian door-stop of painted
cast-iron. 12 inches high.

© Creative Publishing Marine S.A.
Roveredo, Switzerland 1976

First published in French under the title
L'Antiquaire de Marine
by Editions Maritimes et d'Outre Mer

English Translation
© Barrie & Jenkins Ltd. 1976
Translated from the French by Inge Moore

First published in the United States of America in 1977 by
Doubleday & Company, Inc.

ISBN: 0-385-12712-X

Library of Congress Catalog Card Number 76-27604
Printed and bound in Italy by Vallardi Industrie Grafiche - Lainate (MI)

Contents

Midshipman of the Royal Navy
taking a sight with a sextant.
18th century Nautical Instrument-
maker's sign. Painted wood, about
2 feet 6 inches high.

I
Scale and other models

'Small though they may be they have the god-like power of reversing time itself and of recreating within the four walls of a room those epic deeds whose reverberations rouse a ready response in the romantic hearts of those disappointed by the dullness of day-to-day routine.' Thus, almost lovingly, the Keeper of a Museum begins a fascinating essay on ship-models, machines to go back in time, to halt it and to hold it in suspense. Models assuredly are all this—as much by their power of evocation as by the precise detail of naval development which they may express—since effectively they are photographic prints from an age when photography had not been invented. We cannot help being affected by the sight of a model ship and because we still retain that strange, magical, childhood ability to endow toys with a life of their own, we cannot help stepping on board and, on the least provocation, becoming part and parcel of the model itself.

Better still, on these dream-boats we can as and when we please be cabin-boy, passenger or skipper and in the twinkling of an eye can travel from fo'c's'le to quarter-deck, from truck to bilges without a trace of vertigo or tiredness, of lethargy or sea-sickness. With some sea-going experience behind them the highly sensitive and the super-imaginative can even hear the wind singing in the lattice of shrouds, backstays, brails, halyards and sheets, the steady pounding of the engines, the creak of the timbers and the surge of the sea.

But this is to overemphasise the romantic aspect. If I were to attempt a psychoanalytic study of the ship-lover. I should certainly be going beyond the bounds of my subject and out of my depth as well. Surely this heightening of sensibility achieved by a ship-model can be attained by any object which draws its inspiration from the sea?

All I propose, then, is to give you a sort of classified list of all dimensional representations of ships, so that the collector himself can evaluate the technical, artistic or poetic aims of the man who made them, even though at times these intentions are closely interwoven, what is nautically useful being, through some special favour of Neptune, at the same time beautiful, too.

Votive models

When and where did the art of model-making begin? The oldest of which we have any knowledge are undoubtedly those recovered from ancient burials. In those days men had the foresight to surround the corpse with everything which it might need in its journey into the beyond, and they did not forget water-craft. In these ships of the dead the soul could sail into the beyond. This is an exceedingly ancient tradition and thus, in his excavations of Ur of the Chaldees in 1929, Professor Wooley discovered the silver model of a skiff two feet long and dating from 4000 BC. Coming closer in time, the Egyptians did not abandon the custom and outside the tomb-chamber of Tutankamen was found a ceremonial barque intended to convey the Pharaoh's soul across the waters of the dead. The same rule applied in the ancient burials discovered in Scandinavia and doubtless with the same thought in mind the Vikings interred their chieftains in the longships which the latter had steered across the high seas in life. Although these models are highly simplified, they often include a number of details, such as oars or thwarts, treated realistically if childishly. The general shape of these craft is sufficiently close to that of the full-sized vessels of the period as to be of considerable interest to marine archaeologists. Oddly enough, no trace of the ex-voto model exists from the ancient Egyptian period to that of the Middle Ages. This does not mean that none were made. On the one hand the votive offerings of the Ancient Egyptians were miraculously preserved from marauders within the secrets of their graves while on the other one can well appreciate the

Egyptian funerary bark. 2000 BC. About 4 feet 6 inches long.

unhappy fate which would befall such fragile objects from fire, destruction and war, and in the hands of a drunken soldiery, to whom any old wood is good for kindling, of ignorant priests who view them merely as dust-traps, or from the thieving fingers of small boys.

Towards the 16th century the ex-voto model returns, but the spirit behind it is different. No longer commissioned to carry the souls of the dead, their more mundane and prosaic task is to serve as a thank-offering. The patient and laborious toil which went into their making was not intended accurately to reproduce any specific vessel but to provide the medium for unrestrained decorative fancy. The materials employed —gold or silver, chased or stuck with precious stones—express the degree of thanks behind the offering. In the circumstances, understandably few have survived. Time too has done its worst for humbler models—the leaky roof, the smoke of candles and tapers and the faulty supporting string. They can be found, too, restored and rejuvenated over the years by repairers with more of the seaman than the antiquary in them who have brought the rigging up to date in the only style they know. By and large these models cannot be touched, cannot be repaired and cannot even be cleaned so deeply are they imbued with the spirit of the man who made them. This spirit is hard to recapture as antique-fakers know only to well. It is far better to leave well alone, keeping the model under glass in the state in which you found it.

Leaving these ancient offerings aside—they demonstrate more of artistry and of simple-minded craftsmanship than the model generally so-called—let us look once more at more recent examples of the ex-voto model, for clarity's sake from the 18th to the early 19th centuries. Such models as are obtainable from dealers today have not all been stolen from churches or chapels but have often been sold to or exchanged with collectors or dealers by priests with an eye to the main chance. Interest in the sea is comparatively recent and when a church was being spring-cleaned with a coat of white-wash on the walls, dusty old rubbish was happily bartered for a brand-new polychrome plaster statue of Our Lady or one of the saints. This happy state of affairs is now a thing of the past and although they are often quite unguarded these ex-voto church models really are as much priceless treasures as those in museums—and like them are generally catalogued.

The models themselves were made by seamen as a thank-offering to some patron saint or other for having preserved them from the perils of the deep. All, or nearly all

8

Bows of the French warship *Protée*
(1748–1771). 18th century ribbed and planked
scale-model. Length 4 feet 2 inches.

of them can be said to have been inspired by and to show the particular preoccupation of the man who made them. Thus a ship's carpenter would put all his work into the hull, but would neglect the rigging, while a rigger or topman would produce masts and rigging perfect in every detail above a poorly modelled hull and the shiphandler would overexaggerate the importance of yard or boom. Nor would the seaman make any bones about stopping at the waterline, having never seen what lay beneath it. In any case, however fervent the prayers in time of peril, there would be something of a rush to finish the boat and hope that Our Lady would like it all the same.

None the less I should not wish to ascribe absolutely and without exception the characteristics which I have just described to each and every ex-voto. Thank-offerings were made of models which were in every way excellent, in detail, rigging and design, but these models partake less of the peculiar spirit of the ex-voto, and tend far more towards the high-class, scale-model which I shall discuss later.

Earlier I mentioned the rather mongrel type of ex-voto, which seems an excuse to let the decorative artist's skill run riot and which is often rigged in the most eccentric style. I should now like to add a word or two on the caravels which come from 'south of the Border' in whole fleets. They seem typical of a Latin abandon which has been given full rein in monstrous vessels with imitation parchment sails piled by the dozen on every mast one on top of the other, with innumerable square lanterns fore and aft lit intermittently with little coloured electric lights like those on a Christmas-tree. It is difficult to know whether one should regard these nightmare galleons, popular as they apparently are, as examples of the deliberate ignorance and utter tastelessness of commercial enterprise in all its horror, or as the fleeting mark of the affection of an almost mystical love of the sea which lacks the least practical knowledge of it. The ocean is a fabulous element and the countryman tied to his native earth simply cannot imagine what it is like. Perhaps, then, I should remind you of what a wide-eyed Portuguese peasant once announced:

'I know a man, who once met a man, who had seen the sea!'

Vessels entering harbour. Half-block and diorama made by a seaman. Late 19th century. About 2 feet by 3 feet.

The banker *Côte d'Émeraude*, one of the last of the vessels built for the Newfoundland cod-fisheries. The model was constructed *c*. 1930.

11

Sailors' work

A banker at work. Wood and plaster diorama made by a seaman. Early 19th century.

The German five-master *Lothar*. Seaman's scale-model in bottle. Early 20th century. Many of these little models were given imaginary names since their makers' main concern was accurately to depict the rigging and the beauty of a ship under full sail.

Yankee clipper picking up the pilot-boat outside Le Havre. Seaman's half-block diorama of the mid-19th century, the heyday of sail on the North Atlantic routes.

I shall be coming back to the crafts of the seaman on shipboard in the days of long voyages when the watch below was spent turning out those traditional, one might almost call them ritual, objects which include the famous scrimshaw of British and Yankee sailors. However, since we are talking about models, I should like to say something of those made on board ship. They fall into two categories: three-dimensional and framed half-block models.

Sailors' models can be readily identified by their size. They are seldom more than three feet long and the reason for this is quite simple—the space available to the seaman on board ship, a rack specially contrived for the model on the ceiling above his berth. Here the model was secured against the roll and pitch of the vessel, ready to be taken out whenever fair weather allowed work on it to be resumed during the voyage. These models are often highly accurate, simply because the seaman was making an actual copy of the ship in which he served, with the forceful criticisms of his mates to make sure he got the details right. However, particularly characteristic of these models are the materials from which they are made. A softwood such as pitch-pine or deal was used for the hull which was generally solid or only slightly reduced in weight by being crudely hollowed before the deck-planks were put on. The paintwork ran the gamut of the bo'sun's store with black and white for the hull, red and green for the side-lights and varnish for the decks. The seaman would have a

French torpedo-boat.
Steam-driven toy boat made of
painted tin-plate in France,
c. 1870.

American monitor. Steam-
driven toy boat, partially
submersible, *c.* 1870.

14

Japanese iron-clad. Toy
boat made of tin-plate, hand-
painted and with a clockwork
engine with the manufacturer's
name *L. B. France*, depicting
one of the warships which took
part in the Battle of Tsushima,
c. 1905.

The iron-clad *Italia*. Toy
boat made of painted tin-plate.
It is steam-driven and the guns
can be fired, *c.* 1880.

Auxiliary-powered vessel running before the wind in high seas, under fore- and top-sails. Note the top of the main-mast, cracked and just about to fall. Mid-19th century woollen embroidery by an English seaman.

whole selection of threads for the complicated rigging, for running rigging—sheets and halyards—is lighter than standing rigging, such as stays and shrouds. A bit of lead, or a thin sliver taken from the sounding-lead itself, would be used to make anchors, cannon, parrels, caps, skid beams and other pieces of iron-work. A fine chain for the anchor had either to be obtained beforehand or else made link by link from copper wire. Brass wire on the other hand was the thing for stanchions, handrails, davits and capstan-levers. The real expert would make the blocks—and there are more than enough of those on a sailing ship—out of the bones from his dinner plate or from those of the occasional seabird that might be caught. These were the days before special adhesives and it is miraculous that models held together with wood-glue or gum-arabic have survived to today. Over and above the materials themselves it was all a matter of patience and skill, for the tools were of the most rudimentary—a strong knife given a razor-edge on the oil-stone, punches of varying diameter to make the holes and, last but not least, coarse and fine sandpaper. Very seldom do these models have sails, that is canvas sails. The sailcloth on board was far too stiff and coarse, so the sails were made from paper. Paint paper from a nautical chart and it did very well indeed. However, such scraps were like gold-dust on a wind-jammer where charts were used voyage after voyage, the skipper marking the daily run to compare past performance. Sometimes the sails were made from very thin copper sheeting, since this weighed hardly anything. Needless to say no scale-plans were available for the model and all was done by eye and rule of thumb.

When the time came to assemble the finished parts of one of the larger models, out came a cradle to support it while the seaman worked at his ease. However, with smaller boats, which could be flung to pieces by a sudden heave of the deck, sailors used a special technique. Into the point of balance on the underside of the hull they stuck a piece of wood like the cross-bar of a chair. The other end was bevelled to fit into the caulking of the deck and, to keep the model firm on its mount, rigging ran from the mount itself to five or six tacks stuck into the hull of the model. In this way the model could be carried on the mount the whole time it was in the making and only when it was finished would the mount be removed.

The test of a well-made seaman's model is the detailed work which it contains. Some would go so far as to cut out the wheel-grating to imitate the battens: others would copy the skylights of the saloon with pieces of mica. Topmen would take accuracy to the pitch of worming, parcelling and serving their rigging.

Another type of model which was very popular on board ship was the half-block, round which was often built a real diorama. Never very large—under three feet long— these half-block models were fitted into squareish boxes six inches to a foot deep. The backing was smaller than the opening, the sides sloping inwards to give an illusory perspective, and the crude case made of thin pitch-pine boards. The background always consists of a bright blue sky—and the seaman would have to make sure he kept some of the necessary paint in his ditty-box—with fat white clouds, sometimes a few seagulls and often the coastline, with cliffs, houses, a signal-station and a lighthouse as nautical adjuncts. On the base a fairly choppy sea would be modelled from putty or plaster-of-paris and painted green with touches of white for the wave-crests, a dab of white at the cut-water and white for the wake trailing along the hull and far astern. The masts were nailed to the backing, complete with caps and tops. Half-yards, with their swelling sails were braced and trimmed. There was no trouble holding the latter in place since they were carved in high-relief from wood and they all had their brails and sheets. All the stays of the standing rigging were glued to the backing as were the many flags—the ensign, the house-flag and the courtesy ensign, the colours of the country in whose waters the ship is sailing. In the bows there is an impressive bowsprit provided with boom, jib, flying-jib and fore-staysail. This clutter in the bows tended to unbalance the diorama as a whole since there is only two-thirds of the area behind them for the hull and the square lighthouses. The muzzles of cannon stuck out either from painted or real gun-ports. The deck was modelled in some detail and occasionally the stiff figure of a seaman can be seen at his duties there or in the rigging, with a man at the wheel and the officer of the watch on the quarter-deck. To heighten the realism the foreground may be used for another sailing-ship on opposite tacks, for the pilot coming aboard, for a buoy or a lighthouse which the ship is rounding. Often again, and particularly in ex-voto models or paintings of ships, a strip is left at the bottom for the name of the ship, her skipper and the occasion of the voyage. These dioramas were never as completely finished as the seaman could have wished, but they had to be cased in to protect them from damage. Somehow or other the maker would have got hold of a square pane of glass and this was cut to the correct size. Of course he had no diamond for the purpose as the ragged edges show. The whole was set off by a frame made from whatever material was available on board ship. Sometimes, and this was the height of luxury, the sailor had a real picture-frame, and then the box which held the model was made to fit it.

Strange to relate, although the other models which I have discussed disappear with the sailing-ship, these half-block dioramas continue into the early steam-ship era. I can only imagine that the ship under full sail had an aesthetic appeal all of its own and that the seaman found the steam-ship cold and off-putting. However, dioramas go on showing the half-block models of steamers trailing a thick cloud of cotton-wool because the seaman can include within the scene all those old familiar favourites, the pilot-boat under sail, the fishing-smack and the lighthouse.

Ships and dioramas in bottles

While we are on the subject, it seems the place to mention ships in bottles. The earliest are not much older than the 1830s, probably because it was not until then that opaque and dark glass began to give way to clear glass and that the shape of the bottle itself began to change to a shorter and wider neck and a body better suited to holding a ship. The manufacturer's mark and the quality of the glass itself enable ships in bottles to be dated reasonably accurately.

With their love of doing things the hard way, of doing something nobody else

had thought of and of succeeding against all the odds, it is hardly surprising that seamen-modellers should have taken it into their heads to insert through the neck of a bottle something which on the face of it ought never to have got through. We all know how they did it. First of all putty was put in for the sea and the waves were shaped with a metal spatula. Next a rough coat of paint was applied and then the details of the diorama were added—the harbour, the jetty, lighthouse, houses and trees. Now came the turn of the ship itself. It was of course a waterline model on which the rigging had been set, the masts cut down at partner level, yards secured to their masts by their lifts, braced fore-and-aft, and all lying on the deck. The shrouds had been secured to their hounds as had the stays. Hull, masts and yards were already painted. The whole tapering bundle was carefully inserted through the neck of the bottle stern-first and the hull set into the putty while the latter was still wet. Then wire hooks were used to step the masts, which would be slightly raked as was only proper. The stays were taut. A spot of glue at the foot of each mast gave them the right degree of firmness. All that was left to be done was to brace the yards square and glue the shrouds to the shroud-plates. A touch of refinement could be added by setting the sails, starting from the stern and successively setting spankers, mizzens, mains and fore-sails, with the triangular jibs to finish up with. When that was done another touch of white paint could be given to the sea to show the bow wave and the wake. Flags run up, any spot that had been left out was given a dab of paint and when the whole thing had dried and looked satisfactory, the bottle was corked and the cork

Fine-weather model-making on the deck of a windjammer. Photograph taken in the early years of the present century.

The iron-clad corvette *Armide* (1867–1880). Seaman's model in mahogony and bone.

sealed in with wax. Real sticklers would then knit a seaman's cap with a bobble on the end to cover the neck of the bottle and carve a wooden stand for it with the ship's name cut into it. Latter-day ships in bottles carry very little conviction. They are very awkward creatures with yards as thick as their masts and gigantic blocks made from milliner's beads. There is no reason at all for sailors to have allowed such a disregard for scale to creep into their work. Ships in bottles from the best period may be a bit slipshod when it comes to the hull, but on the other hand the rigging is beautifully neat and elegant and this is what collectors will appreciate.

Ships were not the only things which went into bottles and many are the museums which can display dioramas showing the most unlikely subjects. Nor is bottle bound to be horizontal and the Crucifixion might well be modelled in a bottle standing upright.

It is interesting to speculate as to the fate of these masterpieces once the seaman came ashore and also as to the reason why he put so many hours of patient toil into their making with his clumsy hands scarred and calloused by the harsh burn of the rope and nails broken by the stiff canvas of the sails. The sailor is a fatalist. When he came ashore, the model would sometimes come home with him, but unless it was something really outstanding, better than the one they kept in memory of the sailor— uncle or cousin who had made it twenty years before, the piece of work which the sailor brought with him was prized very lightly. Nor were there many collectors in those days. However, these masterpieces were more often than not given to the skippers of sailing-ships as a token of gratitude for some favour as slight as a stick of tobacco, a double issue of rum or the promise of a berth on a good ship. Or else they were left with the good lady who ran the lodging-house where the sailor stayed while he waited to ship out again, often to make up the balance of what he owed her. Then again other models were made with the avowed intention of being offered for sale, as sailors' reminiscences show—and what a paltry price they fetched from the collector or dealer in curios. Yet despite all this, the next time the sailor went to sea, he made sure he had his thread, his glue and his sandpaper ready to make another boat. But it would be a different one this time—the model of the ship in which he now served.

Having got into the habit, once the sailor retired and came ashore for good and all it was not uncommon for him to turn to modelling either as a means of eking out his scanty pension by selling his work to holiday-makers or else simply as something with which to keep himself busy. Now he had at his disposal better quality materials, a wider range of tools and all the time in the world. The fruits of their toil are sometimes very large and such boats can measure up to six feet over all. However they can easily be distinguished from the scale naval, dockyard or ship-owner's models by the sturdy way in which they are built, a sturdiness of the seaman himself. I have personally examined a fair number of them. They are their makers' memories. One of them cost its two builders three years' work before it was completed. What was a stake was no less than a fine square-rigged three-master, copper-bottomed, each sheet being cut from foil, and not a block or piece of tackle missing from bow to stern. The men who made this splendid model were an old sailing skipper and his bo'sun who lived near him in his retirement. Both were as stubborn as they were skilled and their thousand hours of joint toil was punctuated by many a barney over exactly where a pendant or a preventer shroud should go. Work in those conditions could be hardly less than perfect. Nevertheless there are times when the art of the seaman-modeller matches that of the professional and I would not grudge the Americans the splendid models made by Captains Fred Kaatsch and James P. Barker, but it must be stated that what gives a scale-model that touch of quality are proper tools, good plans and the touch which experience supplies.

Prisoners' work

In the same tradition as the sailors' models is the work done aboard the English and Spanish prison-hulks during the Revolutionary and Napoleonic Wars. Nobody will be surprised when I remark that the finest examples of these models are to be found in Madrid, in London—at the Science Museum in South Kensington—and at the National Maritime Museum in Greenwich. No French visitor will bear the slightest grudge against these museums for owning such specimens since they have been preserved as carefully as the relics of a saint—as works of art rather than spoils of war. You have only to read Louis Gareray's *Memoirs* to discover the hair-raising conditions in which the prisoners lived aboard the hulks. Ill-clad and starving, the prisoners had only their talents to barter with their guards for the bare necessities of life. The sailors surpassed themselves and in wood or bone produced models of which the finest goldsmith would be proud. How they must have prided themselves upon their skill! When the boat was finished it was sometimes surrounded by an ornamental balustrade carved with syrens or dolphins. The size of the model did not matter, since the price depended upon the skill of the craftsmanship. Some models are so small that they are mounted behind a huge magnifying-glass so that the detail may be seen. One wonders how many men were involved in each model and whether it was the joint work of a group. I think that undoubtedly it would have been and that a whole watch profiting from the pot of rancid fat, the packet of tobacco or the rot-gut liquor which they received in exchange, would busy themselves with the communal task. Be that as it may, once this odd bargain had been struck, the prison-officers on these hulks were the first to appreciate these masterpieces at their true worth, since they were handed down within their families as priceless heirlooms. Seldom do they find their way into the sale-room. One passing comment: however realistic and detailed hull and rigging may be, these models are always given imaginary names. Can it be that these craftsmen preserved naval secrecy to the bitter end?

In addition to the European collections which I have mentioned, there are two in the United States which contain several bone and ivory models—the Seaman's Bank for Savings and the Rogers Collection (now in the United States Naval Academy Museum). In the latter is the model of a French naval dockyard with a 130-gun ship on the stocks. As usual the keel and ribs are of wood but the planking is bone. 'On the ground, around the ways, are all the guns, boats, masts, anchors, yards and tops ready to rig the boat after launching', we are told in the description. The whole measures 14 by 9 inches.

Building ship models in bone and ivory was a traditional art of Dieppe and Fécamp and it seems very likely that French sailors in prison in Dartmoor, Porchester Castle and Norman's Cross taught it to their English captors during the Napoleonic Wars between 1793 and 1815. The latter proved ready pupils and the art was taken over to the United States by English prisoners in the War of 1812. Those kept on a hulk in the North River at Salem repaired the bone model of the frigate *Constitution* now kept in the Peabody Museum along with the bill for 12 dollars which they presented for putting her to rights.

However, there were also a number of American prisoners on the British hulks, and without making any claim that the art of scrimshaw was imported from Europe, one cannot help but think that the Yankee prisoners took home a number of traditional tricks of the trade and various ideas.

Naval and civil dockyard models

For centuries the basis of all ship-building was tradition. Since there was little development in the various individual types of ship, the shipwrights had all the time in the world to pass the mysteries of their craft to their descendants. Thus there grew up a tradition as to exactly how each sort of ship should be built and, as a result, once the main dimensions—length, beam, draught and depth—had been determined, matters moved of their own accord, since everybody knew exactly what was required to finish the job. Precisely the same thing goes on all over the world today in a lot of little, back-garden boat-yards where they still use timber. What was good enough for fishing-smacks and coasters was good enough for big ships which required a regular building-programme, timbers shaped by the adze and some prior agreement between shipwright and shipowner. This is doubtless the reason for the lack of all documents and plans until the seventeenth century. Precisely what the ships were like before then has to be left to guesswork and deduction. The discovery of the *Wasa* was of incalculable value to maritime archaeology as would be the find of a longship, a mediaeval cog or a Roman galley. However, from about the middle of the century there was a move, stimulated in France by Colbert, to rationalise what had hitherto been instinctive and so to improve ship-design. The first treatises on naval construction were published and with them came mathematical studies of the behaviour of hulls in still and rough water and the effects of pitching and rolling. Argument ranged too over the theories of wind-propulsion and for the first time the notions of the centres of buoyancy, of lateral resistance and of effort and of the metacentre were formulated. And with all this came plans and working-drawings. Furthermore, since

Seaman's model of an early 19th century second-rater. The clumsy repairs made when the model was restored are very obvious, in particular the whaler on the port quarter which has been hoisted back-to-front on its davits and the peculiar way in which the bower anchor has been catted.

the lessons of the past are always invaluable, the plans of bygone ships, such as those of the various East India Companies, were drawn afresh when such ships had proved their worth. In France Colbert commissioned albums in which every ship in the French service was shown in side-view with notes about its dimensions and performance. Spurred by the burgeoning sciences of mathematics and hydrodynamics, naval architects worked at their drawing-boards on plans of great ships of the future, but the dockyards were still run by shipwrights for whom plans were so many lines on a piece of paper. Splendid craftsmen though they were and faultless in their work, they found it hard to conceptualise. Like Saint Thomas they needed to touch and see. Nor were they the only ones. A king or his minister might be able to follow the broad lines of a town plan or of the plans of military fortifications, yet would be completely lost when faced by a plan, cross-sectional drawing or elevation of a ship. For shipwrights and princes alike were fashioned those lovely toys which they could actually handle and from which they could visualise the plans which were being put to them. This is the origin of dockyard models.

Most of these elaborate mock-ups are in maritime museums today, given by the dockyards themselves. With scrupulous fidelity they reproduce the exact volume and scale of the original plans of the vessels concerned. In the first place the hull is constructed in exactly the same fashion as a real hull, with all the individual timbers— stem, forefoot, keel, floors, gripe, stern-post, inner-post, transom, knighthead, square frames and cant frames, beams, girders, shelves and stringers. The fastening is shown, so that the workman could see where it was placed. Sometimes only one side of the hull is planked the other being left bare so that the internal structure can be seen, or else it is covered by planking like a skin which can be removed to show the stowage facilities and the internal arrangements of the vessel. If it is merely a constructor's model, then it stops at this point. If on the other hand it is a model designed to show the stowage facilities, then everything will be in place below decks—casks in the holds, cables in the lockers, spare anchors, ballast, powder in the magazines, cannon on the gun-decks and all the fittings in place. Yet again it may be a model designed to show the lines of the hull and the rigging. In this case although the model will comprise a properly planked frame, the attention given to the timbers will be less scrupulous, while spars and rigging will be shown in complete detail.

It may be said with some truth that the perfection of these ship models is due to their subservience to scale. Perfection is achieved because every detail is in pro-

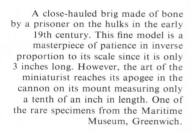

A close-hauled brig made of bone by a prisoner on the hulks in the early 19th century. This fine model is a masterpiece of patience in inverse proportion to its scale since it is only 3 inches long. However, the art of the miniaturist reaches its apogee in the cannon on its mount measuring only a tenth of an inch in length. One of the rare specimens from the Maritime Museum, Greenwich.

portion, perfection which includes absolute accuracy of colour and identity of materials used. Even the sails are miniature versions of real sails, made up 'of the same number of bolts as the full-sized sail, with the same number of cringles in the bolt-ropes, the same number of reef bands and even an identical pattern of splicing round the eyelets at the peak of the sail.

Apart from helping the shipwrights and riggers understand the instructions of the naval architects, these models were also used for instructional purposes in naval academies. Since all the rigging worked in exactly the same way as it would in a real ship it was easy to explain to embryo officers, tacking, heading into the wind, luffing and reducing sail. Later they would join their ships with the sound theoretical knowledge which they would often be unlikely to pick up on board.

However, briefly to return to Admiralty models. These could be used in discussions of the Naval Estimates as we can see in the painting by J. Seymour Lucas now in the Victoria and Albert Museum, London, which depicts the Navy Board gathered round a model while the naval architect from the Royal Dockyard explains its technical points. Having conducted a post-mortem on the victim, various modifications would be made, so that when the original model survives it cannot be accepted as absolute evidence of the design of the ship that was eventually launched. The fact that these models are generally unrigged can be explained on the grounds that there was little development to this side of the ship and it could be assumed by those for whom the model was intended.

I have already mentioned that the vast majority of these models are now housed in museums to which the dockyards have presented them. Nonetheless their fate has sometimes been a little more exciting, as was the case of a number of models in the collection of Colonel Henry Huddleston Rogers which are now in the Annapolis Naval Museum.

Such models were built at the time when Samuel Pepys was Clerk of the Acts of the Navy Board (1660–89). This was a civil service appointment somewhat different from the present day Paymaster General with the result that, 'Pepys considered the

The two gun-decks of the third-rater *Protée*. 18th century 1/50th scale model. Only the finest models have bronze cannon. Often smaller models are fitted with a system of pulleys which allow the whole battery to be 'run back' for loading, the firing-position being the opposite, 'run up'.

models to be the perquisites of his office and took home those he wanted after their Lordships' commissioners had finished their inspections of the scale models proposed for the next year's building programme.'

Pepys bequeathed part of his collection to his clerk and confidant, William Hewer, and, as his will states, 'this bequest was made for the publick good'. Pepys' successor Charles Sergison, Clerk from 1689 to 1719 had a room in his country house in Surrey specially fitted out to receive the models which he had acquired in the same way as his predecessor. This will explain why private individuals today may possess dockyard models by luck of inheritance and also because in less enlightened times our masters put a far looser interpretation upon precisely what was meant by 'the publick good'.

However, not all dockyard models were designed for the technical discussions of Boards of Admiralty. Sometimes their aim was simply propagandist through the influence they exerted as purely decorative objects. They became the toys of the Royal study. At court there was little knowledge of the sea—Forbin or Jean Bart, tanned, sea-booted and with pipe in mouth, would have caused a sensation at Versailles—so that the only way of broadcasting a knowledge of ships was for those Lords of the Admiralty who knew how to push the interests of their service to try to make the grandees of the realm fall in love with these pretty toys. Let them but touch and play with them and that helps to pass the naval estimates.

To carry still greater conviction and to stimulate still more enthusiasm, the vessels needed to be shown under sail, bravely answering the helm. It would take more than the sight of real ships manoeuvering to move the Court down to the coast. The sea was far away and what was more it was cold and windy and provincial lodgings were uncomfortable. There were no such things as seminars in those days. Thus they adopted the formula of putting miniature warships through their paces on artificial lakes under the admiring gaze of princes and great ladies. One of these was a massive thirty-five foot model of a sixty-gun warship which took the waters of the Grand Canal at Versailles in 1680. Built at Rochefort she had a band of hardy mariners concealed below decks to pull the strings (in more senses than one) and tack her from side to side of the artificial stretch of water. In 1685 a galley built to the scale of 1/18 was commissioned in what had now become a little fleet of ships of all types and nationalities. A ship's company had been specially recruited to sail and maintain them and was permanently quartered in a set of buildings known as 'Little Venice'. These seamen numbered not only riggers among their company, but caulkers

Dockyard model of a late-18th century British ship, showing the fixed blocks for the standing rigging and details of the stern-cabin. Most of these Admiralty models are to 1/48th scale.

Dockyard model of the steam engine
which drove the side-wheel sloop *Le Sphinx*
(1859–1873). This fully-working model can
be driven by steam or compressed-air.

and shipwrights as well, since they built and repaired ships and put them together
when they were sent in prefabricated parts.

With the Revolution, the establishment at 'Little Venice' was transferred once
more to the French navy. An inventory taken at the time shows that all that remained
of the little fleet were one of Louis XIV's Venetian gondolas, a brand-new forty-foot
longboat, thirteen smaller ones, a recently repaired row-boat and enough wood for
sixty vessels. It would be fascinating to know what happened to that fleet of tall
ships and also the fate of those from the Château de Vaux and the Château de
Chantilly.

Whatever else it had done this pro-Navy propaganda gave the French upper
echelons a taste for models, with the result that not all those produced by the dockyards went to instruct shipwrights, officer-cadets or princes. An official returning
from a tour of inspection at Rochefort could write: 'Everyone wants a model of his
own and the best hands in the yard spend all their time turning them out.' Grandees'
mantelpieces were decorated by the most magnificent of models, gauges of promised
advancement for some dockyard labourer or foreman.

Sometimes, too, dockyard models are the joint work of teams of state-paid
craftsmen. Real masterpieces in the technical sense of the term, they are works
designed to demonstrate the skill of the journeymen and their fitness for promotion
to master-craftsmen within the hierarchy of the dockyard.

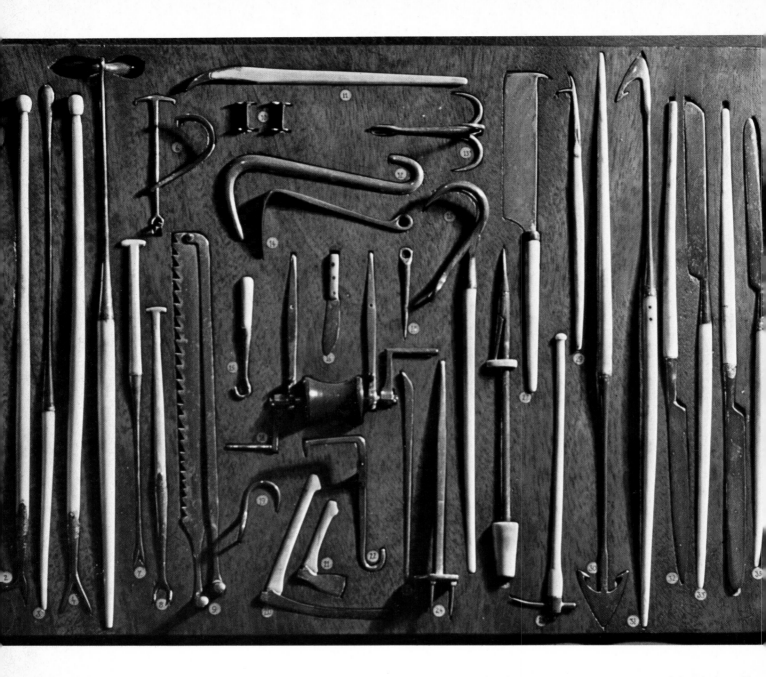

Tools of the whaler's trade—
harpoons, lances, blubber-knives,
etc.—in miniature. Steel, ivory
and bone.

As in the case of ex-voto offering from churches, it cannot be claimed that all the dockyard type of models left the dockyards legitimately. It is not simply, as I have shown, that the grandees regarded thyse models as the lawful perquisites of their office, but it was common practice too for retired shipwrights to build such models. either for pleasure or for profit.

Before leaving the dockyards, I should like to mention models other than those of ships which were also made in them. All sorts of inventions provided the subject for modelling, such as capstans, windlasses, helms, anchors, mooring-systems, not to mention the various installations on the ship. Then there were all the things used in refitting: machines to step the masts, camels and floating docks, the apparatus used in dry-docks, the equipment for raising wrecks. When iron came in to composite construction, structural and assembly mock-ups made their appearance.

I consider two types of dockyard model as interesting as those of ships, the one relating to marine artillery the other to marine engines.

It is relatively easy to identify different types of vessel of different period and of different nationalities from models in museums and from the illustrations in a wealth of printed material on the subject with which the collector is amply provided. I therefore feel that it is pointless to enlarge on this topic. On the other hand the development of marine artillery and marine engines is far less known and although both topics are of absorbing interest, museum collections are sparse and very little on them has been published. In the circumstances it seems essential to give their history in outline so that the collector can form a just appreciation of the extant models in both fields and not lose the opportunity when it offers of acquiring a notable specimen.

The prow of a British first-rater. Highly finished presentation model. Wood, bone, brass and ivory.

Marine artillery: model and full-size

As I shall demonstrate when, in Part V, I come to deal with naval hand-guns, it is difficult to give a description of marine artillery on a world basis. Individual navies progressed at their own rate, each country developing its own weaponry, so that now one is ahead and now another, so that there will seldom be uniformity of armament at any given date. Reservations should therefore be made about any general theory and checked with specialist literature devoted to particular countries.

Naval armament only began to be standardised in the second half of the 17th century—the first French regulations on marine artillery date from 1674. In the 16th century the iron gun cast in England was dominant, but in other countries cannon were cast in bronze with goose-necks or dolphins at the centre of gravity of the piece (normally above the trunnions) for ease of handling. Furthermore these bronze guns were not specifically designed for shipboard but were field-pieces on naval carriages. Bronze was, however, costly and in the middle of the 17th century the Swedes and

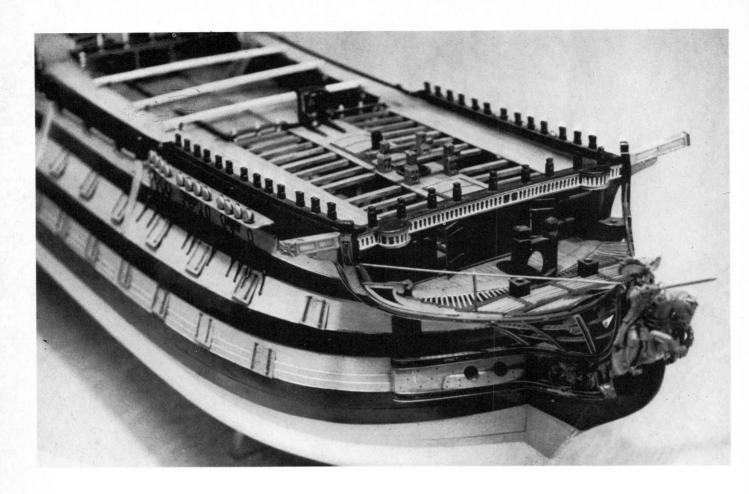

Dockyard model of HMS *Egmont* showing the timbers and intended to be used for the instruction of shipyard workers and foremen. Although the timbers themselves would have been cut and built in the yard by carpenters the decoration and sculpture would have been undertaken by trained wood-carvers working directly from the designs of the artists commissioned to embellish the full-sized ship.

Dutch began to cast iron cannon, so that by the end of the century the proportion of iron to bronze pieces had risen substantially again. The sketch p. 30 shows the names of the different parts of the piece and its carriage. Ornamentation disappeared. The reinforces were designed in accordance with the then knowledge of the strengths of materials. The various astragals were purely functional and it is noticeable that the dolphins have vanished, being far too flimsy on cannon cast from pig-iron. Barrels were cast solid and then drilled out. Originally this process was done vertically, latterly on the horizontal, the barrel alone revolving turned by a toothed mandrel. The most celebrated 18th century iron-founder was the Englishman, Wilkinson. The most immediately noticeable characteristic of marine artillery was the stubby barrel and the large calibre of the piece. A vessel was in any case equipped with a complete range of weapons for the four types of artillery fire it would be called upon to engage in action. Guns of light and medium calibre would be used in the capture of an enemy ship, where this rather than destruction was the end. Light weapons loaded with grape would be used to clear the decks while medium guns charged with bar- and chain-shot would be used against the means of propulsion, 'firing high' to bring down masts, rigging and sails. If on the other hand the object was to destroy the enemy, fire would be directed into her bilges with roundshot of the heaviest calibre or at her freeboard—quarter-deck, poop- and gun-deck—with red-hot shot. Some historians, however, dispute this latter tactic on technical grounds. Sailors spoke of 'firing high' to bring down the masts, of 'firing on the downward roll' to 'hull' their opponents and of 'raking' them. The calibres of the weapons employed were generally 6, 12, 18, 24, 36, based upon the weight in pounds of the cast-iron roundshot they fired.

As well as cannon on wheeled carriages, by the beginning of the 19th century, howitzers and carronades were beginning to come into service as well. These guns were not mounted on trunnions. The barrel had a shoe or sledge mounting, the chase on a bracket and the whole secured to the ship's side by a king-pin which allowed a slight degree of traverse. The recoil of the piece was absorbed by the shoe and light weapons of this type were most usefully employed in small boats until their withdrawal from service around 1850.

Another artillery piece in use from the end of the 18th to the beginning of the 19th centuries was the mortar, with a very short barrel and a very heavy calibre, used for throwing bombs. Two types of mortar were cast either in bronze or iron, one with trunnions so that the angle of elevation could be adjusted to the range of the high-trajectory fire, the other the platform mortar with the barrel set at a fixed angle for which the range was varied according to the amount of the charge.

Another artillery piece which can either be mounted on a wheeled carriage or as a carronade, was the bomb- or shell-gun which came into service around 1820 and was known in France by the name of its inventor as 'Paixhans gun'. For the French version of the shell-gun, the two rear wheels of the standard carriage were removed and a pair of brake-blocks like double butts substituted to absorb by friction the very powerful recoil. The projectile employed was a hollow shot or shell charged with gun-powder and provided with a fuse which lit automatically from the discharge. In weapons of this type, the chamber at the base of the bore is generally narrower than the bore so that the shell is stopped before it reaches the end. This type of cannon went out of service by 1850.

As far as the carriages are concerned, they were made of elm and themselves weighed a considerable amount. Thus, the mounting for the heaviest guns, thirty-six pounders, weighed over half a ton (1,408 lbs) and the piece itself over three tons (7,150 lbs), while the carriage of an 18-pounder weighed just over 800 lbs and the piece over two tons (4,532 lbs). The principal gear used to secure and handle both gun and carriage were the breeching—a thick rope employed to absorb the recoil being secured to the walls of the ship and passed through the breeching-rings on the sides of the carriage and at the base of the piece—and the train tackles, used to run the gun out of the ports before firing, to haul the piece back for sponging out and reloading and to prevent her rolling back during the process.

Obviously very few people are likely to collect 36- or 24-pounders when gun and carriage weigh respectively around four and three tons, but the regulation accessories which went with the pieces can be found and it is worth mentioning a number of them. They include the powder-horn for pouring the priming into the vent, and it

The toy boat belonging to the the Prince Imperial tacks across the lake at Chantilly under the skilled control of two sturdy seamen of the French Navy. Portion of a stereoscopic photograph, c. 1865.

12-pounder carronade with trail. Admiralty scale-model.

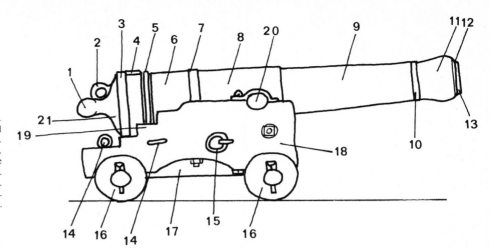

The parts of the naval cannon: 1. Button. 2. Breeching-ring. 3. Base-ring. 4. Vent and vent-field. 5. Astragal. 6. First reinforce. 7. First reinforce-ring. 8. Second reinforce. 9. Chase. 10. Muzzle astragal. 11. Muzzle swell. 12. Muzzle. 13. Muzzle-moulding. 14. Eye-bolt. 15. Breeching-ring. 16. Wheels. 17. Bed. 18, 19. Cheeks. 20. Trunnion. 21. Cascabel.

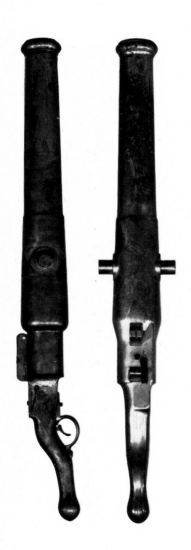

Standard bronze swivel-gun. Side and above views. Lacks lock. Early 19th century.

may or may not have an automatic measure made of brass; the vent-bit and vent-auger for cleaning the vent and piercing the cartridge-bag; the reamer for forcing the priming into the vent; the lead vent-cover to prevent premature discharge during laying. Then there is the board with the number of the gun and the names of the crew; the bed, a pyramidal block of wood wedged under the quoin and used in gun-laying; the quoin itself for laying the gun; the wooden handspike and the iron turnspike for manhauling the wheels of the carriage and raising the breech; the powder barrels (two to the gun) to hold the charges or cartridges, the latter being first made of parchment and subsequently of cloth. The powder-barrels themselves were made successively of wood, canvas, brass, tinplate and leather. Other accessories included the lintstock, a wooden pole to carry the slow-match; the sponge, either sheep- or boarskin; the rammer, a cylindrical block of wood on a handle; the gun-ladle, used for removing charges which had failed to ignite; the worm, a sort of corkscrew on a long handle, for clearing the wads after a misfire; the match-tub used for lighting the lintstock, and the battle-lanterns which lit the gun-deck when the ship was in action.

In the powder-magazine were the powder-chests made of red copper and sealed with screw-tops to keep the cartridge-bags dry. Around 1830–40 an important accessory became standard issue and this was the hammer-lock for igniting the charge by means of a percussion-cap fitted to the vent. By about 1840 the lock became a permanent fixture on the piece and was covered by a copper or tinplate hood. Firing mechanisms were nothing new, for well before 1800 flintlocks had been used to ignite the charge on the principle of the musket or pistol, although in the case of the cannon, the trigger was replaced by a lanyard which the gunlayer pulled.

As far as shot are concerned, apart from the solid shot of regulation calibre, there was a wide range of deadly projectiles; bar-shot (somewhat like a pair of dumbbells), chain-shot (called angels) and sawn-shot which was a cannon-ball quartered, each quarter being fastened by a rod to a ring in the middle so that the whole thing would expand after it had been discharged.

When these three types of shot came whistling through the air, you had to watch out for your masts and rigging!

Finally there were the anti-personnel weapons, grape-shot and case-shot, a bag of lead musket-ball on a circular wooden plate to fit the bore of the piece.

Besides the pieces mounted on carriages, the vessel would be equipped with light mobile weapons, swivel-guns, derived from the culverin. Their trunnions fitted into pivots, called pedestals which were mounted on the bulwarks. Although the swivel-gun was a light weapon, it should not be confused with the blunderbuss, a hand-gun which I shall describe in its place.

However, besides the standardised armament of warships there was the incongruous medley of weapons to be found on merchantmen. Until about 1830, traders had still to fear the attacks of the Barbary corsairs in the Mediterranean and of the Malay pirates in the Straits of Malacca. Ships sailing in these waters did not merely

30

arm their crews, but carried light-calibre guns of every description, bronze or iron, mounted on carriages or pedestals, to frighten off attackers. And here is seems worth noting that the ports painted on the sides of merchant vessels in the days of sail were due to this very fear of pirates. From a distance a vessel with gun-ports could only be a warship. At least as far as pirates were concerned, and they would make themselves scarce.

And while we are talking about *ruses de guerre* as well as about models, I might mention the famous Dieppe lugger, the *Somnambule,* which was sunk in action on 18 October 1810. Her port beam was painted completely black, but down her starboard side was a yellow line of gun-ports. In dirty weather, if she went about, her opponent tended to think it was a fresh vessel coming to her help and would break off the action.

While we are on the subject of merchant naval armament I should mention alarm-guns shipped on merchantmen and on fishing-brigs and schooners as well, to fire as signals in fog.

Returning to marine artillery where we left it in mid-nineteenth century when the first experiments with breech-loading were being made and when barbette-turrets and casemates were replacing the old broadside batteries.

From then on the wealth of new inventions is amazing: methods of sealing the breach, fixed mountings, recoil-brakes, ammunition hoists, gun-laying systems, revolving turrets with mechanical or hydraulic controls, armour-plated cupolas, all, naturally the subject of scale dockyard models made for demonstration as well as instructional purposes. Side by side with these official models can be found masterpieces of skill built by boilermakers and engineers as well as the models civilian inventors found so useful to persuade the authorities to take up their brain-children.

Up to 1850 it is still possible to collect not merely models but real light-calibre muzzle-loading guns, but thereafter and apart from models or actual ammunition, no single piece of marine artillery is fit to be given house-room. This becomes a matter for the Government. National museums have the space and, in France, right of pre-emption from the Navy.

The age of highly mechanised artillery leads naturally to a discussion of a range of models peculiarly attractive to the collector—marine engines and their adjuncts.

Marine engines

The history of marine propulsion is generally unappreciated and I shall therefore outline its main points so that the collector can not only better enjoy extant models but identify such as he has the good fortune to discover.

Early 19th century model of 24-pounder carronade run out and with all its equipment complete—tub, rammer, cartridge-bag, sponge and quoin. Note the hammer-lock firing-mechanism by the vent.

On the same principle that the 5-barrelled pistol had used from wheel-locks in the 16th century, the duck's foot, its five barrels fanning out and loaded with grape-shot was used experimentally by the French Navy from 1792 to 1814. Undoubtedly similar diabolical weapons were carried on slavers to put down any rising by the negroes which they carried.

19th century powder or cartridge box. Standard model with air-tight screw lid and triangular key, made of brass and copper, both non-sparking materials.

The first successful experiments with a steam-driven boat worthy of the name were made by J. C. Perier on the Seine in 1775. The crude steam-engine with the piston-rod connected directly to the paddle-shaft, worked at the lowest of pressures.

In 1783 the Marquis Jouffroy d'Abbans' *Pyroscaphe* successfully sailed upstream on the Saône. A complicated system of cogs and gears transformed the reciprocating movement of the pistons into a circular movement to drive the paddles.

Contemporaneously—in 1787—the American, James Rumsey experimented with the principle of what would nowadays be termed jet propulsion and his success on the Potomac encouraged him to demonstrate his vessel in 1793 on the Thames.

In 1801 the Scotsman, Patrick Miller's *Charlotte Dundas* went into service on the Clyde Canal. She was a stern-wheeler like the old Mississipi steam-boats.

Back in the United States, Robert Fulton enjoyed better luck there than in France with his *Clermont*, a side-wheeler, which reached 4.7 knots in trials on the Hudson River between New York and Albany. His vessel was a 100-tonner and so far from being an experimental model was successfully employed in regular service as a river-boat for a number of years.

But official recognition awaited use of the engine at sea in an East-West Atlantic crossing against prevailing winds and currents made by the British *Rising Star* in 1821, the West-East crossing having been made by the American *Savannah* in 1819.

All engines and boilers of this period bore the stamp of the genius of that great Scottish engineer, James Watt. He had set land propulsion under way, marine propulsion was yet to come. The inertia of the weight of the vessel and the resistance of the hull to the water had first to be overcome. From 1820 beam engines were the standard equipment of most steamships, but the rise and fall of this heavy beam well above the waterline threatened the stability of the vessel and it became better to use the oscillating cylinder engine with its lower centre of gravity and so disposed that the piston connected directly with the paddle-wheel crankshaft. An ingenious system of side-valves let in the steam. Engines like this were fitted in the first all-iron paddle-steamer the *Aaron Manby* (1822) and the huge *Great Eastern* (1856), both of which flew the Red Ensign. Meanwhile the propeller had been invented in 1837 after innumerable abortive projects and experiments.

Its use demanded higher speed than did paddle-wheels and with nothing better than the oscillating cylinder engine to hand, of which the working speed could not be increased, ingenious systems of multiple gears were invented and these were put into the *Great Britain*.

It was essential for warships to have their engine-rooms well below waterline as a protection against small arms fire. A variety of athwartships arrangements were carried out with double reciprocating and oscillating pistons working at right angles the one to the other. Such equipment was installed in the American frigate *Princeton* as well as in the celebrated *Monitor* (1862). Other systems of right angle drive transmission were effected with worms and gears which only raised acute problems of wear and tear and faulty obturation for the horizontal cylinders. As the design of boilers improved and they provided a head of steam which could be recovered after the piston had travelled down the first cylinder the idea of double, triple and quadruple expansion engines was born. One such engine was successfully fitted to H.M.S. *Duncan* in 1871.

Each step in this fascinating development can be traced by means of scale models correct to the last bolt and rivet. Feed them with steam and they will work perfectly. Made by skilled engineers, these models were generally submitted with the working drawings and were intended not merely for experiment but to influence the dockyard in their choice of prototype.

After tests made with such a model, in 1894 Sir Charles Parsons built his *Turbinia*, the first experimental vessel with a steam turbine. One can easily imagine the surprise her speed of 34.5 knots caused the Admiralty at the Spithead Review in 1897.

The earliest direct-drive turbines suffered from the defect that power could not be increased without at the same time increasing the diameter of the turbine, as also from the tendency to break down because of excessive centrifugal force. Turbines of reasonable diameter, but of very high speed, were therefore produced which drove the propeller-shaft via a reducing-gear.

As far as the internal combustion engine is concerned, the first of them saw the light of day in Hull in 1888 and it was driven by petrol. Outboard engines which people think only came in after World War II, go back in fact to 1910. Broadly similar to present-day models, they were an American invention of the Swedish engineering genius, Evinrude. A collection of the various types produced over the years is housed in a warehouse belonging to Outboard Marine at Ghent. The invention of the German, Diesel (1893), was soon taken up by the shipbuilders. The first marine diesel-engine was produced in Paris in 1902 by the Société Sauter-Harlé, better known for the mines which they supplied to the French Navy. The first ocean-going vessel with a diesel-engine was the Dutch tanker *Vulcanus* (1910).

To round off this resumé of marine engines, we should observe the extraordinary progress made in boiler-design, from James Watt's first model in 1780, a plain copper cauldron the shape of a cocktail-shaker, closely related to Denis Papin's boiler and only just sufficient to raise the steam to drive a locomotive. Very soon the notion was adopted for marine engines of increasing the steam-pressure by running the smoke-tubes vertically inside the boiler itself (John Fitch's, James Rumsey's and Robert Fulton's systems). These smoke tubes were, however, very second best since they caused heat-resistant deposits to form on the inside of the boiler. To raise steam-pressure still higher, the boiler with vertical water-tubes was invented in 1842, and this was followed in 1878 by the horizontal-tube boiler. The only really satisfactory boiler built on these principles was the French Belleville inclined-tube boiler of 1872 which was used in the Royal Navy as well up to 1901. Other systems, such as the Thornycroft and Yarrow, were to follow, while the Niclause boiler (1862) was built on entirely different principles as was the Babcock and Wilcox boiler of 1889 which was later installed in the ships of the U.S. Navy.

Engine and boiler are the primary elements, but there are a host of secondary ones as well and these essential mechanisms were all modelled to scale. As well, then, as models of boilers you have models of combustion-chambers, condensers, safety-valves, and even telescopic funnels designed to regulate the 'draw' of the furnace and ultimately the steam-pressure itself.

Amongst all this mechanical equipment are to be found the countless experiments undertaken on the paddle-wheel and propeller. As concerns the former there is the invention of the cycloidal movement and of variable and retractible paddles. As concerns the latter there is the development of Archimedes' screw (which was practically ineffective) into the multi-bladed variable-pitch propeller.

I shall close my survey of the mechanical appliances on board ship by a mention of the countless systems employed for capstans and steam-winches once so very necessary to haul in the chains with their massive links and anchors weighing several tons which had to be heaved off the bottom. Nor should I forget the large number of remote control systems produced, from voice-pipes to servo-motors, absolutely essential to move the rudders, the latter requiring under hand-operation in the old days no less than eighty burly deckhands—this is no exaggeration—heaving on the handspikes.

Ship-builders' scale models:
scale-models from shipping lines

I now leave the naval dockyards which produced so many scale-models of ships, marine engines and artillery to return to the medium-sized civilian yard which built for individual shipowners or for shipping-companies. You cut your coat to suit your cloth and that did not allow for any frills. Whether it was a steamer or a sailing-vessel, the hull alone concerned the buyer and the builder. Rigging could be left to a sketch on a piece of paper, for in the long run masts were masts and yards were yards.

Concern for the hull was concern for the waterlines, although these were judged by the naked eye. Since both beams were exactly the same they would save money by simply making a model showing one side only. These half-block models of ocean-going ships would be glued and screwed to a panel of wood some four feet six inches or six feet long. Sometimes the hull, waterline and upperworks were painted, at others simply varnished. More often than not this half-hull was carved from a block of wood composed of individual planks glued together, each plank of the exact thickness to represent a yard or a metre in the model. When these half-blocks were simply varnished the layers of wood might alternate mahogany and deal, dark and light, so that from stem to stern waterlines and buttock-lines could be clearly seen. The decks of these sailing craft were just as utilitarian. A summary of the lay-out ran

Model of a cylindrical boiler of the early days of steam propulsion. Early 19th century.

from fore to aft—windlass, main deck-house, galley, small deck-house amidships, chart-house on the poop, hatchways and ventilators. Masts were no more than stumps cut off a few feet above the partners. All was spare and neat and built for taking measurements with a pair of dividers. The only luxury allowed was the engraved brass plate bearing the name of the ship, her dimensions, the name of the yard, the date she went on the stocks and the date on which she was launched. One of the high-spots of the Hamburg-Altona Museum is the impressive collection of half-block models bequeathed by Ernst Dreyer of vessels built in his yards between 1840 and 1859.

These half-block models generally remained in the possession of the yard. They had been produced to show the lines of a particular vessel, but subsequently helped potential customers to choose the type of ship which they required. Other, more modest verions are to be found too, which were more clumsily put together in the little yards along the coast which specialised in building wooden fishing-boats. Here, more than anywhere else, the fishermen, their customers, preferred to see what the boat would look like with their own eyes rather than read a plan and the shipwright could add a bit here or take off a bit there while following the general line of the half-block.

Splendid illustrations of the hydrodynamics of hull-shape, these half-blocks provide mural decorations in many yacht-clubs. They are a reminder of the triumphs —and the tragedies, too—of the yacht whose name is engraved on the mount. All these half-blocks date from a period when yachtsmen still had the means to have their boats designed and built, this being before the days of the class- and series-boat, before 1914, even, which marks an abrupt halt to custom-building. In the New York Yacht Club is an impressive collection of these half-block models. All carefully preserved and varnished, they retrace the story of the golden age of American yachting and are invaluable instruction for naval architects today.

If the cheese-paring owners of sailing ships made do with dockyard models, there were always the more prosperous steamship companies to go far beyond the utilitarian bounds of these half-blocks. A company's image is nothing new and shipping companies furnished their waiting-rooms with superb scale-models of their latest vessels. The board of directors could take a healthy pride in them and those who visited their offices either as prospective passengers or shippers had tangible proof before their very eyes that their lives or goods were in safe hands. Particularly noteworthy are models of steamers as long as nine or even twelve feet overall. Although hitherto neglected by collectors in favour of sailing-ship models, serious interest in them is beginning to grow. The accuracy of detail, the variety of materials employed and microscopic size of some of the working parts all specially made and hand-turned and finished comprise the true worth of these splendid craft, recalling as they do the world's great steamer-routes in the golden age of P. & O., Cunard, Norddeutscher-Lloyd, Lloyd-Triestino, Messageries Maritimes and the French Line, to mention only some of the companies which still survive.

Amateur and professional modellers

In my discussion of votive, seaman's and dockyard models, I have said something of the spirit in which some of them were made. A symbol for the creator of the votive offering, poetry for the seaman and an exercise in accuracy for the shipyard worker: these will be the three goals to which the modeller will be drawn according to his own temperament.

The most rough and ready ship-models, but those with the strongest emotional overtones must assuredly be the ones which children make. I do not know if any museum of popular art has a collection of these amazing playthings, but if you place yourself in the shoes of the children who designed them, you will always find something to learn from these weird and wonderful steam and sail lay-outs. It is especially interesting to see what has particularly impressed the young boat-builder, whether it be the colour of the hull, the gun-turrets (a cork and a couple of nails), or the torpedo tubes made from empty aluminium cigar-tubes. Although they are the toys of the poor, what riches of the imagination are theirs.

However, as they grow older most modellers lose this power of the imagination. Even by the age of ten children like the exactness and the rigidity of the plans in their modelling magazines, although their own drawings and models fall far short of this

Model of a late 18th century galley-stove. Notice the iron plate like a stuffing box at deck level, designed to prevent water leaking round the stove-pipe. Galleys were located in the tween-decks and bows.

realism. They generally go about modelling ships with more concern for accuracy than realism. Long before the days of plastic construction kits, there were wooden kits on the market some more lavish than others, from 'which model ships could be built and what is more which gave the modellers a far greater freedom in the process. You had to sandpaper, polish, drill, screw, and nail and use far more of your own initiative than you need for plastic models for which paint and glue are often all that you want. The fittings, too, varied to suit your pocket. Real blocks, complete with sheaves, or a real bronze anchor cost the earth. Really skilled modellers made them themselves. However, one should be fair to the firms which make special fittings for scale-model ships; their catalogues are a dream and I sometimes wonder if there can really be more than a handful of customers for the non-standard items which they list and which must have cost a small fortune in patterns, moulds and castings. I think particularly of ornamental scroll-work with its festoons, foliations, twirls and arabesques of such imaginative design that nobody but an accomplished engraver could execute them.

But of all these amateur models the most interesting without a shadow of doubt are those built from scratch from plans either taken from a treatise on naval architecture or else supplied by a modelling club. In this case all the techniques I have already alluded to come into play according to the time and the skill at the modeller's disposal. The best of them are inspired by the dockyard models to be found in museums, models which show the ribs and planking. Some are so obedient to the discipline of scale-modelling that they carry it to observing the different thicknesses of ropes and shrouds—an essential if the finished model is to be true to life. Everything must be made from scratch since there are no such things as prefabricated parts for models like these. Anchors and cannon must be cast and the barrels turned and bored; wire must be twisted and special machines used to make the ropes, for no commercial brand corresponds exactly to scale with the original of which the model is an accurate reduction. Titanic work for which precision tools are an essential.

However a half-digested appreciation for the need of realism sometimes may have monstrous results. Some years ago I was always being told about a retired skipper who over the years had been building a wonderful model of a sailing ship in steel as the real windjammers had been built in their closing years. Intrigued I paid

This clean and functional model was built for a shipping company. It depicts the three-masted, square-rigged wool-clipper *Loch Etive*, in which Joseph Conrad served.

35

Half-block dockyard model of a four-master showing the disposition of the upper works and the water-line of the hull.

a visit to the artist and his model.

There I was with the slightly crazy builder of a nine-foot model which was enough to make the eyes jump out of my head.

True enough, steel was used throughout and the hull plates had been hammered out one by one on the anvil and then well and truly riveted to the ribs. But the plates were a mass of dents, the rivets were gigantic and instead of the flowing lines of a clipper you had something which looked more like an old fashioned cauldron. He had everything including the kitchen sink! The stern-post carrying the rudder was solid steel; the marine engines were all there; the boiler behind the crew's quarters worked with a wood fire and the steam which it generated turned a capstan which raised and lowered the anchors. But this monstrous capstan was as wide as the fo'c'sle and the copper steam-pipes running from it to the boiler had a scale diameter twice the size of a seaman's head. Blocks and winches, too, were all there and all of them worked. Chain stays were made of real chain and wire shrouds of real wire, but I should not have wanted to sling my hammock aboard a ship like that when—still to scale—you could have had a block the size of a lorry-wheel falling on top of your head from the rigging. To match the capstan, the rudder quadrant filled half the quarterdeck and would undoubtedly have withstood the stern-battering seas off Cape Horn. I never saw the sails designed for the yards, but I have no doubt in my mind that they were made of as stout tarpaulin as ever covered hatches. It was all good solid work and the old boy's boat must have weighed nearly a ton. He had been working at it for the past three years and was not a little proud of his masterpiece.

Museums employ professional modellers for restoring existing models and adding new ones to their collections. Here again the professionals are the people who make the models for the shipping companies which I have already mentioned. This involves long and complicated work which may take two or three craftsmen anything up to a year to complete and is consequently extremely costly. That, however, is a mere drop in the ocean by comparison with the price of a real liner or giant tanker.

Other craftsmen specialise in building model yachts. Liking to see photographs of their boats under full sail—Beken of Cowes owe their success to their humble beginnings taking snaps to order—owners are just as happy to have a model. Here again are all degrees of finish from the solid hull to the model complete in every structural detail. Sometimes too they incorporate flattering dioramas in painted plaster-of-paris of the boat scudding at ten knots over a wild and foaming sea.

The art of the diorama is a direct descendant of the seaman's cased half-block and ship-in-a-bottle, as well as of those scenes produced in shipyard models of careening, raising wrecks, or stepping or lowering masts. The diorama recreates in miniature the full-size scenes shown in wax-work museums and provides an excellent way of evoking atmosphere. In museums throughout the world I have seen such scenes as these depicted: the gun-deck of a warship in action, pirates boarding their victim, rousing the watch, washing the decks, hand-to-hand fighting, Admiral's inspection, or launch coming alongside.

Some dioramas reproduce famous paintings in high relief or depict such stale subjects as Columbus sighting the New World. I have also seen static models driven by clockwork or electric motors of ships heaving and pitching amid the tossing waves.

Also to be included among the works in high relief are the historical figurines in various sizes which provide important evidence in the development of naval uniforms.

The realm of modelling is boundless and it is hardly necessary to cite the work of jewellers and goldsmiths, such as the scale models from Dieppe made of ivory in which technical skill vies with detailed accuracy. Mention should also be made of working models whether driven by sail or by power. As we have seen they go back a

long way, from the fleet at Versailles in the days of Louis XIV, and the tradition lives on. Miniature naval battles were arranged in Paris in 1899 and in London in 1913 when faithfully built models sailed on specially prepared and decorated pools. Cannon fired and by prearrangement certain ships actually sank.

Coming nearer home, the trainee skippers of the giant tankers learn to steer these monsters in special tanks where everything is built to scale, from the tanker—reduced model though it is which none the less may run to twelve to fifteen feet in length over all—and in which they sit at the wheel—to the piers, harbour lights and buoys which mark the channel. Hard though it is to classify it as such, the fifty-four foot whaler *Lagoda* housed in the New Bedford Museum at $\frac{1}{2}$ scale must be one of the finest scale-models in the world. Other museums have been quick to bring real ships within their walls. One thinks immediately of the Swedish Ship Museum with its *Wasa* and its *drakkars*, of Greenwich with its 19th century tug, of the Munich Museum where a North Sea fishing-boat may be seen and of the Science Museum at Milan where there is a sailing coaster 120 feet long as well as the entire bridge superstructure of the Italian liner *Conde Biancamano*. These last two were miraculously saved from the breaker's yard at La Spezia.

To return to working models: when from the end of the 19th century naval dockyards began to build special test-tanks they gave the lie to such great mathematicians as Euler and Bouguer who had claimed that no useful technical conclusions for full-scale ships could be drawn from tests made upon models. Nonetheless comparative tables were drawn up to take account of the density of seawater which must always affect the hull-performance of a model more strongly than the real ship as well as formulae to cover relative speed and acceleration.[1] Hydrodynamic tests were therefore carried out in tanks upon the hulls of fast-moving vessels. However, as far as the collector is concerned, these bare and functional hull shapes are disappoint-

Dutch barge or *bojer*. A 17th century model hollowed from a block of mahogany correct to the smallest detail of the rigging. Notice the care which the modeller has taken to depict the panelling and carving which turns this rather clumsy type of craft from the fishing-boat or coaster (its usual role) into a comfortable yacht.

[1]Thus the speed of the model, v, equals the speed of the real boat, V, divided by the square root of the scale, e, and is expressed:
$$v = \frac{V}{\sqrt{e}}$$

ing and without the decorative appeal even of shipyard block-models. I shall therefore pass to the working models produced by amateurs and shall first deal with sailing ships.

This type of ship must obviously be more stoutly built than a model designed for the drawing-room or the museum. The hulls are either carved out of a solid block of wood or better still from a lamination of successive layers of wood strongly glued together and then hollowed out to provide better buoyancy with a lump of lead along the keel, like a real yacht, to ballast it. Rough and ready though the rigging generally is, its function is to provide the requisite sail surface and it can be adjusted to suit the circumstances. Some models include automatic steering devices which are sometimes complex and always interesting. Generally speaking, however, these models, because of their rough and ready construction, are far more attractive from a distance running under full sail before the wind than from close up.

The same cannot be said of power-driven models. While there is something attractive about a boat however rudimentary under sail, what a dead and sorry sight is a floating mechanical vehicle more or less, driven by its propellor in a straight line across the water. This is why builders of power-driven models take such pains over colour-schemes and details to give them a bit of character. And so they have lights which work, guns which fire, funnels which belch smoke and to crown it all sirens which shrill. Clockwork and electric motors are dull enough as are those noisy little monsters driven by petrol engines designed for model aircraft. There is assuredly far more charm in the marine steam engines for models, especially when they are built from scratch with every part hand made and not prefabricated. The boilers are heated by alcohol—or gas-burners.

Radio-controlled models are too fresh upon the market to be classed with antiques for the collector, but their day will undoubtedly come as it has for the earliest crystal-set of the 1930s.

Toy boats

I now leave the realm of craftsmen's models to explore that of an industry which has an attraction all of its own. The industry is that of toy-boat manufacture and the specimens of the vintage years are as fraught with romance as with very real nautical and artistic qualities.

When we were children we all of us had lead soldiers in our toy-cupboards. If the future infantryman needed forts and pill-boxes and field artillery, the budding sailor would command squadrons of warships made of metal and with revolving gun-turrets. The best known firm to produce them during the inter-war years was undoubtedly Dinky Toys, yet they were not the first to be placed on the children's market. Their ancestors were the flat or slightly moulded lead silhouettes, painted and mounted on a stand which had appeared at the end of the 19th century. They were in fact versions in metal of coloured paper shapes mounted on wooden blocks. All varieties have become all the more scarce because a broadside of marbles or building bricks fired by a small and warlike boy is proportionately that much more destructive than anything of which the real 15-inch naval gun is capable.

Such interesting and evocative objects as these little models can be are only six inches long at the most and are strictly waterline.

The most luxurious toys remain the tin boats of the vintage years. The secret of their quality seems to have been lost. They were manufactured round 1900 both in France by Radiguet and Jep and in Germany by Bing, Märklin, Schöner and Plank. In the latter country it is generally supposed that this harvest of naval toys was due to the seeds planted by the Kaiser, stout protagonist of overseas imperialism. If, as he had announced, the future of Germany lay upon the high seas, there remained the task of awakening the seaman's vocation in the hearts of German children. This could not be done unless the toys themselves were reasonably detailed and accurate models. Nearly every vessel in the High Seas Fleet was reproduced as a toy. It is easy to imagine worthy old retired admirals being called in as technical advisers by the toy-makers and inspecting the moulds for the tin parts. The results are surprisingly true to life. Although frequently out of scale—something which does not upset small boys —and sketchy where a detail is hard to bend, mould or model in tin, all the minor details of scuttles, ports and rivets were painted on. The superstructures are often made of copper and comprise turrets, guns, ladders, handrails and flagstaffs.

Of course all this works. In the first place there is an engine in the bowels of the

Full-sized wooden patterns used for making the moulds from which various items of marine equipment were cast. Included here are an alarm-gun, a gear-wheel and the blade of a screw with its boss. Cannon were cast solid and then bored out with a special drill.

ship. To get at it, the central superstructure was removed—it came up in one piece. In France it would usually be a steam engine worked by methylated-spirit burners or else a primitive electric motor, Gramme's ring, worked by a battery. In Germany it was usually a clockwork engine.

This was however only the start. The guns were real guns which would fire gunpowder. Many of these toys were 'programmed' so as to leave harbour, fire a broadside, turn thirty degrees to starboard, fire a broadside from the second turret, make another turn to port and return to harbour. Submarines with adjustable hydroplanes were 'programmed' to dive, fire a torpedo with a cap which would go off if the nose struck any object. In order to dive the submarine was provided with a simple ball attached to the vessel by a long rubber tube, or else the trick was done through such chemical mixtures as tartaric acid or bicarbonate of soda.

Thus there is this advertisement in a 1915 catalogue: 'Scientific and mysterious toy enabling the child to make his acquaintance with fascinating physical and chemical phenomena. The little boat makes a series of dives and surfacings of its own accord. The submarine torpedo-boat with all accessories, 5 francs and from 6 francs 95 centimes upwards. For details write to Messieurs Clement et Cie, Directors of the Submarine Torpedo-Boat Company.'

This shows not only how seriously such toys were taken, but also that they were by no means cheap for the period. Their present-day price would of course make them toys for young princes.

Although tin models continued to be produced between the wars, they were unfortunately clumsy, degenerate, botched jobs like motor boats. Better by far to choose instead of them those commercial amalgams of painted tin allegedly of those boats which were then in fashion. Their merit is at least that they stimulate the imagination. We shall come upon them again at the end of this book with all the other items of nautical *kitch*, a fantasy world inspired by the sea.

If you collect ship models you will give yourself any number of archaeological and constructional headaches. On the one hand there are the problems of identifying the type of vessel, the country from which it came and the sort of craftsman who made it. So many ships bear names which do not appear in naval records or in the lists of such underwriters as Lloyds or Veritas—*a priori* evidence that there will be neither plans nor sketch to help replace any missing parts. Then as in the case of pictures there come the problems of restoration which is an art in itself and which should always be left to the specialist. Nevertheless, should the collector himself attempt it, the first thing he must do is permeate himself in the spirit in which the original model was made. This is essential if he is to avoid anachronisms. Each model, diorama or toy has a trick of workmanship peculiar to itself. Sometimes too there are painful decisions to be made as whether to sacrifice the original rigging which is so completely broken-down and tangled that it cannot be mended, and replace it by modern shrouds, which however well rigged, are always going to clash slightly with the rest of the model. Then you must hide the cheat by artificially aging and soiling. The rich patina of the rare woods used in those lovely models of yesteryear is hard to match. There are all sorts of pitfalls involved in repainting, but, as they say, nothing is impossible to the valiant heart, and ship models are worth every minute spent in their construction or restoration. They cannot but grow upon us all the more as a result.

A World War I U-boat. Early 20th century tin-plate toy made by the wellknown firm of Märklin.

II

The sea depicted

Throughout the ages artists have found to an extraordinary degree a source of inspiration in the sea. It has given them themes of infinite richness and variety. Sea and sky are ever-changing; ships cross the waters at different trims to match the changing weather conditions; there are countless bits and pieces of tackle aboard any one ship and these change with the ages; superstition and credulity invent fabulous creatures, while the seamen's yarns conjure up the very scenes in the mind of the imaginative listener. Graphic artists have not remained unmoved by such lavish wealth, whether they were completely free to express themselves as they would or were tied to the restrictions of a particular craft. The subject of my second chapter is the way the sea has inspired artists and my endeavour will be to disinter the whole range of forms this inspiration took.

Marine painting

I am purposely omitting marine painting by the great masters from my gallery. Indeed, although it is possible in certain so-called minor genres to speak of schools and to trace developments from one painter to the next, the personalities of the masters are so overpowering that their works can only be studied within the frame of a detailed monograph. I therefore thought that it might be worthwhile to list, however incompletely, those painters whom I would include within this category, from earliest times down to our own day, namely:

Van Aaken, known as H. Bosch (1450–1516); P. Bruegel (1544–1628); H. C. Vroom (1566–1640); A. Willaerts (1577–1664); F. Napoletano (1590–1629); Claude Gellée, known as Lorrain (1600–82); Van de Velde the Elder (1611–93); J. de Toledo (1611–65); S. Rosa (1615–73); A. Cuyp (1620–91); R. Mooms, known as Zeeman (1623–68); J. Van de Capelle (1625–79); J. I. Van Ruysdäel (1628–82); L. P. Verschuier (1630–86); L. Backhuisen (1631–1708); H. Van Minderhout (1632–96); W. Van de Velde the Younger (1633–1707); A. Strock (1635–1710); L. Smoute the Younger (1671–1713); J. B. Van Loo (1684–1715); A. Manglard (1695–1760); F. Guardi (1712–93); J. Vernet (1714–89); L. N. Van Blarenberghe (1716–94); C. H. Brooking (1723–59); J. Reynolds (1723–92); C. P. Crépin (1772–1851); J. M. W. Turner (1775–1851); A. L. Garneray (1783–1857); T. H. Géricault (1791–1824); C. Corot (1796–1875); E. Delacroix (1798–1863); T. Gudin (1802–80); J. B. L. G. E. Isabey (1804–86); J. B. Jongkind (1819–91); G. Courbet (1819–77); E. Boudin (1824–98); T. Monticelli (1824–86); C. Pissarro (1830–1903); E. Manet (1832–83); J. M. Whistler (1834–1903); W. Homer (1835–1910); E. de Martino (1838–1912); C. Monet (1840–1926); A. T. Ryder (1847–1917); J. Ensor (1860–1969); P. Signac (1863–1935); A. Marquet (1875–1947).

The work of these painters is either partially or completely devoted to marine painting, while some, indeed, were appointed official Naval Painters, among them Vroom, both the Van de Veldes, Verschuier, Smoute, Vernet, Crépin, Garneray, Gudin, Martino, Signac and Marquet.

Another reason for omitting these masters is the price to which their works have risen, making it a virtual impossibility for the private individual to acquire an example nowadays. When they come onto the market their paintings are purchased almost exclusively by museums, the only bodies with the necessary funds at their disposal. Since the object of this book is to guide the individual who seeks to build up a collection of marine antiques, I propose only to discuss those items which are likely to be available, together with similar objects displayed in museums and which act as references for purposes of comparison and dating. It is in any case no dishonour for the painters whom I shall subsequently discuss if they are not among those whom I have just listed. I personally attach a great deal of importance to paintings which record the technical details of seamanship, which tell a story or which are quaint. These are all qualities acceptable within this field, but in general scorned by easel-painting. It is highly likely that in the immediate future this type of graphic self-expression will follow the pattern of 'primitive' painting, rising to prices which nobody would have suspected both on grounds of originality and of rarity.

The public at large is unaware that schools of marine painting have been in existence since the 17th century, most frequently coming into being in ports or in those areas where shipping activity was intense and where it effectively provided the sole theme of an artist's work. This was the case of the Neapolitan school, of schools in Dutch and English ports and of the Hudson River school in the U.S.A.[1]

There is always some discernible mannerism in the work of these local artists by which they may be identified in their treatment of sea, sky, landscape, background or shipping. However, what is so striking is the evidence of an eye accustomed to the sea. Here are painters with an astounding technical knowledge of seamanship and an overriding concern for realism, and their work provides some of the most valuable evidence for naval historians.

The precise detail of rigging, the exact colour of a hull or design of a flag are so many pieces of fresh evidence in the overall picture of naval history. Some idea of their value may be gained from the examples given in this book and the captions which accompany them.[2]

We should not, however, lose ourselves in general considerations of the intentions of these artists, the conditions under which they worked, their techniques or the reputation which they enjoyed in their lifetime, for all these properly belong to the biography of the individual painter. When we come to their choice of subject we find that it is as vast as the sea itself: departure and home-coming, tempest and squall, sailing through ice-floes, whaling, wintering in the Arctic.

But first I would tackle three truly original aspects of marine painting—ship portraits, ex-voto paintings and paintings on glass—categories which deserve specific and detailed discussion.

Ship portraits

From the beginnings of oil-painting until the 18th century, portrait-painters existed in some numbers in the towns. Not only the high and mighty of this world liked to see themselves on canvas, but anybody else with a modest substance. The family portrait gallery was traditional among the townsfolk as a forerunner of our modest, present-day photograph albums.

It was only natural that as the landsman had his nearest and dearest portrayed on canvas, so the seaman should want his ship to be painted, the ship being a living thing for those who devoted their lives to her. It is impossible accurately to date the beginnings of this art and technique or to state definitely where in the world the first marine portrait painter hung out his shingle, or which was the first skipper to take the craftsman's claims at face-value and to commission a portrait of his ship. Nevertheless it does appear likely that the earliest broadside paintings of ships cutting through

[1] John Wilmerding, *A History of American Marine Painting*.

[2] The fact that Yankee whalers were painted white for their entire maiden voyage is only known from a painting by Charles S. Raleigh.

the blue sea under a press of sail go back to the late 18th century. Often these paintings are neither signed nor dated, but they do have a strip at the base of the canvas on which the names of the ship, the skipper, and sometimes the circumstances of the voyage are written, and it is from the letter forms and spelling of these that the date of the painting may be surmised.

Furthermore, the background, be it seascape or harbour, shows whether this is a painting by a north European or Mediterranean artist. Among all the European artists who painted the portraits of ships, the four members of the Roux family of Marseilles are most famous.

The story of this family of painters is an extraordinary one and it illustrates the nature of these ship portraits and of the art of the painters who were commissioned to supply them.

In the early years of the 19th century, between the church of the Augustinians and Fort Saint-Jean in the Old Port of Marseilles the cream of the world's sailing craft were tied up alongside, ships from the Far East, from Africa, America and Northern Europe. A forest of spars and bowsprits rose proudly above the red brick of the quayside and overshadowed a mass of people who in one way or another and to a greater or lesser degree lived from the sea—shopkeepers, pedlars, seamen, deckhands, sightseers all crowding round to watch the arrival or depature of the ships.

The ground-floors of the houses which stretched to either side of the town-hall housed innumerable shops, their windows decorated with tropical birds, tortoises, guinea-pigs, exotic objects which roused dreams of distant voyages and far-off, cinnamon-scented isles.

Then there were the watchmakers, jewellers and hatters, the shop with the sign of the Negro's Head belonging to the master sailmaker Revest, commerce which flourished as fresh crews and fresh vessels fed it from day to day.

Had you walked along the row of shops you would have come upon a narrow window in which dreams and reality lived happily together. The brass of compasses, barometers, quadrants, telescopes, logs sparkled against a background of many-coloured flags and sea-charts. Painted wooden figures of two merchant marine officers, cocked hat on head, telescope tucked under the arm, quadrant in hand, stood on either side of the entrance.

This was the shop which belonged to Joseph Roux, since 1750 'Nautical Instrument-maker'. Here in 1766 was born Joseph Ange Roux, who with his three sons was to create in France a new species of painting—ship portraiture—which was to remain in fashion until photography came in and in which a number of painters, such as Adam or Baugean known as Simone, were to achieve their differing measure of fame.

Young Antoine Roux was a natural draughtsman. He worked in his father's business assembling precision instruments, but in his free time he would wander around the harbour sketching and was noticed by officers from English ships which in those days used to land their cargoes of spices from the Indies or textiles from the Levant. As a result he took his first lessons in watercolour-painting and was advised to specialise in painting ships, since pictures of this sort were by now highly appreciated in England.

The young man was a glutton for work. Over a hundred of his sketch-books survive where, cheek by jowl with studies of hulls or rigging, are all sorts of fascinating jottings about the ships and the happenings of the time. In these sketch-books can be traced the growing assurance of a talent founded upon the sensitivity and accuracy which were to be so characteristic of the work of Antoine Roux the Elder. Great skill in execution, a profound knowledge of naval architecture and seamanship and an immense capacity for work soon brought him mastery in his chosen field. Roux continued in his father's trade, but at the same time accepted commissions for ship portraits from owners and skippers and even, so they say, from ordinary seamen who wished to thank their patron saint by a votive offering. Soon he had gained a solid reputation.

It is also said—and one must accept that in those days business and inclination went hand in hand—that foreign skippers were quite prepared to go out of their way to call at Marseilles to have the portrait of their ship painted. As soon as a watercolour was finished it was hung in the window of the Roux shop and, when the Exchange closed, dealers would take a stroll to examine the new masterpiece.

Apart from the freshness of the colour and the technical precision, Antoine

A Dutch whaling fleet in Arctic seas. Picture made up by 16 Delft tiles. This form of pottery became established in Holland from the 17th century and special patterns were produced for export. Sometimes pictures with a maritime theme were painted on single tiles.

43

A fresh breeze off the English Channel.
Early 19th century oil-painting, unsigned, but
clearly the work of an artist familiar with
matters nautical. Note the accuracy with
which the handling of the vessels is depicted
as is their technical detail. This concern does
not override the pictorial effects which are
seldom if ever found in paintings by seamen.

Roux's originality lies in his composition. Unlike the work of so many other painters, his ships are depicted in a way peculiarly their own, at sea in a variety of weathers so that, in addition to the beauty of the vessel herself, you have the sauce of a lively scene taken from the life. Often, too, upon the same watercolour the same ship is shown from a number of different and flattering angles.

The period of Britain's continental blockade gave Roux many opportunities for depicting incidents of naval warfare, lively scenes with short captions written in a copperplate hand in white upon the black border which often runs along the base of his watercolours.

Typical examples are: 'The brig *Dubourdieu*, Captain Mordeille, boarding the English three-master *Loyalty*'; or else: 'The privateer *L'Hirondelle*, Captain Pontus, armament 2 four-pounders, ready to board and take the 300-ton *Arrow*'. Antoine Roux had plenty of eye-witnesses of the action to help him, which was just as well, since his critics were all professional seamen who would not have allowed a single mistake. All details, then, are shown with exceptional accuracy.

Antoine Roux died during a cholera epidemic in Marseilles in 1835, leaving three sons, Mathieu Antoine (1799–1872), Frédéric (1805–70) and François Jeoffroy (1811–82).

About this time Mathieu-Antoine set up in business in the port in a nautical instrument maker's belonging to one of his uncles, to continue his father's tradition of business and painting. A large number of his watercolours survive, but he was apparently less popular than his brothers.

Frédéric Roux met the painters Carle Vernet and his son Horace at a very early age and the two of them persuaded him to study in Paris. There at the age of twenty the young man found himself in the famous studio of this great painter where he soon developed into a brilliant watercolourist. However Roux's independent temper prompted him to strike out on his own as soon as he possibly could. In 1830 he settled in Le Havre where he opened a nautical instrument business. Following in the footsteps of his father and his brother, he soon gained the reputation of a marine artist, particularly among the skippers of American sailing ships which frequented this busy Channel port at that time. Despite a wide circle of customers whose commissions he was unable to fulfil, his instability and greed for fresh adventure took him on many a voyage to Russia and Norway from which he returned with invaluable views of landscapes and harbours. He visited Marseilles once, before returning to Le Havre where he died in 1870.

The third and youngest son, François Roux, was of an equally strong character. He, too, began in the nautical instrument business, but in 1860 he handed his interest to a nephew to devote himself exclusively to painting, dividing his time between Paris and Marseilles. Although he was completely self-taught, François Roux reached a high degree of skill which is best exhibited in massive canvases. His work, with its scenes of life on board ship, its details of bows and sterns, its portraits of warships and merchantmen, is a living history of a hundred years of change in naval architecture and an unique source of documentation.

Specialising in portraits of warships, François Roux was given a flattering appreciation at the time of his death from Vice-Admiral Paris: 'The French Navy has lost an artist of whom it may be said that he depicted it with the greatest accuracy and elegance.'

Despite the retrospective exhibition organised in Marseilles in 1882, these four great painters were completely forgotten in France for nearly a century. The sketchbooks of Antoine Roux the Elder and the best work by the Roux family is to be found in the U.S.A. and especially in the Peabody Museum in Salem, Massachusetts, which has patiently built up this unique body of work into one of the finest collections in the world.

A paragraph in *L'Illustration* for 18 December 1926 revealed to the French public the existence of the Marine Research Society, the occasion being the publication of the society of an illustrated pamphlet devoted to Antoine Roux and his three sons. It was interesting to be told that a few watercolours were preserved in the Musée de la Marine (housed in the Louvre in those days), in the Musée du Vieux Marseille and in the Museums of Nice and Draguignan. Through their publication the American society had saved the Roux family from being utterly and completely forgotten.

Ship portraiture, so well developed in Europe and especially in England, France

Gilder's stamp with nautical subject. 18th century bronze bookbinder's tool.

and Italy by the beginning of the 19th century, was to be given a fresh lease of life by the golden age of the Yankee clipper in the Gold Rush, from 1850 onwards. To the nautical public of the time all those prestigious ships designed by Donald MacKay for the San Francisco passage via Cape Horn were 'crack-ships'. Fabulous sums were wagered on them and their portraits were all the rage, for this was the era of performance figures and competition under sail. The victory of the schooner *America* over her English rivals in a race round the Isle of Wight in 1851 was the opening shot in the great battle of yachtsmen.

The discovery of gold in Australia set the clippers racing once more for Sydney and Melbourne with their impatient passenger-load of emigrants. Like the Yankee clippers, these magnificent greyhounds of the seas became the subjects of paintings and of mass circulation engravings. The golden age of commercial sail navigation marks the high-point in ship portraiture. Although it continued in England and the United States until well into the 20th century its subject matter grew ever more predominantly to be yachting, for from then on yachts were the sole representatives of the great tradition of sail. On the one hand there was no longer anything very spectacular about the performance of commercial sailing vessels—rock-bottom freights hardly encouraged owners to rig their ships as they had done in the fabulous days of the Opium, Tea and Wool Races—and on the other, ocean-going ships were mighty cargo-carriers and sail was dying, to be replaced by coal-burning engines. The last of the ship portraitists were to paint steamers so long as they had paddle wheels, auxiliary sails and an ornate superstructure. Shipping still danced along in its plumes even if they were plumes of smoke. Successors to the Dutchmen Vettewinkel, J. Plaat and J. Morel, to the Belgian J. H. Mohrmann, to the Americans James E. Butterworth and Thomas Birch, to George Ropes, J. Hughes, James Spurling, Yorke, Walters, Salmon, Lane, and Bradford in England and Pellegrin, Cosini, Montardier, Morel-Fatio, and Lebreton in France would be the painters of steamships, men like the Frenchman Edouard Adam or the Americans Antonio Jacobsen and Reuben Chappell.

The American whaling tradition did, however, provide Charles S. Raleigh, one of the last painters of sailing ships, with his opportunity and since he was in any case a remarkable personality the story of his life should be told as an accompaniment to an account of his work as a painter.

Born in England in 1830, Raleigh went to sea at the age of ten as a cabin-boy. He remained at sea from 1840 to 1870 until he was put ashore sick at New Bedford after a long and exhausting trip from Rio, having made up his mind to sling his anchor and marry. However, he had to make a living and he was soon to be found working for a firm of 'House Decorators and General Painters'. These were the days of New Bedford's prosperity and Raleigh's brush found plenty of work on the rich homes of the wealthy ship-owners. However, this wealth itself was due entirely to the phenomenal activity of shipping in the harbour. Thus Raleigh often exchanged the flat-brush of the housepainter for the camelhair of the artist.[1]

Within a few years he had established himself as a portrayer of ships, in some sense indeed a court painter, the court being composed of hardy whalers. This was to be the beginning of an extraordinary burst of artistic creation which produced some 1,100 pictures devoted to the nautical history of his time. Although he himself was no whaler, but a seaman from a wind-jammer, circumstances soon made Raleigh specialise in this field. His customers were pernickety in matters of detail, but always able to advise him as he worked on the painting.

This too was the great age of travelling shows, touring museums of curiosities which moved from town to town to offer their attractions to the idler. Between 1847 and 1848 two artists, Benjamin Russell and Caleb P. Purrington, had painted a 'Parorama of a Whaling Voyage round the World' which measured no less than 1,275 feet in length. Following this lead upon a more modest scale, Raleigh was to paint a panorama 197 feet long between 1878 and 1880 which he called 'Panorama of a Whaling Voyage in the Ship *Niger*'. It comprised a series of 17 realistic panels 6 feet by 11, but did not achieve the fame which he had expected during the lifetime of its painter.

[1] History records plenty of seamen who became artists. Geerit Groenewegen (1754–1826) was originally a ship's carpenter. After losing a foot in an accident, he turned to painting and has left a splendidly engraved series of 84 contemporary Dutch vessels, forming historical documentation of the first order.

The American three-master *Hope* being towed out of the port of Marseilles by her whaler in a dead calm. Water-colour by Antoine Roux, *c.* 1860.

Raleigh was a regular work-horse of painting with the ever-itching brush, for apart from the portrait of ships which he turned out, he decorated his own house and at the same time continued his business interests in the same way as the Roux, who were at one and the same time marine-painters and nautical instrument makers. Thus the trade card of this artist-craftsman a few years before his death bore the legend: 'Charles S. Raleigh, House, Sign, Carriage & Ornamental Painter'.

Raleigh, who died at Bourne in 1925 at the age of 94, remains the most sincere and authentic American painter of ships. Today his work has been given the accolade which it deserved. The seventeen panels of the voyage of the *Niger* are now displayed on the walls of the Whaling Museum in New Bedford. The Curator has devoted a short and meaningful publication to Charles S. Raleigh as illustrator, and this in fact forms the basis of the foregoing.[1]

Then photography appeared and painted portrait was replaced by the sepia print, far cheaper and capable of almost infinite duplication, the latest gadget of the day. The yachting world began to neglect its portrait painters, for marine photography had been turned into a real art by men like Beken of Cowes or Rosenfeld and W. R. Macaskill in the United States. Other humble but talented photographers, too, went to work to record for posterity those superb sailing vessels of whose imminent disappearance they were no doubt the heralds. This was certainly true of Wilhelm Hester of Tacoma and Seattle on the Puget Sound in 1900. He had emigrated thither from Germany some twenty years earlier with his camera and tripod tucked under his arm and would have been doomed to complete oblivion had not the San Francisco

[1] Philip F. Purrington, *Four Years a' Whaling,* illustrated by Charles S. Raleigh.

This water-colour, its details heightened in Indian ink, has all the ingenuousness of the simple pictures seamen painted to tell a story and to commemorate important moments in life at sea. Hence the caption at the foot of the picture reads: 'The *Espérance* of Bordeaux, Captain Alquié, aground in the Bay of Bengal, 12 May 1818'. Unsigned.

museum in 1960 sent one of its assistants to look over a collection of negatives which had turned up in an old barn. It was real treasure trove. Week after week Hester had photographed the cream of sailing fleets of Europe and the New World. Like so many of the photographers of the time he had the true painter's eye and his work has composition and real character.

This is also true of Albert Cook Church of New Bedford. Son of a pilot from Buzzard's Bay and a talented photographer, Church has left us an unforgettable visual record of the last American whaling fleet.[1]

But the last men to paint the portraits of ships were undoubtedly the crews of

windjammers. Everything aboard these craft was done in the time-honoured way, as we have seen in the case of ship-models. Similarly tradition prescribed that inside the lid of the sea-chest—the seaman's trunk—there should be a picture of a ship. Now, although a fairly presentable model can be hewn from a piece of wood, canvas, brushes and oil-paint are not always so easy to manage. This is readily apparent in

[1] Two of these collections of photographs are well-known—*Whale Ships and Whaling* and *American Fishermen*. One might remark that, well-organised though he was, Church could not be everywhere simultaneously, and that photographs taken on the high seas at various places on the globe at the same time are due to whalers to whom Church gave the necessary instructions and equipment when they put to sea.

the resultant work of art. In the first place the brushes often seem to have been coarse and the palette of four or five primary colours is crude enough. The all important object was to depict the sails swelling in the wind and to put all the details of the hull in—ports painted correctly, beading, bow and stern decorations. The sea is shown stiff and angular. With no thin brush, the rigging is often drawn in pencil with a ruler and then more or less clumsily filled in with black oil paint and a split reed or nail. The mount is coarse canvas sail-cloth with the disadvantage of cockling when the paint dries. The pictures were of no great size—roughly a foot by eighteen inches—so that they could be nailed inside the lid of the sea-chest. The subjects of the paintings

were always the same. More often than not it would be one of the crack ships in which the artist had served, or if need be and this were not strictly true, he would so prevail upon himself as to carry conviction with his shipmates.

Those who were least handy with the oil-paint would touch up and colour a newspaper or magazine cutting or else make collages out of all kinds of material.

Just as booksellers 'break up' an illustrated volume to sell the plates separately, the sailors' heirs have not hesitated to use their old sea-chests for kindling wood and all that remains are the somewhat ingenuous paintings which once lived inside the lids, saved from the stake, without stretchers or frame, simple scraps of painted canvas still bearing the four holes left by the nails which once secured them inside the sea-chest and later to the wall of the house.

Apart from these utilitarian or decorative efforts, few sailors painted pictures of ships for the fun of it. Somewhat clumsy portraits of vessels will either be votive offerings (often painted ashore) or else the work of naval officers. In those days people were fair hands with the pencil, especially in the Navy, where drawing was a test which carried top marks in the examinations. The art was useful for taking the outline

Painted on sail-cloth, this painting of a four-master is intended to go inside the lid of a seaman's chest. Unfinished. The artist doubtless intended to add the standing and running rigging. Notice how the royals and top gallants and the inner jib are reefed as she runs close-hauled in a fresh breeze. Practical details of trim, such as these, would only be known to those who had served aboard the windjammers. Early 20th century.

of coastlines, entrances to harbours or prominent sea-marks, for you did not always have a draughtsman from the Hydrographic Department on board.

Ex-voto paintings

In manuscript illumination, as in ex-voto painting, the artist's imagination often oversteps the bounds of strict historical accuracy. Although the vessel depicted in this 16th century miniature painted on glass is somewhat exotic, it does serve to confirm what we know of naval architecture and ship-handling of the period.

Superstition is as old as mankind and it is only natural that sailors should not have been immune to it, particularly since the sea with its unknown worlds below the surface and beyond the horizon would seem the ideal breeding-ground for mystery, legend and fable. So many books have been written about 'the mysteries of the sea' that I shall not attempt an original study or a rehash of the topic. Scylla and Charybdis, the Sirens, the great sea-serpent, the Black Hand and the Flying Dutchman are themes which die hard. The map-makers of the Middle Ages enjoyed lightening their learned labours with a world of imaginary creatures. If they do not detail the precise

position of any one fabulous monster they stud their maps with enough of them as if to remind sailors that the sea has always been the realm of the imaginary.

The prows of Egyptian ships were decorated with an eye to ward off the evil influences of 'The Wicked One'. The Chinese look on a boat as a fish, and of course it must see. The eye painted on the stem watches the course, just as the *phong*-bird which spreads its wings over the stern helps the ship to keep the poop clear of a following sea in a storm. A dolphin's tail or a sheepskin nailed to the boom drives away the perils of the deep. Storms are stilled by rich offerings made to the raging sea, but when all is lost and old magic and spells prove ineffective, there is nothing left but to get down on your knees and promise your patron saint some precious gift once you are safe and sound and ashore.

Thus the faith of simple and deeply religious men gave birth to the ex-voto offering. The oldest known examples go back to the 16th century and are small wash-drawings of ships. They are to be found in an area round Naples fastened to the walls of little chapels facing the sea and built on some wild headland to which sailors used to go on pilgrimage.

From the 18th century the ex-voto marine painting is a real work of art on wood and then, from the 19th century on a properly mounted canvas. They are seldom larger than eighteen inches by two feet, since space on church walls was limited and the artists who painted them undoubtedly felt more at home on a smaller canvas. These painters comprise all sorts and conditions of men, even the occasional sailor, and especially a group of professionals ranging from the most appalling botchers to real masters. An appreciable number of great painters of the Italian Renaissance began their careers in back-street studios turning out religious pictures for a living. A number of good marine painters have followed in their footsteps and practised as members of the ex-voto trade, chief among them being the Roux.

Nevertheless all these painters were ever so lightly sprinkled with salt water. They were told what had happened at sea, the ship was described—supposing that it had sunk and the donor had survived—and the painting took shape. It could be shipwreck, fire at sea, chase by the foe—in the Mediterranean they would be Turkish or Barbary corsairs—an engagement with a better-armed opponent, wreck—off-shore, riding out a gale with a storm-anchor at sea or avoiding the enormous wave which is about to break over the stern and poop the vessel. Men can be seen kneeling on the quarter-deck praying to the Virgin or to some saint and then the miracle takes place. In one corner of the painting there is a gap in the stormy sky and there stands Our Lady haloed in clouds of cottonwool and gilt, holding the Christ-Child in her arms and gazing down in pity on the sailors in distress.

As seamen as a class became more literate, they obliged the ex-voto painter to set a descriptive panel at the foot of the picture just as they did for ship-portraits. Comprising four or five lines of writing, black on white or vice-versa, it told the name of the ship and the hero of the adventure, and the dramatic circumstances of the vow, closing with the ritual letters V.F.G.A. *Votum fecit, gratiam accepit*, 'He made a vow and received a favour from Heaven.' Such was custom.

By the end of the 19th century religious faith was growing weaker. Either steam-ships were safer or else they no longer inspired the painters. Be it as it may, ex-voto paintings have become fewer and fewer if one goes by the engraved plaques in seamen's chapels, sober squares of white marble in which, as is now the custom, the words are incised. Sometimes these marble slabs have a scene cut on them in low relief. For example there is the marble memorial in Canterbury Cathedral dedicated to the men of H.M.S. *Kent* who fought in the Battle of the Falkland Islands in 1914.

The paintings which infrequently appear upon the market are not all stolen, despite the thefts from churches which latterly have been on the scale of organised looting. Sometimes the pious memorials owe their newly-won lay status simply to a passion for order on the part of the verger. The state of these paintings is not improved by the dark and damp corners in which they have been hung. Nearly all of them will need relining by a sound and sensitive picture-restorer who is capable of replacing missing paint-work in the spirit of the original.

Painting on glass

This very special category of painting seems to date from the 17th century. Known today as 'fixé sur verre', 'peinture églomisé' or simply 'églomisé', we do not have to accept the word of the experts that these latter terms are derived from a man called Glomi, who was thus the inventor of the technique.

This technique originally consisted of cutting the design into a coat of paint and in filling the furrow with a contrasting shade. Some glass-paintings which use this technique merely give the effect of a shadow theatre in black and white, but as skills improved with the years, so the picture is really and truly thought out beforehand from back to front.

But it will provide a clearer idea if we discuss marine paintings on glass, these more often than not being ship-portraits.

Hull details are the first to be painted in—sides, beading and ornament: then comes the shading for the curve of bow and stern, and finally the overall colour of the hull. Turning next to masts and sails, the first thing is to draw in the shrouds and main ropes; then add the shading which gives the sails their shape and finally apply the coat of cream for the canvas. Last to be painted are the flags, device first and background later, and only then is attention paid to the sea. First the white caps on the crest of the waves, then the darker blue of the troughs and last of all the general mass of colour. Finally the clouds in the sky are shaped before the blue background is applied.

If some small detail is forgotten and has to be added to the foreground, the outline of that detail has simply to be scratched in the coats of paint which have already been applied and then filled in. This in any case is the way in which the line of wake is shown creaming along the hull and dropping astern of the vessel. The materials used in the painting are not oil-paints alone, but can include water-colours, gum-arabic, wash-colours, varnish and bitumen. Occasionally the glass-painting achieves its effect by mounting several sheets of glass within the same frame, with a space between each to show perspective and to give the illusion of standing out in relief.

But whatever the method employed to produce them, these works of art are so very fragile that it is easy to see why they are so rare.

The chosen themes of these paintings are similar to those of the ship-portrait and indeed to the process lends itself particularly well to the subject. At the foot of most of these glass-paintings, too, a fairly full descriptive text is to be found, more clearly written perhaps than those of the ship-portrait, but from their technique highly prone to the classic error of the *S* or *N* reversed.

There were schools of glass-painting just as there were schools of the normal marine painting. A study published by the curator of the Antwerp Museum, which holds a particularly rich collection of these glass-paintings, mentions a painter called Wenzislaus Wieden as the founder of the Belgian school in the 14th century, followed by Petrus Weyts and then by an anonymous artist who signed a large number of works with the initials P.N. However, it would seem highly probable that the art of glass-painting was Belgian, or rather Flemish, soon spreading to and copied in neighbouring countries without ever becoming a true speciality in the country of its origin.

As with other media, so schools of glass-painting may be identified by the overall tone of the painting and the peculiar manner in which sea, and sky are treated and in their decorative, stylistic or realistic spirit.

In the 19th century paintings, with their realistic treatment, the overriding concern of the artists would seem to have been to get every smallest detail of the ship correct. The sailors who commissioned the paintings appear to have been unable to leave anything to the painters' imaginations and hence their work is all the more important to the naval historian as a source of technical information.

Only once in a blue moon is a steamer the subject of a glass-painting. Either it was not in itself an inspiring object or else its stay in port was too short for the artist to make his sketches preliminary to painting the glass. Be it as it may, by the beginning of the 20th century this type of painting had become very rare. No doubt the artists who undertook the work went over to painting the glass panels for magic lanterns, where a very similar technique was employed to that which they had used before.

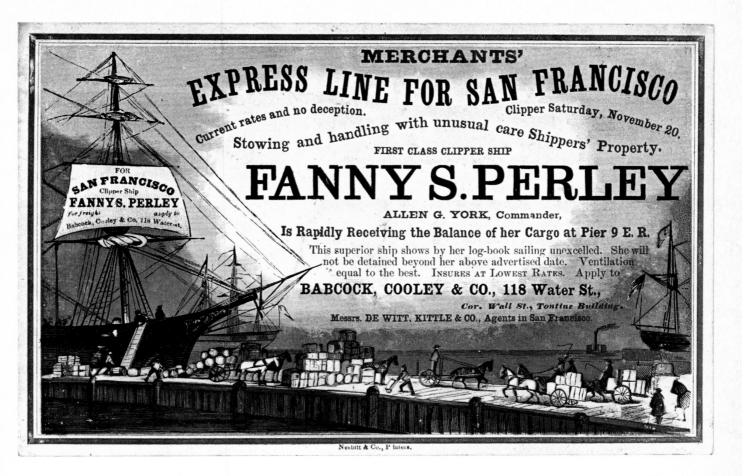

Posters, trade and other cards

Having dealt in some detail with the three major categories of marine art, I do not propose seriously to enter into the technicalities of all the forms of graphic expression which have drawn their inspiration from the sea and comprise what might be termed marine iconography. They are far too numerous for this and I would therefore propose merely to list them as suggestions for the new collector or as fresh branches in existing collections.

Original drawings include plans of ships, ports and docks, tinted drawings of marine engines with enlargements of details and colour symbols. These are often decorative works of the highest quality.

Designs for ornamental work on ships and showing figure-heads and stern scroll-work belong to the same family as the famous studies by artists like Puget, Ozanne and Caffieri.

By comparison with this original work, the province of printing is of course far richer and there can be no argument that the most spectacular examples are posters. Ancient posters of the 17th and 18th centuries comprise in the main proclamations, notices of conscription for sea-service and of the sale of prizes and their cargoes taken in the hey-day of the privateer. These posters are purely typographic, printed in black on white and lack the eye-catching qualities of the illustrated poster which appeared in the middle of the 19th century in the days of the clipper ships. Then advertisers did not know which way to turn in the circumstances to attract the emigrant and his money aboard a vessel which the rats had left already and which would founder in the harbour mouth. Then the most pitiful ocean-going bark was depicted by the nameless image of some superb clipper or else by some proud figure-head which would create trust and confidence. Very often these would be provided by a woodcut enlargement of an illustration or a tail-piece taken from a book. However the

19th century sailing card announcing the departure of the American clipper *Fanny S. Perley*. Such handbills were an established feature long before the California Gold-Rush, but it is only then (in the 1850s) that, with so many ships competing for the migrant trade, advertising became an essential element to survive that competition. The very first posters from the Gold Rush are particularly interesting because of the importance of the matter printed on them. It gives the pioneers full information as to their sea passage, their arrival at the placer mines and the incentive they have to take shares in the company which has chartered their ship.

53

UOEU · FAIT · A Mᵗᵇᵉ · DAME · DE ·
GRACE · PAR · LE · CA ᵖⁿᵉ IEAN · LE · GRIX ·
DE · HONFLEUR · ET · SON · EQUIPAGES · LE 21 · ᴹᴬᴿˢ· 1754

This ingenuous 19th century ex-voto painting was offered by Captain Jean Le Gris to Our Lady of Grace, Patroness of Seamen, whose ancient chapel stands on a headland facing the sea above Honfleur. Ex-voto paintings, traditional to Catholic countries may be found on both sides of the Atlantic, as well as on Mediterranean coasts.

lettering of these posters is what is really breathtaking. The wood-cut capitals show infinite stylistic variations and all in impeccable taste. It is as though the cream of the world's graphic designers rallied to the United States at the time of the Gold Rush. Sometimes these posters are printed in several colours. The printed text is always fascinating to read and recreates a century later all the excitement of setting off for California. It also provides invaluable information as to freight rates, company regulations, shippers' contractual obligations and even to time-tables, which must make one pause when one remembers that these were voyages under sail.

Then, with the progress of printing and engraving methods, the poster loses its disciplined beauty. Six-, eight- and ten-colour lithography degenerates into a wishy-washy mess. Artists such as Toulouse-Lautrec especially were to put a serious stop to such wasteful tendencies which weakened the medium. But at the same time as the typographic element was becoming impoverished, the visual elements were enriched by a fresh tendency to tell a story. The true motivation of the public can be discovered at a time when advertising techniques were coming into being.

The shipping companies were engaged in a war to the death on the passenger-carrying routes of the North and South Atlantic and the Far East. Invention was strained to lure customers aboard the liners. Cunard and Norddeutscher Lloyd boasted the luxury of their floating palaces. It was so difficult to tell whether you were on land

or on sea that a young passenger is supposed to have asked his parents: 'But where is the boat? I want to see the boat.'

Posters for Far Eastern lines tended to favour the exotic. Immediately in the background behind the ship are palm-trees, junks and friendly natives smiling in adoration of the god-like European colonists.

Equally interesting are the recruiting posters put out by the naval authorities in various countries. Stressing the good pay and good food in the Fleet, they urge young men to sign on and then to sign on again. They show warships and uniforms accurately. Wartime naval posters are much more rare.

Less obviously attractive, but textually interesting, are the medium format posters for regattas and similar events as well as exhibitions and pamphlets on matters relating to the sea.

The theme is in any case so vast that it has been used for commercial advertising and I know of some notable collections of posters which use the theme of the sea to push a particular product.

The sea, too, has its full share of attention from those highly coloured engravings which used to be printed for children to cut out and stick in scrap-books and which are known in France as 'Images d'Epinal'. The widest variety of subjects are depicted graphically if naïvely, ranging from pages of sailors from cabin-boys to admirals,

The sailor's farewell is a commonly treated theme of popular prints as well as straw boxes and rolling-pins. The seaman's life was one long series of homecomings and departures so it is easy to understand the popularity of this sentimental motif, especially in the old days of sail, when a voyage might sometimes last for several years and when the perils of the deep reflected these tremendous ocean-crossings. This 19th century wool picture is the work of an English sailor.

55

Glass painting depicting the square-rigged Belgian three-master *Sainte Aldegonde* with all sails set. Attributed to Carolus Weyts, *c.* 1863.

broadside views of all the warships in the Fleet, parts of ships to cut out and glue together and scenes of famous sea-fights. The engravers are touchingly ignorant of technicalities, but the effects their woodcuts achieve are pleasant enough. They are close relations of that whole category or popular art which includes folders depicting battles at sea or deeds which won the Empire, playing cards, certificates of various more or less official descriptions issued by clubs and Friendly Societies and, stemming from the latter, printed certificates for those who have crossed the Line.

In this tradition are the celebrated Japanese prints from Nagasaki, an art-form which persisted from the mid-17th until the second half of the 19th century. Nagasaki being the only harbour open first to European and later to American ships, Japanese artists isolated in their island were so struck by the unusual shape of these foreign vessels and by the strange costume of their crews that they felt it vital to portray what they had seen, spreading the pictures abroad to let others know what they had seen and felt. The prints are naïve, pulled on cheap paper and with an often lengthy explanatory text to accompany them. Among them the arrival of the first English steam-ship to Japan is shown in black and white most picturesquely. Used only to junks, the artists were so overwhelmed by all this machinery that they minutely described every part of the boat, explaining what it was used for and its size in somewhat ludicrous prose. This popular art-form was used for propaganda and, most

effectively for political indoctrination, being copied for the same purpose by the Chinese on the intervention from time to time of the European Powers with their combined squadrons.

In the days of such artists as Lebreton and Morel Fatio, and between 1830 and 1840, woodcuts of nautical subjects reached their peak, so successful in fact were they they were promptly and shamelessly copied line for line in breach of all copyright with merely a change of flag on the part of the plagiarist. Thus the shipping advertisements appearing in the American press from 1850 onwards use cuts originally engraved twenty years earlier in Europe and particularly in France. This has, however, always been the case with successful mass-circulation illustrations on religious or sentimental themes with popular appeal which are taken over by each country by a simple change of uniform or flag.

However, it now seems appropriate to make a special place for a great American illustrator, forefather of modern Pop Art, in the days before photography had come into its own and when the popular artist had, thanks to a new romantic and realistic style, to be able to depict excitement and drama. The person concerned was N. Currier, Lithographer and Publisher of No. 2 Spruce Street, New York, whose productive period extends from 1834, when the west was still wild and woolly and Texas belonged to Mexico, to 1888, the golden age of the machine in the United States. This great publisher put his name to some 700 engravings, of which 300 are devoted to that supremely adventurous element the sea.

Among these 'colored engravings for the people' sold at popular prices from 5 to 25 cents—and never more than 3 dollars!—are to be found all the favourite themes of the mass-circulation illustrated magazines. The publisher himself defined them as 'views, political cartoons and banners, portraits, historical prints, certificates, moral and religious prints, sentimental prints, prints for children, country and pioneers, home scenes, humor, lithographed sheet-music, Mississippi River prints, railroad prints, piracy, emancipation, speculation, house prints, sporting events. . . .'

Sailing card advertising the departure of the Yankee clipper *Stars and Stripes*, Robert Cleaves, Commander, *c.* 1860.

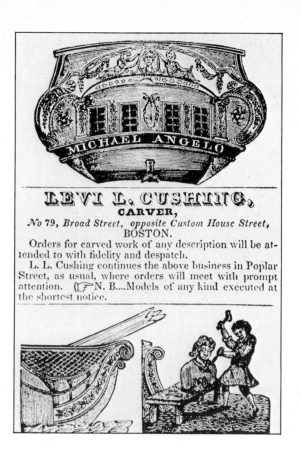

Advertisement from an early 19th century Boston newspaper proclaiming the skill of the carver Levi L. Cushing. The name, Michael Angelo, cut on the transom is doubtless intended to give prospective customers an inkling of the carver's talents.

As far as the marine prints are concerned, one cannot do better than to quote from the preface of a book published some years ago and devoted to Currier and his partner Ives.

> In the Marine prints, just as in the pictures of other phases of national life at that time, Currier and Ives gave the American people what they wanted and succeeded in handing down to us true and vivid pictures of those great ships and the hardy men who sailed them.

It must be admitted that the men whom Currier and Ives commissioned for their marine prints were artists of some ability, and particular notice should be taken of such names as Charles Parsons, James E. Butterworth, J. B. Smith and Son and D. McFarlane. The earliest lithograph to achieve best-seller status depicted the wreck of the steamboat *Lexington* in Long Island Sound on the night of 13 January 1840. Copious captions accompanied the plate and swarmed with those dramatic details for which the readers were so avid. This was, of course the age of the Mysteries of London and Paris and the popular music-hall songs of such entertainers as Macky. It is obviously impossible to list in this book by name all the prints published by this famous firm, but it includes portraits of such famed clipper-ships as the *Nightingale, Red Jacket, Dreadnought, Comet, Great Republic* and Donald McKay's masterpiece *Flying Cloud*; nautical events such as the sea battles of the War of 1812, the victory of the schooner *America* at Cowes in August 1851, or the Great Ocean Yacht Race from Sandy Bay to the Needles from 11 December 1860 to 25 December 1865, between the three statuesque square-rigged schooners *Henriette, Vesta* and *Fleetwing*; or again shipwreck or dramatic whaling incidents.

Some of these fine popular engravings now fetch several hundred dollars each, and although this type of picture was copied in a number of countries it does not diminish the importance of Currier and Ives as pioneers in this field, both by the sheer scale of their production and by their keenness as publishers.

To conclude this survey of marine prints I would like to remind the reader of two categories, the one—postage stamps—already established, the other—post-cards—on the way to so being.

Marine philately is far richer than is generally believed. Thematic collections show how early nautical subjects were used on stamps. Obviously the net must be spread widely enough to include antiquity, voyages, discoveries, distant islands, maps, and ship-building within the theme before coming down to our own day with stamps depicting contemporary ships, generally issued to mark their launching. Nor does philatelic interest stop there. Postmarks and covers have a nautical interest even when the stamps themselves are of a non-nautical subject. For example, there may be letters despatched from post-offices on liners during their maiden voyages or else letters covered by the postmarks of all the great ports of the world as month after month they chased those elusive wanderers, the sailors to whom they were addressed.

The post-card is still with us and still flourishes. Although it is less than a hundred years old, this does not prevent its inclusion nowadays in the charmed circle of things which people collect. Any shot taken in a harbour or on board ship has a vast interest. Photographers seem to have had to an unusual degree the art of combining picturesque detail within the general composition. Every post-card is a miniature painting with plenty to find under the magnifying-glass. In addition, up to 1914, they were produced by a process particularly suited to short runs and known as 'phototypie' which gives them a fine grain very like the surface of an original photographic print. Furthermore, the messages written on the cards, the postmarks, the news they give of life at sea are all small pieces for the jigsaw of social history. Obviously, as with postage stamps so with post-cards fine collections have been built round a chosen theme such as the fighting fleet or the merchant service, fishing or yachting, port life, voyages or life at sea.

Seals with marine subjects

If the postmarks of the world's great ports set the mind wandering with dreams of voyages and adventure at sea, this is almost their sole merit for the design of most of them is particularly austere, comprising as it does the name of the post-office and the date in the most utilitarian of lettering. The same cannot be said of the seals—wrongly termed stamps—of the departments of state concerned with the merchant service and the fighting fleet. There is the added advantage, as well, that aside from the impression on paper, the seal which made it is a finely engraved object.

Seals go back to Classical Antiquity, when the Romans used the stones in their rings—*annuli signatorii*—to seal their letters. Theodoric, King of the Goths, sealed his letters with the incised pommel of his sword. At first only such symbols as the lyre, the anchor or the trophy of arms were engraved on these seals; portraits were to come later.

The term seal is in any case a mediaeval name and its used now spread to church and state as a means of authenticating documents by the impress of a mark upon wax and the wax so marked is what is really meant by the word 'seal'. Later, wax seals were customarily reserved for letters patent and other official documents to which particular importance was designed to be given. In government offices the seal became the ink-stamp. Officials wishing to validate any written document would stamp and sign it. Finally, and side by side with the ink stamp, came the dry stamp demanding a double seal, one cut in intaglio the other half in relief so as to leave its impress on the paper. However, these functional engraved plates, mounted in a punch are utilitarian and graceless things.

Let us therefore return to copper seals which seem to have originated in the Middle Ages.

Whether intended for use with wax or with ink, the seal was, unlike medallions or tokens, engraved in intaglio and seldom any other shape than oval or round bearing the name of the government service or department, commercial company or club round the rim and in the centre some appropriate decorative design, a ship, an anchor or some other marine emblem, or else a coat of arms. The latter are generally to be found upon the personal seals of high dignitaries granted the right to use their private monograms in the exercise of their duties, as for example, Cardinal Richelieu and various High Admirals of France.

Sometimes there would be a change of government and there would be delays in providing the various departments with their new paraphernalia. Seals had to

Three faces of a triangular seal of the period of the French Revolution which bear philosophic and nautical subjects. Translated, the legends round them read: *Liberty makes me faithful; Hope sustains me; Where will it take me?*

Various official French seals. From left to right and from top to bottom: Marine Impériale (Second Empire); Secrétariat d'État à la Marine (Third Republic); Régates de Cancale (late 19th century); Service des vaisseaux du Roi (French Monarchy); Inscription Maritime, Quartier de Lannion (Third Republic); Trésorier des Invalides, Port d'Antibes (Third Republic); Bureau des Revues et Armements, Saint Servan (Napoleon); another example of the seal of the Inscription Maritime showing the attempt to erase the Imperial eagle after the restoration of the Bourbons.

Reverses of two commemorative silver medallions: *right*, Louis, Duke of Vendôme, General of the Galleys, 1746; and, *left*, General de Tessé, Grandee of Spain and General of the Galleys of France, 1750.

continue to be used in the transitional period, but with the device of the old regime altered or erased. This is what happened to the stamps of the Navy Department when the Napoleonic eagles were gouged out after the restoration of the Bourbons.

Through these stamps the stories of regimes and institutions can be followed and vanished corporations can be resurrected, such as the fishmongers of the various great ports whose seal bore a fish. Similarly, naval archeologists can rediscover the image of the famous *kogge*—the most popular type of merchant vessel of the period—upon the seals of the Hanse towns. The ownership stamps which the major departments of state affixed to books, plans, drawings and maps sometimes help to establish the dates upon which they were received. However, in any case these seals, ancestors of the hated rubber stamp of today, are always finely engraved and give the collector the chance to build up notable thematic collections as his fancy dictates.

Private seal of Colonel Edward Pope, first Collector of Customs, New Bedford, 1789–1801.

Silver commemorative medals: Chamber of Commerce of the Department of the Charente-Inférieure (*left*); Chamber of Commerce, La Rochelle, 1771 (*upper centre*); Académie Royale de Marine, 1778 (*lower centre*); Reverse of medal on left (*right*).

61

Medals and tokens

The branch of numismatics concerned with coins and medallions is too closely connected with the depiction of nautical subjects to be ignored in a book such as this. Scholarly studies by many authors have always included examples of this sort. Most of the world's great maritime museums, and especially those at Paris and Greenwich, hold collections of naval commemorative medallions. These are historic items of which anyone might be proud.

They comprise pieces of metal struck to commemorate either an actual event or its anniversary. In the commonly accepted sense of the term, medallions also include medals awarded as prizes in competitions or as awards for gallantry or long service and good conduct.

All these medals and medallions are of concern to the collector for they impinge in part upon nautical matters: equally falling within this same category are the engraved metal discs which certain classes of harbour or dockyard worker wore fastened to a chain round his neck and which served as security passes.

Religious medallions should be excluded. They may be characterised as decorative and prophylactic and without historical interest.

In Europe medallions were first struck in the 15th century, in the precious metals gold and silver and roughly the same size as the largest coins. The earliest French specimen commemorates Charles VII's final victory in 1461 over the English armies of occupation which are seen taking to their ships. Medallions are pleasant things and grew in demand so that in the end they were moulded to the detriment of the quality of engraving. Only at the Renaissance were medallions once more struck with a more regular and delicate design.

Soon governments acted against the spate of commemorative medals. In most countries organisations were set up to regulate the design, the legend and the number of these minor works of art which were issued. In France, the Académie des Inscriptions et Belles-Lettres, founded in 1663, has this duty to act as the legal depository for such things. On the one hand the Mint thus obtained the exclusive monopoly of striking all medals, while on the other the State could by these means ensure that the medals so struck bore nothing seditious. These arrangements have had the advantage if nothing else, of preserving complete collections of medals in the various mints so that it is possible today to follow the course of history, and especially naval history, as a series of great events each depicted visually with the appropriate date and legend.

The variety of subject-matter so treated is amazing and comprises not merely war and battle, but peaceful voyages, with medals to commemorate the institution of new shipping routes, important anniversaries, the endowment of institutions etc.

Then there are the campaign medals awarded to naval officers and ratings which bring back a whiff of the wars and expeditions in which they were involved—the Baltic, the Black Sea, Mexico, Tonkin. . . .

Tokens, or counters, were originally pieces of metal, ivory, bone or shell used, as their name implies at a time of illiteracy when few were able to read either letters or figures, to perform mathematical calculations. Even Pythagoras himself found it easier to use counters, and similarly the beads of the abacus retained their popularity through the ages.

The use of tokens survives today in that species of paper money and counters used in some games to mark the score and pay at the end, or which waiters in some restaurants use as a private system of accounts at the till.

It is hard to settle precisely when tokens were first issued although it was no doubt some time during the 16th century. They were then given as rewards, as wages or as gifts for services rendered. They were often struck in very considerable quantities. For example at the New Year festivities in 1683 Louis XIV ordered the distribution of eight hundred gold and twenty-six thousand silver tokens to his entourage! It became the custom to strike them annually to commemorate the historic events of the year. Nor was their issue confined to the State; town corporations and tradesmen's guilds each had their own tokens. Our interest lies in matters nautical and these are represented by tokens issued by harbour authorities, insurance companies, workers' guilds, all of the greatest historical interest when taken, of course, together with the official tokens struck to commemorate naval battles, appointments as General of the

Above and *below* Tokens issued to shareholders attending the annual general meeting of the Compagnie Générale Transatlantique.

Galley, etc. As a whole they make up a chronological series of souvenirs in pictures. The legends engraved upon them often express some sort of message or philosophy which the token itself is able to spread harmlessly but efficiently.

There are also tokens issued by some companies to those attending their annual general meetings as a stimulus to the shareholders to attend, and this practice continues.

Most tokens are round and struck in the same way as coins. Some are however octagonal and some rare specimens are engraved. Many tokens seem to have spent a busy life in pockets or purses since they are as worn as any coins. Clearly this is both because they could in fact be used as money and also, as many experts have been at pains to point out, because of the prestige which they conferred upon their possessors. A token received as a reward distinguished a man as much as a club-badge does nowadays, and no doubt people got just as much enjoyment in producing and passing them round at social occasions. A reminder: the obverse of a medallion or token is the side which has the head or the subject engraved upon it, the reverse (*vulgo* tails) is the other.

As in the case of medals, it was not long before the Mints acquired the sole right to strike tokens, which enables us to see a complete run of them today.

III
Nautical bibliography

The good seaman's library

This chapter will come as a surprise to those of my readers who think of nautical antiques predominantly as things used on board ship, as models or as an object evocative of the romance of the high seas. However, I propose to confine myself here to printed and manuscript books, documents and maps, the latter, with their visual and decorative elements, being the only objects (together with ships' log-books) which some people will admit to their collections.

Nevertheless it is only by the aid of books and manuscript material that the objects of the daily life of the seaman come to life in any real sense.

All collectors are something of historians and ethnologists, for it is inevitable that they should make every effort to discover the history of the objects they so passionately amass. In any case too many people now enthusiastically collect books about the sea for me not to feel tempted to interest my readers in the subject.

Good nautical libraries are, however, far less common than good collections of nautical items. A library is the work of a life-time, perhaps even of several generations, and if you have not had the good fortune to be able to loot the shelves of a family library or to have been given some sort of introduction to the art of the book, you may find yourself bewildered by the sheer numbers and variety of books about the sea. In order to know what books to keep and what criteria to apply, one must have recourse to some specialist in the field, even though he himself may be dismayed by the problems of classification faced by large libraries or official archives. As far as the present chapter is concerned, I have had the good fortune to enjoy the guidance of heads of rare book collections, archivists and palaeographers whose love of the sea has not been overridden by a love for printed books or manuscripts. Thus the whiff of salt air is far stronger than the dusty smell of paper when they invite us to take a trip among the folios, incunables and palimpsests which treat of nautical matters.

Books about the sea

From the very beginning sailors have been drawn towards books as a means both of enshrining their adventures and discoveries and of imparting their knowledge to those whose profession is seamanship. Sometimes both types of book run together, at others they are separate. Accounts of voyages seldom lack practical instruction, while instruction itself may be illustrated from personal experience.

The earliest printed works on navigation appeared in the 16th century in the Low Countries and in England, both sea- and freedom-loving countries which did not try to keep secret their sea-routes like the Spaniards and Portuguese. The first books to be printed were the ones which would be the most useful—portulans, pilots or rutters, ancestors of our modern sailing instructions—and they guided the mariner along the long sea-routes to the East and West Indies and the Newfoundland Banks.

Simultaneously, since trade and navigation are often synonymous, appeared codes of practice and collections of laws, regulations and customs to guide the merchant mariner through the shoals of the law.

These, as one might well imagine, were followed almost at once by treatises on navigation, ship-handling and ship-building, that inseparable trio which comprise the main concern of the seaman.

As knowledge expanded, books became outdated and new ones were needed to demolish false theories, put the finishing touches to new ones and publicise the most recent inventions. But the intellectual disciplines to which seamen are subject are as wide seemingly as the oceans themselves, and the infinite variety of subjects to which seamen have devoted their lives and their talents is an established fact.

Law books

First editions of Royal Orders in Council, Decrees and Regulations were published in generous formats, handsomely printed in legible type and with engraved head- and tail-pieces, often incorporating nautical motifs.

Booksellers' catalogues list Orders in Council somehow like this, for example:

ORDERS IN COUNCIL: 7 items dated 27 September 1776 bound in one vol., contemporary half-sheep, mottled. Raised bands. Paris, 1776, 4to.
1. Royal Order in Council to regulate the administration of the Fleet and Dockyards, 160 pp.   2. To regulate the duties of naval officers at sea, 23 pp.   3. Port officers, 4 pp.   4. Disbandment of the administrative officers' and naval clerks' department, 4 pp.   5. Establishment of Commissioners in General and Ordinary for Ports and Harbours, 8 pp.   6. Establishment of Commissioners and Syndics for naval recruitment, 4 pp.   7. Establishment of a Controller of the Navy, 4 pp.

However, collected volumes of such Orders are rarely collections of the individual first editions but subsequent reprintings of their texts. An early and well-known example of this is the fundamental work on the Spanish maritime code, the *Consulado de mar*, printed at Valencia in 1539.

Some works of law and custom require illustrations to make them intelligible. Typical of these is Duhamel du Monceau's *Traité des Pêches*. It is illustrated by the copper-plate engravings of the period (that of Diderot's *Grande Encyclopédie*) which are all of a high quality.

Dictionaries of sea terms

Dictionaries generally consist of an alphabetical list of nautical terms with their definitions and some examples of their use. Graphic illustrations are only incorporated in the 19th century, and even then only as a supplement to the printed text. Typical are those in each volume of Bonnefoux and Paris' dictionary (Volume I, 'Sail': Volume II, 'Steam'), where they comprise folding plates at the end of each. The plates themselves are a mass of little line drawings reproduced by copper-plate engraving.

Among the best-known dictionaries are: Willaumez' *Dictionnaire de marine* (Paris: 1820); Lescallier's *Vocabulaire des termes marines anglais et français* (Paris: 1777); Falconer's *An Universal Dictionary of the Marine* (London: 1769), and Roding's *Dictionnaire universelle de marine, allemand, danois, suedois, hollandais, anglais, français, italien, espagnol et portugais* (Hamburg: 1794).

The arts and sciences of the mariner

Etchings, steel- and copperplate-engravings all achieve a clarity of definition which the earlier and clumsy woodcut strove in vain to equal until the 19th century.

However, the disadvantage of the first three intaglio processes lies in the fact that plates and text cannot be printed together, since printing from movable type is a relief process. The copper-plate necessitates special equipment, its own ink and press. These separately printed plates were inserted in the book without a great deal of reference to the text they served to illustrate and this sometimes impairs their usefulness. Woodcuts, employing the relief process are a different matter altogether. They can integrate text and illustration and were used from the very beginnings of printing from movable type until the start of the 20th century.

The earliest treatises on navigation (G. Fournier's *L'Hydrographie,* 1643; R. Norman's *The Safeguard of Sailors,* 1590; Bleau's *The Light of Navigation,* 1612) contain woodcuts placed in juxtaposition to the nautical matters which they illustrate. It must, however, be said that the thickness of the line sometimes makes it difficult to interpret the cut, since the technique of engraving with the grain of the wood was far from its perfection. It may also be presumed that the engravers enjoyed displaying the contrast of black and white provided by the genre and indulged the vagaries of personal style.

The need accurately to depict technical detail enforced the copper-plate upon the 18th century as is the case with Nicolas Bion's *Instruments*, Berthoud's *Chronométrie* and Borda's *Cercle à réflexion*. However, when it came to head- and tail-pieces or cuts for the title page, these were still engraved in wood so that text and illustration could be integrated and both taken from an identical pull of the same press.

Title page of Father Fournier's
Hydrographie, 1643.

Hydrographic works

Books on hydrography are basically of two sorts: collections of maps and charts, and manuals of pilotage.

Although the collections of maps are often in a large folio format, they cause a raised eyebrow when compared with modern charts, since they are essentially works of reference and do not appear to allow a detailed course to be plotted upon them with pencil, protractors or parallel rulers. For that purpose seamen have since Elizabethan times taken to sea large sheets of paper unmarked except for the lines of latitude and longitude. Known nowadays as plotting sheets, these as it were unsullied canvases would take the daily note of the recorded position. Some bound or loose collections of maps contain individual charts which may have the north-pointing arrow at an angle to the page so as to allow the drawing to remain within the rigorous limits imposed by the format. This arrangement can be found in a number of works such as *Neptune François, ou recueil de cartes marines levées et gravées par ordre du Roi* (Paris; 1693), *English Pilot* (London; 1732), *Neptune Oriental* . . . .

These collections most often aim merely to identify various countries and to give a limited number of bearings. However, when it comes to harbours, then they run to very considerable detail and give soundings, warnings of dangers to be encountered and the like.

When the huge double-elephant folio maps came on the scene in the early 19th century, these collections bowed out. Printed from copper-plate blocks, the map now became a real instrument of navigation upon which positions could be noted precisely and courses marked. Since the plates themselves were dated, the various naval hydrographic departments were constantly improving and up-dating these charts in the light of fresh knowledge.

Despite this, plenty of seamen, particularly in the coasting trade, made do with a single 'rutter' containing charts of the areas in which they normally sailed. For his landfalls and making harbour he had his pilot-books. These latter derive from the portulan which was not, as is commonly believed, the chart of the mediaeval seaman, these being called 'maps on vellum'. In fact the portulan is a handbook of coastal navigation and as such describes the shoreline and its approaches. It contains rough sketches of harbours and anchorages and those features of the coastline which, seen in silhouette and from far out to sea, enable the sailor to spot the position of the entrance to a port or the mouth of a bay. Admittedly seamen in those days needed a strong dash of luck to identify the shifting shadow of the shoreline. That is why the crudities of the woodcut gave way in the 18th century to the silhouette of the coastline engraved in the corners of sea-charts, themselves engraved on copper-plates.

The pilot-book (or nautical manual) became a handbook detailing the dangers, the currents, tides and port-customs.

Books on naval tactics, ship-handling and ship-building

By the middle of the 18th century books in these classes had become quite common and with them those splendid large engraved plates so superbly decorative in themselves. The working drawings in treatises on naval architecture by such writers as Chapman, Charnock, Furttenbach, Lescallier, Duhamel du Monceau or Vial de Clairbois are of such exceptional historical and artistic value that in recent years they have been re-issued in facsimile editions.

Engravings of signal-flags and ensigns printed in black and white were coloured by hand in the regulation shade so as to be easily recognised.

Before the invention of colour printing, hand colouring was of long standing. Many an atlas or collection of voyages has had its plates touched and coloured which gives them so much of their value.

Books of voyages

By the end of the 18th century the great voyages of scientific discovery round the world had begun with such men as Bougainville, Byron, Cook, Vancouver or Krustenstern. These voyages were systematically financed by all the major sea-powers. The scientific instruments at the disposal of their seamen allowed highly accurate surveys to be made from now on and we shall see how at that particular point in time

Title page of the narrative of William Schouten, who discovered Cape Horn in 1616, published after he had completed his voyage round the world.

66

De architectura navale (1629), by Joseph Furtennbach, was the first
treatise on naval architecture to be published in the German language.
A line for line translation of the title-page reads as follows
Architectura navalis
or concerning the
Building
of ships used on the high seas
and in coastal waters.
This treatise shows in simple style the
certain and sure methods which must be used to
build gallies, galleasses, galliots, brigantines, feluccas, frigates,
liudos, barkettes, piattas as well as nefs, polacres, tartanes,
barcones, caramuzzales, and standard barks, such as
you may meet with in times of peace and war
in all sea-ports.

Joseph Furtennbach, De architectura navale, Plate 10. The author's
caption, referring the reader to the key letters in the cut, is written in
the conversational style belonging to such treatises.

Left: Title-page of *Arte de Navegar* (1545) by Pedro de Medina and the finest Spanish work on navigation. The author, who was with Cortes, may be said to have been the founder of the literature of seamanship. He was entrusted by the King with the examination of pilots and sailing-masters for the West Indies, taught navigation and was held in high esteem as a cosmographer.

Although very popular with the successors of Columbus, it was not the earliest book on navigation, the honour belonging to a Portuguese work published in 1506, *Regimento do Astrolabio et do Quadrante* prepared by Prince Henry's pilots from the mathematical tables drawn up by Abraham Ben Samuel Zacute of the school of Salamanca in 1496.

The full-page woodcut map in the text of Medina's book may be taken as embodying the results of Spanish discoveries up to 1545.

Right: A typical woodcut from the *Arte de Navegar*.

A pamphlet by Captain George St-Lo which continues within, 'Proposing a sure method for encouraging navigation and raising qualified seamen for the well manning their Majesties fleet on any occasion in a month time . . .'

Consulado de mar (Valencia, 1539), one of the most famous collections of the customary law among seamen in the Eastern Mediterranean and an important source for the modern law of the sea.

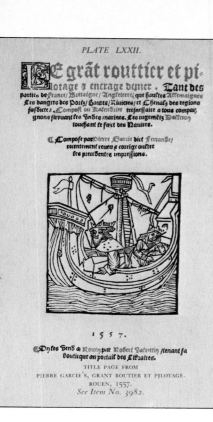

PLATE LXXII.

TITLE PAGE FROM
PIERRE GARCIE'S, GRANT ROUTIER ET PILOTAGE.
ROUEN, 1557.
See Item No. 3982.

Le grand routier de Garcie (Rouen, 1557). One of the earliest books on navigation, it relates for the most part to the English Channel. The author is also known as Pierre Ferrande. The woodcut on the title page shows the voyage of a king and a queen while other woodcuts in the text depict headlands, coastlines, etc.

Joost Hartgerts, *Oost Indische Voyagien* (Amsterdam, 1648: 16 parts in 1 vol.). So rare that it is virtually unknown to bibliographers, this extraordinary collection of voyages is sometimes called the Dutch De Bry or the Dutch Hulsius, for in beauty of execution and in intrinsic interest, it rivals both of those famous collections.

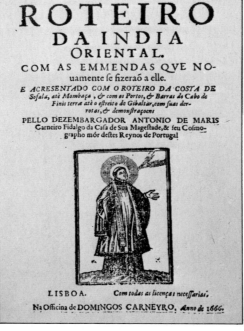

Antonio Maris Carneiro, *Roteiro da India Oriental* (Lisbon, 1666). This book, compiled by the Chief Cosmographer of Portugal, contains detailed instructions to pilots for the voyage from Portugal to India and back.

navigational instruments take the shape in which we know them. This is the age of timekeepers and quadrants. Purely geographical survey of unknown lands always went hand in hand with work in the fields of ethnology, botany and zoology undertaken by the scientists who were members of the expedition. Alexander von Humboldt's *Voyage aux régions équinoxiales du nouveau Continent* (1812) is typical of the sort of work which they produced.

On their return from such an expedition, the crew not only landed with a fabulous collection of charts, plans and surveys of the area which they had explored, but also with sketchbooks full of drawings of the natives, of plants and animals, of local scenery, of scenes of daily life. All this mass of drawings, texts and figures cried out for publication and thus accounts of the voyages of Cook, La Pérouse and Dumont d'Urville appeared with their engraved plates and separate volumes of maps.

Naturally publications like these were translated and re-issued in several different countries.

If we are to be comprehensive we must not forget the 16th century forerunners of these discoverers. Although less known, they are no less essential sources of

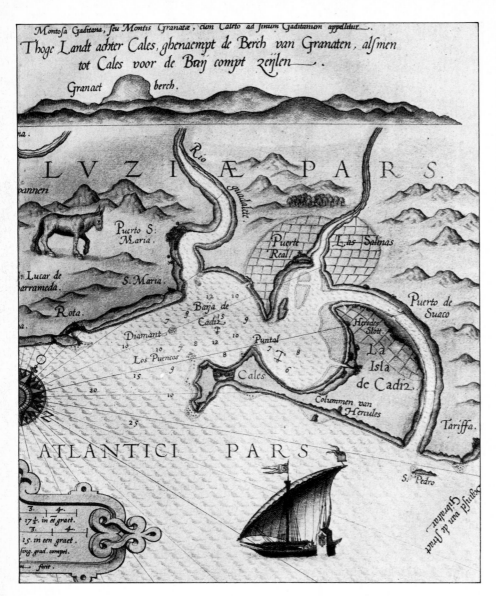

Montosa Gaditana, seu Montis Granatæ, cum Caleto ad sinum Gaditanum appellitur.

Thoge Landt achter Cales, ghenaempt de Berch van Granaten, alsmen tot Cales voor de Bay compt zeijlen.

Granaet berch.

LVZIÆ PARS.

Puerto S: Maria.

S. Maria.

Rio Guadalete

Puerte Real

Las Salinas

Puerto de Suaco

Lucar de barrameda

Rota.

Baja de Cadiz

Diamant

Los Puencos

Puntal

Cales

La Isla de Cadiz

Herodes Slott

Columnen van Hercules

Tariffa.

ATLANTICI PARS

S. Pedro

Mont van de Strat Gibraltar

This chart, taken from Wagenaer's *Speculum nauticum,* showing landfalls in the Bay of Cadiz, allows us to appreciate the knowledge and hydrographic symbols of that time. Comparing it with modern charts of some four centuries later one notices particularly how seamen of the 16th century needed the faculty almost of second-sight if they were to make use of such charts since artistic licence always overrode hydrographic accuracy. The coastline depicted above the plan is especially revealing of the aims of the artists employed on the *Speculum.* Nevertheless these first manuals for the coasting seaman were a decisive step in the direction of modern hydrography. A start had to be made somewhere!

Title page of the *Speculum nauticum* published in English translation as *The Mariner's Mirrour* and especially interesting in showing a complete range of the navigational instruments used by the seaman at the end of the 16th century. Published between 1584 and 1585, Lucas Jansz Wagener's work is the first sea atlas and coastal pilot from Gibraltar to Bergen. Manuals for coastal pilots were first written by hand and only printed after Wagener's book had been published. The latter is of exceptional quality, so many 'rutters' being no more than a series of very sketchy coastlines and views of anchorages. In the 17th century, charts were often inserted in pilots' manuals.

information for land and sea exploration. Among the most celebrated are Richard Hakluyt's *The Principal Navigations* (London; 1598-1600), Georg Spilbergen's *Speculum orientalis occidentalisque* (Geelkercken; 1619) and Jan Huyghen van Lintschoten's *Navigatio ac itinerarium in orientalum sive Lusitanorum Indiam* (Amsterdam; 1596).

Archives and manuscript material

In the widest sense, archives comprise all those original documents which form the basis for historical research. Logically, then, our survey should have taken them first since books are, or ought always to be, based upon them. Behind the few hundred pages of a book are in fact thousands of individual documents analysed and read at the cost of long and arduous research. Nobody but a professional could hazard a voyage through these countless documents from the past. The select list of nautical writers which I have provided above will enable lovers of the sea to build their knowledge of its history upon sound foundations, and if I now broach the subject of naval archives it is not so much to rouse a historical vocation as to help collectors on the one hand to identify interesting documents which may come their way, and on

Teerste Deel vande

PARS PRIMA

Speculum nauticum super navigatione maris Oc
cidentalis confectum, continens omnes oras mari-
timas Galliæ, Hispaniæ & præcipuarum partiu
Angliæ, in diversis mappis maritimis comprehensu
vna cum vsu & interpretatione earundem, accurata
diligentia concinnatū, & elaboratū per Lucam Iohan-is
Aurigarium.

Spiegel der Zeevaerdt, vande navigatie der Westersche
zee Innehoudende alle de Custen van Franckrijck, Spaig-
nen, en tprincipaelste deel van Engelandt, in diuersche
zee caerten begrepen, met den gebruijcke van dien,
nu met grooter naerstic heijt bij een vergadert,
en geprachzeert Doer Lucas Ianß Wagenaer

Cum Priuilegio ad   decennium, Reg. Ma.tis
et Cancellarie   Brabantie.
1. 5.   8 3.

Ioannes à Doetecum Fecit.

Ghedruct tot Leyden by Christoffel Plantijn.

71

the other start to research into particular points concerning items in their possession—their origin, provenance and the authenticity of the signatures or other marks which they bear.

In any case, apart from these strictly utilitarian reasons of immediate interest which bring the collector to consult naval archives, there is a very special interest in the archives themselves which are real collector's items themselves when they comprise such original manuscript material as ship's log-books or personal reminiscence or depositions. For this reason I shall first describe the sort of material which is to be found in the principal official naval archives before I go on to indicate how varied are the manuscripts of nautical interest which the collector can come to unearth in the course of his forays.

Naval archives

In all the major maritime countries naval records are kept either in one central archive or in a number of provincial depositories. In the case of France there are the five maritime provinces with their headquarters at Cherbourg, Brest, Lorient, Rochefort and Toulon. The documents are those that have survived the chances of war, fire and pillage, and the archival material varies from one depository to the other. Then, certain government departments ancillary to the navy have also preserved their records. Researchers will therefore need a bit of luck and a certain amount of serendipity if they are to light upon the documents they need for their studies. Their task however, will be considerably lightened by those remarkable lists of manuscripts in numerical order, produced by the patient labour of successive curators and their staffs.

Copies of these numbered lists are kept in the Bibilothèque Nationale in Paris and the student would be well advised to consult them before setting off to conduct his researches in one of the great ports.

Whenever you read through these long lists of documents, you are always struck by the care the French Navy took meticulously to catalogue its men and materials, as if it expected from one moment to the next to have to provide a full situation report or an order for general mobilisation was likely to be given at any minute. Yet this is

Head-piece to an 18th century *Ordonnance royale* concerning the Navy. Nowadays their place in France is taken by the *Journal Officiel*. These *Ordonnances* were printed in very small numbers since they were intended only for the information of the Admiralty officials concerned.

Title page and frontispiece of a German seaman's discharge book (*size:* 115 × 185 mm). Through the well-thumbed pages of this little book the adventurous sea-going career of Gerd Seeberg of Bremen may be followed, with the dates and names of the ships in which he served, the duties he performed and the pay which he received. The continuous discharge book which all seamen must carry nowadays is similar in principle. Handed down like holy relics from one generation to the next, such discharge books are the rarest of treasure-trove on the antiquarian bookseller's shelves.

not really so surprising when you look back on European naval history from the 15th to the 20th centuries and see how periods of peace alternate with periods of war with bewildering rapidity.

In such conditions it is no wonder that those responsible for naval recruitment should have kept so jealous an eye upon the seamen whom it had enlisted to ensure that they were within hailing-distance when the fleet needed manning. This underlying concern partly explains the amount of 'bumph' generated by the recruiting department, and it also explains the attempts made to smooth the hard life of the sailor. While certain maritime powers only knew the system of the press-gang, forcible enlistment by recruiting-sergeants not very different from what the merchant service was later to call 'shanghai-ing', in other countries care was taken to train seamen in times of peace aboard the merchant- or fishing-fleets, to ensure that they were paid a living-wage in peace and in war, to see that they were not recalled once they had completed the term of their engagement and to pay retirement pensions through the pensioner's department.

This accounts for the sailor's paybook, a regular private dossier, and also accounts for the existence of ship's articles. The articles kept on the ship concerned carry a description of the vessel, a complete list of all her crew, with names, ages, ranks and terms of service, and notes of the occasions of their being taken on or struck off the articles whether through leave, sickness, death, loss overboard, desertion or capture, together with the consular stamps from all the ports at which the ship called during that particular voyage.

A true copy of the ship's articles, its duplicate, as it were, was kept ashore and remained on file in the recruiting department.

Now that we have got on to the ship's papers, we might briefly glance at the main

Bill of lading of the 18th century Spanish vessel, *La Purisima Concepción*, for a voyage to Honduras.

official and private commercial papers which a ship's captain would keep in his sea-chest. They would comprise the Certificate of Registry, issued in France by the Customs authorities, the Clearance Certificate issued annually by the Customs and validating the Certificate of Registry, the ship's articles, the log-book, the charter-parties (contracts for loading the cargo on board the ship) and bills of lading or detailed lists of the goods in the holds.

The chances of a seafaring life sometimes scatter material of this sort after a vessel has been sold or condemned to the breaker's yard and these are documents of permanent interest to the collector. Other choice items which may appeal are the seaman's book of the merchant service or the pay-book of the naval rating, which provide a real *curriculum vitae* of the mariner. Other fine examples include officers' certificates, the 'tickets' of masters of ocean-going vessels, coasters of various sorts, trawlers or the like.

Apart from such major archives as we have mentioned, the private archives of shipping and insurance companies and municipal and other local record offices also contain matter of nautical interest.

Naval records

Manuscript material, whatever its form, is historical evidence and as such properly belongs to a public record-office. I have shown how these depositories contain handwritten reports, drafts, minutes, both the originals and the copies of correspondence, with now and again a seaman's book or a set of ship's articles bringing up the rear, along with passports, discharge certificates and notes of seamen's debts. However, I suggest that a far more entertaining class of writing is involved when I come to treat of what might be termed 'library' manuscripts, for when freed from the trammels of officialese, their authors can give free rein both to what they have to say and to the way in which they say it, and sometimes they provide a bonus by way of calligraphy or illustration. Furthermore, as none of this has been sifted by engraver, publisher or printer this is all so rich and raw and direct that it

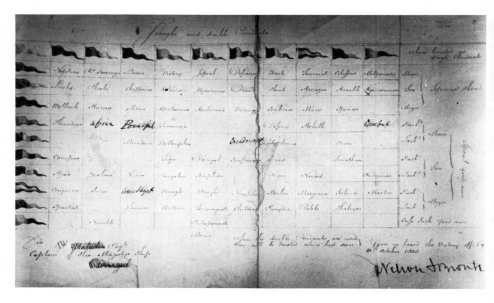

Below: Plate from page 35 of an *Instruction for the Ships of War,* issued in 1793. The caption reads: 'The changes in the motions and positions of the enemy or strange ships are to be made known as follows: viz . . .'. This type of document is particularly valuable in any assessment of naval tactics of the period. The instruction, signed by Admiral Howe, was complemented by two manuscript leaves of 'single and double pendants' (shown right) and of the 'Order of sailing' of the different ships in the British squadron. The manuscript is signed and approved by Admiral Horatio Nelson, from the *Victory*, in Cadiz Roads, on 10 October 1805—eleven days before his death at Trafalgar.

cannot but delight the collector of nautical items.

If you ask what you are likely to find in such manuscripts freed from the constraints of official language and presentation, I can only say that you are likely to find anything from the diaries of cabin-boys on their maiden voyage to the off-the-record confidences of admirals unburdening themselves to whoever may chance to read what they have written.

Some idea of what I mean can be obtained by this brief quotation from the catalogue of the Historical Branch of the Admiralty in Paris:

Private and official diaries of admirals.

Log of the captain of *La Fleur de Lys* (details of armament carried, tactics employed during voyage).

Fighting Instructions for the fleets of the French Republic with signal code for use under way and at anchor.

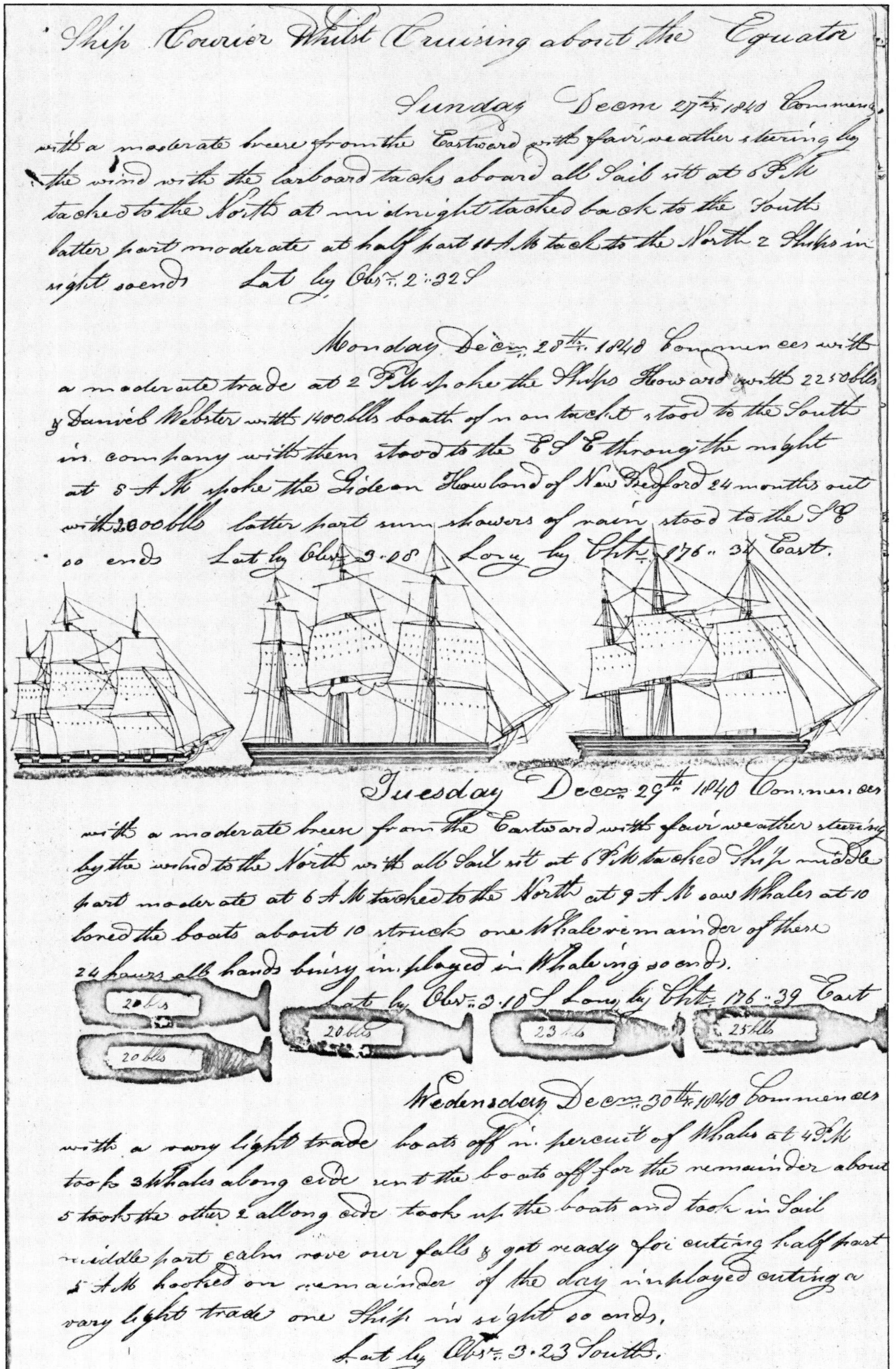

Ship Courier Whilst Cruising about the Equator

Sunday Decem 27th 1840 Commences with a moderate breeze from the Eastward with fair weather steering by the wind with the larboard tacks aboard all Sail set at 8 PM tacked to the North at midnight tacked back to the South latter part moderate at half past 11 AM tack to the North 2 Ships in sight so ends   Lat by Obs. 2:32 S

Monday Decem 28th 1840 Commences with a moderate trade at 2 PM spoke the Ship Howard with 2250 bbls & Daniel Webster with 1400 bbls both of us on tacked stood to the South in company with them stood to the E S E through the night at 8 AM spoke the Gideon Howland of New Bedford 24 months out with 2300 bbls latter part sun showers of rain stood to the S E so ends   Lat by Obs 3:08   Long by Chit. 176:34 East.

Tuesday Decem 29th 1840 Commences with a moderate breeze from the Eastward with fair weather steering by the wind to the North with all Sail set at 8 PM tacked Ship middle part moderate at 6 AM tacked to the North at 9 AM saw Whales at 10 lored the boats about 10 struck one Whale remainder of these 24 hours all hands busy employed in Whaling so ends.   Lat by Obs 3:10 S Long by Chit 176:39 East

20 bbls
20 bbls
20 bbls   23 bbls   25 bbls

Wedensday Decem 30th 1840 Commences with a very light trade boats off in persuit of Whales at 4 PM took 3 Whales along side sent the boats off for the remainder about 5 took the other 2 along side took up the boats and took in Sail middle part calm rove our falls & got ready for cutting half past 5 AM hooked on remainder of the day employed cutting a very light trade one Ship in sight so ends.

Lat by Obs. 3:23 South.

Page from the log of the American whaler, *Courier*, fishing near the Equator, longitude 176°E, in December 1840. The skipper's copperplate epitomises the self-control and inner harmony of these Quaker captains, rough seamen with the faith of another age which they exercised so patiently and painstakingly across the Seven Seas in those endless whale-hunts which only terminated when every cask in the hold was full.

Cruise of the battleship *Le Marengo* (September 1883-August 1884). With photographs.

Ship building. Collection of papers.

Papers written by the naval historian Jal.

Report on the gale damage to the sea-wall at Cherbourg.

Pharamond Blanchard. Sketches of shipping and seascapes made at Saint-Jean d'Ulloa. Pencil sketch books (1837–1838–1839).

Extracts from the log of a cruise with a vindication of occurrences therein.

Engineer's note-book.

Historical sketches.

Log of a voyage from Tahiti to Saint-Malo.

Letters from Jacques Blin, a prisoner at Brest, to Citizen Bourgeaud (1797).

Imperial Navy. Steamships. Log of the Captain, officers and cadets aboard the training-ship *Jean-Bart* (1866).

Sketch for a book entitled *The Sea-Gunner's Catechism.*

Circumnavigation of the World by the Corvettes L'Astrolabe *and* La Zelée *under the command of Monsieur Dumont d'Urville,* written by a naval officer or rating.

Log of the *Diligent* (1733–1735) with sketches, drawings and notes on trade.

The horrible sufferings of the French prisoners from the hands of the English (1798).

Short account of what occurred to the sloop *L'Anémone* two leagues from La Tour des Arabes and of the passengers who escaped massacre (1798).

A new method of calculating the longitude.

Ledgers from slave-ships.

However, I am sure that the following makes some of the most interesting reading:

'Log of my second cruise. When it is over I shall tell you where I went. I cannot do so now. All the same I hope to come home if the Devil doesn't get me. Aboard *L'Océan* off Cap Martin in the Mediterranean, 9 November 1757.' Autograph manuscript of Yeoman of Signals Champclos. His log is followed by notes on the frigate *La Pléiade* and the third-rater *Le Téméraire* and was used as an account book while Champclos was a prisoner-of-war in England in 1759.

Among all these first-hand documents the log-book stands on its own. These are the private journals which supplement so admirably the official logs, the bare and unadorned style of the latter often failing to convey the atmosphere of the voyage to those who were not of the ship's company.

Numbers of these logs have been handed down in the families of their writers and appear in booksellers' catalogues. Here are a couple of well written specimens which would appear to contain interesting material:

Log-book. Cruise of the frigate *La Vestale* to Brasil, Chile, Peru and Bolivia in the years 1829–1830–1831 and 1832, by Monsieur de Nourquer du Camper, Commodore of the Pacific Squadron. Manuscript on paper. 66 leaves. Small folio in modern paper wrappers. Waterstains. Highly interesting manuscript neatly written in a clear hand and illustrated by a number of watercolour sketches.

La Vestale set sail for Rio de Janeiro in June 1829 and arrived there on 4 August after fifty-two days at sea. The author has provided sketches of Cape Frio, Rat Island and the Bay of Rio in which the frigate was moored until 1 September. *La Vestale* then put to sea for the Straits of Magellan. There are descriptions of the coast and the islands, and sketches of Tierra del Fuego and Patagonia made while on course for Valparaiso. There is a very detailed account of General Prieto's attack on the city in December, and of the events leading up to it, including the engagement between the English frigate, *Thetis*, and a Chilean brig-of-war. A chapter on trade follows. In May 1830 they set sail along the coast to Callao and thence on 1 September for Coquimbo. There follows a chapter entitled 'Description of the land visible since 29 September from our anchorage in Coquimbo Bay', and it comprises maps of the bay, sketches of the coastline and drawings of English, Spanish, Chilean and Peruvian shipping. On 11 October they set sail for Valparaiso where *La Vestale* remained at her moorings until March 1831, when she set a course for Callao once more. There is an account of what occurred during the Revolution in Peru in April. On 29 May the frigate *L'Herminie,* Captain Villeneuve-Bargemont, arrived from France to replace *La Vestale*, and on 7 August the latter set sail for Rio de Janeiro. After encountering a violent storm she docked there on 21 September. A detailed description of the Bay is given, and then, on 27 November, they set sail for Brest. The end-leaves of the manuscript are used for a watercolour drawing depicting the wreck of the brig *Les Amis* on the southwesterly side of La Grande-Magne in Haiti, on 1 August 1833.

Log of a voyage to the East Indies. Manuscript on paper. 241 pages. Small folio. Contemporary marbled paper wrappers.

This is an interesting account of the voyage of *Il Granduca de Toscana*, a merchant ship of five hundred tons burthen, with ten cannon and a crew of fifty-one, bound with a cargo for the East Indies. She set sail from Marseilles on 22 February 1787 and returned in March 1790, having called at Leghorn, Cadiz, Trinidad (to which the author devotes a three-page description), Mauritius (where he resided), Cochin (25 December–24 January), then Bombay (where he was involved in a number of engagements in the locality) and finally Pondicherry and Mahé, whence he returned to Europe. Throughout the log-book there are numerous notes on fish seen or caught as well as on birds.

However good the story which some of these logs tell of voyages in merchantmen or cruises aboard warships, none can equal the colour or the feelings aroused by those journals kept aboard two classes of ship—the whalers and the slavers.

In both may be found undiluted adventure. The whalers were often at sea for three years before returning to their home port, every cask brimming with whale-oil, and they experienced not only the hazards of sailing impossible seas, but the surprise of putting in to some port of call in a forgotten corner of the globe. Thus day after day you follow all the ins and outs of the pursuit of the whale—the boat smashed in the jaws of a sperm-whale, the smack of the creature's tail which causes the loss of the best harpooner, the maddened finback ramming a hole in the ship's side. Such occurrences would be illustrated by little marginal ink-drawings, clumsy in all conscience, but accurately and vigorously drawn. Then page after page come the little black silhouettes to show the whales taken or escaped despite a ruthless hunt.

Elsewhere one comes upon the mutineer marooned like some Selkirk or Robinson Crusoe upon some island, with a musket and a bag of tools. Then there are the tallies of full casks and estimates of profit and loss, since the main object of the voyage was to earn a living. Once more the account of day to day life on shipboard is resumed with the scattered note of such items as the cook being given a flogging, or of a mutiny brewing in the ship's company, the bo'sun being put in irons, reduced rations of water being served out and the crew awarded a hundred strokes at the pump night and morning. Sometimes a personal note intrudes and we can see something of the writer's state of mind when the catch is poor. Typical is an entry from the log of the *Minerva Smyth* of New Bedford on a whaling voyage in 1856:[1]

Oh dear, this is very hard times. No whales and no prospect of any . . . . What shall we do, the worms eating up the bottom and the people the top . . . . This day my mother's unfortunate sone John is 36 years of age and when he comes to look and see what an unprofitable and useless life he has led it causes him to blush with shame. 36 yrs. of sin and guilt have done very little for the good of my fellow beings that my place had better been filled by a better man. Yet I feel anxious to linger out a few more years in the hope of there being a change for the better, for I am sure that I cannot easily change for the worse. The greatest trouble with me at present is the want of whales to fill up Mr. Robinson's old sugar-box, the *Minerva Smyth*.

Up to 1815 the slavers lived the same adventurous life as their cousins the whalers. Their logs contain the same humdrum records of storms or flat calms at sea. As they near the Doldrums the voyage seems endless. Water becomes short; scurvy rages below decks and a score of negroes have to be thrown overboard as hopeless cases. Ten strokes of the cat are awarded to a young black for insolence, forty to the ringleader of a group of others.

But after 1815 the slaver's life becomes even harder. Cruising frigates give them chase and then, to gain speed, the ship must be lightened. Often their cargoes are thrown overboard and the most outrageous tricks are played on boarding parties to persuade the officers in charge that the brig is an honest merchantman, although below decks is still heavy with the stench of the two hundred wretches who lived there for weeks chained like beasts.

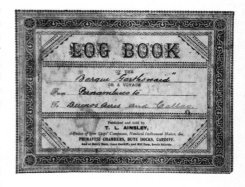

Log of the voyage from Pernambuco to Buenos Aires and then round Cape Horn to Callao, made in the early years of the century by the English sailing-ship *Garthsnaid*.

[1] From the collection of log-books of the Marine Historical Association, Mystic, Connecticut.

IV

Navigational instruments

The pilot's tools: navigating by dead reckoning

When young Jim Hawkins in *Treasure Island* held the old parchment map open, counted ten paces due east, altered course, counted another ten paces due north and discovered where the booty had been hidden, all he was doing was steering by dead reckoning on dry land. But then, the plan of the treasure's hiding place had been drawn by and for seamen.

Once mariners left the shoreline out of sight over the horizon, their first concern was to discover the means of making a safe return to their home port. To this end they observed as best they could the direction in which their ship sailed and the distance which it travelled and for their return journey it was enough to steer the same course and travel the same distance in reverse. Then, as the range of their discoveries widened and these discoveries were mapped, mariners could, by drawing a line between their home port and their port of call, measure the course which they were to steer and the distance which they would have to sail. From then on it was simply a matter of setting sail, trusting that the compass was accurate and that the run of the ship correctly logged, or else there was always the risk, when several days out of sight of land, at best of losing track of one's position or at worst of running on the rocks.

In default of reckoning your position by celestial observation, steering by dead-reckoning (course and distance) was for long the only means available to the seaman. Then latitude could be determined by shooting the sun at noon with the astrolabe and, much later with the advent of the chronometer, the longitude could be measured by a method employing sightings of the stars. Navigation by dead reckoning had become navigation by celestial observation.

In fact, however, you still steer by dead reckoning today, at least when sailing between two fixed points determining the course. Furthermore, in modern ships the bearing is so accurately known and the course so precisely followed, while speed is so exactly shown by the number of revolutions of the screw, that paradoxically, despite all the aids which Decca, radar, sonar, gonio and even space-satellites bring, this primitive method has never been followed so surely.

However, as we have seen, accurate navigation by dead reckoning is a matter of instruments: the compass for direction and the log for speed. Now centuries separate the first fumbling attempts and today's near perfection of these two essential tools for the steersman. I therefore propose to trace the steps in and behind the fascinating story of their development.

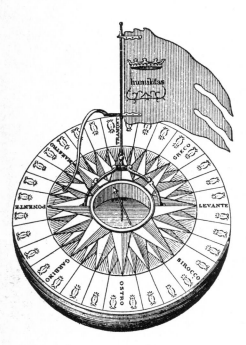

16th century Provençal compass, imported from Venice and deriving directly from Chinese models.

The lodestone, magnetite, in a more or less decorative mount was a piece of pilot's equipment and was used to re-magnetise compass-needles. This richly decorated example belonged to the French Admiral d'Estaing.

18th century heavy bronze dolphin-type binnacle.

Direction finders: the compass

The sea compass seems to have evolved from that legendary steel needle cased in a straw and floated on a bowl of water. With a few magic passes of his lode-stone the pilot would revive the magnetism in the needle before asking it to tell him where the north lay, as it swung on the top of the water, as the vessel wallowed before the next wave tossed her and threatened to spill the bowl completely. Having in that brief span discovered where the north lay, the position of the ship could now be determined by reference to the prevailing wind, supposedly constant, or by the stars, so that a certain course could be steered 'by wind' or 'by stars'.

The ingenuity of some long-forgotten man suggested mounting the needle on a pin. The argument rages as to whether he was the traditional Chinese, or whether, as some would claim, he was a Scandinavian and the compass, brought by the Norsemen to the Mediterranean, travelled to the Far East with the Arab seamen; but the fact remains that after 1200 all treatises on seamanship describe the sea-compass. At that time the needle was mounted on a pin centred in a wooden disc itself divided into 32 parts each of 11° 15′ corresponding with the directions of the main prevailing winds in the Mediterranean—tramontane in the north, Greek in the northeast, sirocco in the southeast. These parts, the points of the compass, remained current until the end of the sail-era, since steering to a half-point was accurate enough for navigation under sail.

The primitive form of compass, inconvenient as it was for use at sea, was in all respects like the compasses made in China up to the end of the 19th century. However, an ingenious craftsman, allegedly from Amalfi, succeeded most cunningly in mounting a thin card on a magnetised needle and the sea-compass was born. Generally the needle would be replaced by a blunt lozenge of steel wire, the longer diagonal marking the north-south axis, either stuck or stitched to the card. This system of mounting

Dry-compass cards. *Above*, the printed card and the parallel arrangement of magnet bars. *Below:* the ultra-light Thompson card, printed on Japan paper, silk thread holding the bar magnets and the cap. *Bottom right:* agate cap and ruby centre-pin to reduce wear.

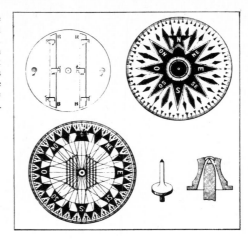

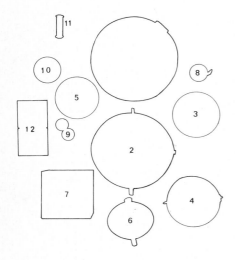

1. Late 19th century large windjammer compass. The card, printed on very light paper, is signed 'John Bruce & Son, Compass-maker and Adjuster—27 Wapping —Liverpool'; 2. Liquid steering compass, central buoyancy support and Cardan suspension. English, unsigned, early 20th century; 3. Small French liquid compass, unsigned early 20th century; 4. Small French dry compass with engraved card. Unsigned, early 19th century; 5. 17th century Chinese sea-compass with astronomic dial; 6. Bearing compass used for land surveying. Italian, signed 'Ferdinando Grazzini' and dated '1747'; 7. Liquid boats-compass with Cardan suspension. Nantes, unsigned; 8. French travelling compass, signed 'Lenoir', with case. 19th century; 9. Small English travelling compass with protective lid. Victorian era; 10. 18th century Chinese compass; 11. 19th century French Navy 15-second hour-glass; 12. 18th century hydrographic compass with wooden case and engraved card.

proved so effective that it was still in use on compasses dating from 1805.

The compass cards were hand-drawn at first and this provided an excuse for such elaborately decorative twirls as sometimes to interfere with their legibility. The accuracy of a scale marked out by hand left much, too, to be desired and from the end of the 17th century they were engraved and printed. In the days of the French monarchy and beyond, the north was always represented by a fleur-de-lys. This symbol was, in the 18th century, the cause of an amusing misunderstanding on a Pacific island. A French expedition found a native tattooed from head to foot with fleur-de-lys and immediately jumped to the conclusion that they had been forestalled by an earlier expedition which had reconciled these noble savages to the French Crown. They were cruelly disappointed. The natives were distinctly unfriendly and the fleur-de-lys they had judged so beautiful as to tattoo its design upon their bodies must have come from a compass card washed ashore from some wreck.

From the 13th century, compass-cards had been mounted in turned wooden bowls with lids. From the 16th century they were set in brass bowls hung on gimbals so as to remain unaffected by the movement of the ship. To make the card even more sensitive the volume of the magnetised steel bar, lozenge or needle was increased, but the excess weight resulted in increased wear by the cap uoon the pin. The head of the latter soon became blunt, thus interfering with the free rotation of the card. To combat this, agate caps and ruby-tipped pins came into use. They did not become worn so easily and provided a highly sensitive card.

Until the 19th century the printed card was glued to a mica disc since this was not liable to distortion; however, attempts were made to find a lighter substitute and these resulted in the invention of what is known as Thompson's card. From a hard stone cap, banded by a brass ring, a network of strong, thin silk threads runs to hold a light crown of aluminium wire on which a silk paper card is glued as well as the magnetic element below it, comprising six or eight steel needles set in parallel groups.

Improvements to the dry compass could hardly be taken further. As we have seen, the only way of improving the directional force of the compass was to increase the size and hence the weight of the needles. It then occurred to manufacturers in order to compensate for this increased weight (and hence increased wear) to enclose the cap in a float and to immerse the card in a liquid which would carry the weight of the whole. The liquid compass was a strange throw-back to the very first sea-compasses—the needles in a straw floating in a bowl of water. First produced at the end of the 19th century, this type of compass was not generally adopted until after World War I. The liquid used is generally a mixture of water and either alcohol or glycerine, to avoid freezing. To compensate for the expansion of the liquid, the base of the bowl is provided with accordeon flanges and the base itself often consists of a round polished glass so that the compass can be lit electrically from below. This in turn requires a transparent card of vegetable ivory or galalith. These compasses are criticised for the slight drag which affects the card when the vessel yaws, but this drag is more than compensated by the directional power of the heavy magnetic component, comprising two heavily magnetised steel bars sealed in brass tubes.

Liquid compasses proved wonderfully efficient on small boats subject to sharp and rapid movements. The popular dory-compass from Newfoundland and Iceland, with its octagonal wooden case, may have started life as a dry compass but soon became a liquid one round 1920. Towards 1870, use of iron in shipbuilding raised the problem of compass deviation which was so considerable as in some cases to amount

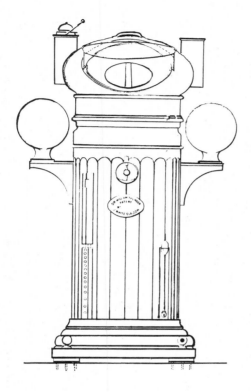

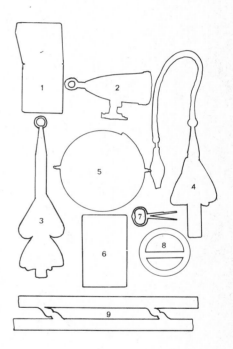

Early 20th century Steering and bearing compass on a Thompson binnacle with correctors and globe lanterns.

to 90°. Some process had to be discovered to reduce or even eliminate it. This method is compass adjustment, which naturally leads to a discussion of the way in which compass cases were suitably mounted aboard ship.

On wooden ships the earliest binnacles were rather like low, glazed cupboards with three compartments, two compasses set side by side and lantern in the middle to illuminate them, set before the helmsman. This developed into an elegant carved wooden stand and this in turn into a gilded bronze affair of which the most widely imitated was the English version of three tritons joined back-to-back.

Since no serious problem of compass deviation was encountered aboard wooden ships, the binnacle was no more than a stand for the compass bowl, but the scale of compensation defined by Lord Kelvin meant that on steel and iron ships the binnacle had a strictly utilitarian role to play. All unnecessary ornament disappeared from the 1880 Kelvin-Bottomley binnacle which was to provide the pattern for all subsequent models. The sober dignity of the teak or mahogany box and the polished brass cover both attract and charm, while on either side of the cover a pair of brackets for oil lamps served to illumine the compass card at night. Compensation was effected by a number of separate elements. The box itself was divided into cells to hold the permanent supply of magnets used to counter the constant deviation caused by the ship's plates. Other compensators in the form of iron globes compensated for the further deviations caused by the ship's course taking her into a fresh magnetic field. The thick brass pedestal, too, contained iron slabs adjustable both as to quantity and height to correct the different deviations occurring in the different latitudes in which the ship sailed. This was called the Flinders Tube after its inventor.

Although the gyro-compass was first used on merchant ships at the beginning of the 20th century, magnetic compasses with their Kelvin binnacles are still kept in

1. Zenith watch with second-hand and rewind-indicator. Issued to destroyers in the early 20th century; 2. Merchant-ship's log-counter. French-made; marked 'E.V.', early 20th century; 3. Walker log with built-in counter. Three dials showing tens of miles, miles and tenths of miles. Only the five-bladed screw turns. Late 19th century. Not in general use; 4. Standard pattern log-screw signed 'Walker Harpoon'; 5. Windjammer's dry compass signed 'G. W. Lyth, Stockholm'; 6. Sliding-gauge of a 19th century stigmo-graph, signed 'W & S Jones, 30 Holborn, London'; 7. Dividers for pricking the chart. 19th century; 8. Circular protractor for plotting on the chart, signed 'F. Robson & Co, 46 Dean Street, Newcastle on Tyne'; 9. Standard pattern parallel rulers in ebony and copper for plotting courses on charts. 19th century, English, unsigned.

One of the earliest patterns of bearing compass. For horizontal sights only.

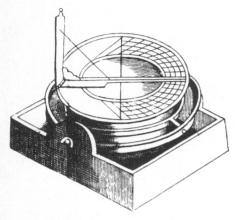

18th century bearing compass allowing star-sights. Cardan mounting but the azimuth circle has yet to be given its central position.

Early 20th century English-made taximeter for bearings. Signed 'Heath & Co. London'.

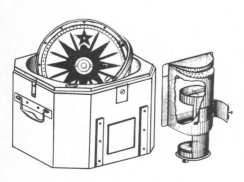

French Navy-pattern liquid boat's compass with oil lantern for illumination, c. 1870.

reserve. Although lit electrically, oil lamps are still there for emergency use.

Some pieces of navigational equipment derive directly from the dry or liquid magnetic compass. Chief of these is the bearing-compass which serves two purposes. When within sight of land it is used to take bearings on sea-marks, known points on the coast in relation to magnetic north. These bearings enable the ship's position to be plotted precisely on the chart. At sea, the bearing compass is employed to measure the angle between a given star and magnetic north, that is, to give the magnetic azimuth. This enables the deviation of the steering-compass to be calculated.

The simplest form of bearing-compass is undoubtedly the one described by the Jesuit, Fournier, in the 17th century in his *Hydrographie*. This is a square box holding the compass, with slits cut in the opposite sides and provided with cross-hairs for sighting. In the 18th century two-armed sight-vanes with cross-hairs and central pivot came into general use as is evidenced by the brass studs to be found in the middle of the compass-glasses of the period. By gently raising and lowering the arm carrying the cross-hairs the observer was able to measure the sun's azimuth from the shadow falling on the compass-card. However, until the 19th century, it was standard practice that when the steering compass was so placed as to prevent a direct sight of the stars to be taken from it, for a sight-vane mounted on a fixed scale of copper to be used for the purpose. A typical example of such an occurrence would be when the steering-compass was mounted in a covered wheelhouse. What is more, a steering-compass is a costly piece of equipment, whereas with the sight-vane and fixed scale placed on the quarter-deck with a clear field for taking sightings of sun and stars, checks with the steering compass allowed deviations in the latter to be detected. These fixed scales are the forerunners of the modern taximeter.

An instrument of the greatest rarity today is the azimuth or vertical compass manufactured in England by Ralph Walker in 1793. Provided with an imposing and highly perfected azimuth circle, this ultra-sensitive compass was supposed to be able to solve the problem of longitude since it was able to measure magnetic variation almost to the tenth of a degree. The process proved ineffectual since so little was known at the time of the laws of magnetic deviation on board ship, and slight as this

Overhead or 'tell-tale' compass, which generally hung above the captain's bunk and enabled him to check the course being steered by his ship without his having to go onto the bridge. This finely decorated 18th century example came from a French warship. The card is marked 'Port de Toulon'.

85

Magnetic compass with bearing-recorder.
Late 19th century, English, signed 'Newton
Brothers Hull'.

Dry compass binnacle on a wooden
mount carved and painted by Jacob
Anderson to represent a young American
sailor. This unusual example was produced
by the famous New York firm of nautical
instrument-makers, Negus, round 1875, for
the clipper *N. B. Palmer*. This sermonising
binnacle—'Mind your course' is written on
the sailor's hat—nearly caused a mutiny on
board, enraging the helmsmen who
suspected the statue of the evil eye.
Accordingly, the binnacle was replaced by a
conventional model in polished mahogany
and the T. S. Negus Nautical Instrument
Company presented the controversial piece
of equipment to the New York City Museum.

was aboard a wooden ship, it was still enough to throw all the calculations out. Nevertheless, Walker's instrument was so good as a bearing-compass that it remained standard issue in the Royal Navy from 1795 to 1819.

Another ship's compass was the hanging-compass, so prized by collectors of curios. It was quite simply a cabin-compass designed to hang from the beams and to be read by somebody below and therefore from back to front. If you look at the compass-card from this angle east will be to the left and west to the right of the north-south axis.[1] A cross-bar running diametrically from one side of the reversed compass-bowl to the other carries the pin on which the cap for the card fits. There is a glass lid to the bowl which hangs on gimbals. The particular use of this compass, which was more decorative than accurate, was to allow the skipper to keep an eye on the ship's course while resting on his bunk, and the fact that it allowed the master to keep things under his surveillance from behind the scenes as it were got the hanging-compass its nickname of 'tell-tale compass'.

[1] As far as the conventional signs for the cardinal points are concerned an international convention of 1920 states that on compass cards they must be printed NSWE, and from that time on, French models carry a W instead of an O. It is common knowledge that it was Lieutenant Commander B. W. Diehl, USN, who brought in the convention of graduation from 0° to 360° around 1900.

Regulation French Navy
steering compass. These models
were generally used in pairs.

Among compass oddities mention must be made of the Mariner's Recording Compass of which an example was made by David Napier of Glasgow and fitted to the *Great Western* in 1848. Other makers produced similar instruments to all appearances similar to the steering-compass on its wooden box with its copper cover.

A specially treated leaf of silk paper was placed under the compass-card and therefore followed every shift of the latter whether caused by an alteration of course or by the vessel yawing in rough seas. A piece of clockwork (made entirely of bronze and therefore non-magnetic) released a thin pin at regular intervals to pierce the paper. This pin moved out automatically from the centre of the compass-card until in twenty-four hours it had travelled along an axis to meet the lubber-line on the rim of the compass bowl. By tracing these hundreds of pin-pricks you could follow the exact course steered by the vessel in any given twenty-four hour period. This follows almost the same principle as the manual notations of the traverse-board, that memory-bank I shall mention later.

Log ship. *Left:* the log ship, a triangular weighted board. *Above:* the log reel used to reel the line in and to let it out when measuring the vessel's speed. *Lower right:* pintle to hold the crow's foot, and bull's eye mounted on the line and used to release the crow's foot when line and ship were swiftly and smoothly hauled inboard.

Speed through the water: logs and related instruments

As we have seen the second factor in navigation by dead reckoning is the run of the boat, the distance travelled as a result of her speed through the water (own speed +wind-drift) taken together with the drag on the vessel caused by the currents (tidal-drift): when allowance has been made for both these factors, the true run of the boat can be determined.

First let us take the speed which the ship herself generates from her sails or her screw.

This speed cannot be guessed at a glance, unless the boat's performance under all conditions is known precisely. For this reason, from the 16th century onwards, Dutch manuals of seamanship laid down a practical and simple method which consisted of measuring the length of time which it took a log of wood cast over the bows to pass the length of the ship and fall astern. If the overall length of the ship was known, a simple rule of three would enable the speed of the ship to be determined. Although the marine time-keeper had yet to be invented and hour-glasses were in general use, the Dutch had produced a clumsy sort of clockwork instrument with a spring and a bell fixed on top which was known as a 'log-timer'. The works were set going as the log was thrown overboard and it struck the seconds on the bell. There were 14- and 28-second log-timers. Painted, engraved or printed tables, conveniently small, converting the time into knots (nautical miles per hour) were currently used on board ship. They were generally to be found on the backs of snuff-boxes or snuff-rasps, thus combining business with pleasure, and their appearance has given them their name of Dutch Shoe.

The inaccuracy of these two methods—the human eye and the log of wood—was replaced in the 17th century by a new form of log. This was the 'ship', a weighted plank secured by a crowfoot to a long line known as the log-line. This weighted float —the ship'—was thrown over the stern and the line was allowed to run out until a sand-glass emptied, and when it had done so, the line was hauled in and its length recorded. Very soon the sand-glass adopted was the half-minute variety, for the log-line was knotted at fixed intervals determined on the principle enunciated by Gunter, that is, if the ship travelled at the speed of one knot it would travel a distance of one nautical mile (6,080 feet[1]) in one hour (3,600 seconds).

In thirty seconds the ship would therefore travel 50.75 feet. This is the theoretical knot, but, because the log has a tendency to forward drift, the practical distance between knots was settled as 44 feet 6 inches. In practice, when measuring speed by use of a log, a length of line known as the strayline was first paid out over the stern

[1] The length was not really fixed until the second half of the 19th century when the exact length of the nautical mile was measured, being one minute of longitude on the equator.

so that the 'ship' would be clear of the vessel's wake and only when the first knot had been paid out was the sand-glass started and all subsequent knots counted until the sand had run out.

Because the log only gave the ship's speed at one particular moment in time, it had to be heaved every watch so as to obtain an average. Thus very early on, attempts were made to produce a revolution-counter which would enable the course sailed to be determined. The French for this is 'Sillage' or 'seillage' and these instruments are sometimes called sillometers. All sorts of systems were put forward, the first, in 1776, being William Foxon's log. It was tested by Cook, but proved unsuccessful. The revolution-counter, mounted on the taffrail, was all right, but the rotor which turned in the water was an Archimedes screw, a geometrical spiral which Frederic Sauvage and countless other inventors were to attempt unsuccessfully to adapt to marine propulsion.

Around 1800, Gould's mechanical log came on the market at Boston. This was a milometer which was submerged and towed. The counter was activated by a variable pitch propellor which was adjusted by hand to the known average speed of the ship. The Peabody Museum has an example of this type. Use of this log does not seem to have spread very widely and it was soon superseded by Edward Massey's log (1802), although the latter was constructed on the same principle of the rotor and submerged counter. This fixed-blade rotor, very similar to the screws on present-day logs, proved first-rate in practice. In 1805 it was tested by the Royal Navy and became very popular when it was manufactured commercially. Round 1850 Thomas Walker began making logs under licence from Massey. In 1851 he patented his own 'Harpoon the first of the famous series of Walker Logs. This was soon followed in 1863 by the 'A1 Harpoon', a compact log incorporating counter and rotor on a spindle. As with Massey's, it had the disadvantage that it had to be hauled up every time it needed to be read and there was always the risk that the larger fish would be attracted by the glitter of the screw-blades and swallow rotor, counter and all—a costly business. Thus the Walker company patented the 'Cherub' in 1879, comprising a counter mounted on the rail with torque-free line, flywheel and propeller towed astern. More powerful models followed; the 'Neptune' in 1899 and the 'Trident' in 1905. Meantime, in 1902, Walker had produced an electric log which did not come into extensive use commercially until 1924 under the name of the 'Electric Trident'. Electrical impulses from the counter were relayed from the stern to a dial on the bridge. In 1903 Walker's bought up the Massey company.

In France, various models were produced, based upon the principles employed by Walker. Fleuriais, who had invented a bubble sextant for taking sights when the horizon was obscured, made experiments with an electric log in 1880. His rotator was towed under water and comprised four arms with a cup, like those on an anemometer, at the end of each. The tests proved inconclusive.

Although the towed screw log is standard equipment on board ship, it is seldom used.

A far more accurate estimate of the distance run is provided by the revolutions of the ship's screw corrected by various factors including the state of the hull.

One of the earliest examples of the mechanical log, signed by William Foxon of Deptford, 1772. These computers were fixed to the taffrail and recorded the turns of a helix towed behind the vessel. Three dials showed tens of miles, miles and tenths of miles. The basic principles of the geometrical helix presumed to turn in the water like a screw measured inaccurately and the fragility of the instrument led to its abandonment. James Cook used a Foxon log of this pattern in 1776. *Above:* The log in its case. *On preceding page:* Uncased to show mechanism.

Fleuriais's experimental electric log. Each turn of the cupped spokes, dragged behind the ship, transmitted an electric pulsation to a counter from which their proportion to the distance run could be determined. Nonetheless it took half a century for the idea to achieve practical expression.

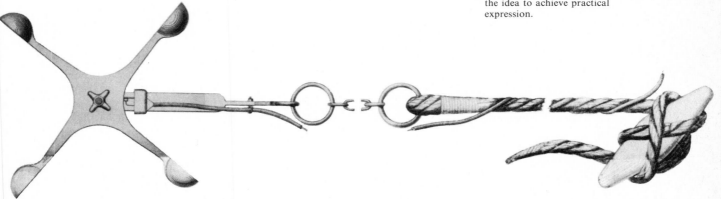

Pitometer logs which work on the principle of air compressed in a tube by the speed of the vessel through the water have now been replaced by electronic logs which react to the water flow caused by the forward movement of the ship.

Plotting a course

With the compass to provide a magnetic heading and the log the distance run in nautical miles, the navigator could plot his position on the chart. His plot was based upon dead reckoning. Various means enabled him to ascertain magnetic variation based on calculations starting from observations of the azimuths of the sun and the stars at their rising and setting. (Remember that magnetic variation is the angle of difference between true North and the north to which the compass needle points). This variation is very seldom nil and itself alters from year to year and also from place to place, the latter being one of Columbus's discoveries. Cape Aghulas ('Needles') near the Cape of Good Hope reminds us that on this spot in the days of Vasco da Gama, seamen found that compass North and true North were identical and that there was a nil variation. Until then the vagaries of the compass had been blamed upon the idiosyncrasies of the binnacle, clearly an easy way out of the dilemma.

Once magnetic variation had been established, the first step had been taken to enable a magnetic heading to be transformed into a compass heading when plotting a course. When iron and composite construction ships came into service in the 19th century allowance had to be made for another compass error—deviation—and we have seen how Lord Kelvin's discoveries provided the corrective for each bearing.

However, as anyone with any practical experience of sailing knows, there was also the problem of the drift caused by the action of the wind upon the sailing-vessel. Drift was apparent to the naked eye by comparing the line of the wake with the line of the ship's axis. Thus a traverse board or a semi-circular gauge mounted on the stern gunwale was sometimes used to record it. The unknown factor remained the drift caused by currents. Pilot-books and nautical manuals of the period tried to indicate them. The Gulf Stream and the tidal currents of the European seas were known, but those of the oceans were an enigma. After several weeks at sea, the strength and direction of these currents completely falsified any notion of position to such an extent that a vessel might find itself off Land's End when it believed it was entering the Straits of Gibraltar. It was only around 1850, when the American Maury brought out his pilot charts, that all the exact data for navigation by dead reckoning could be set out in one place. But here, as elsewhere, these charts came onto the scene very late in the day, since accurate plotting by sextant and chronometer already enabled the navigator to correct his position and to check his reckoning.

The earliest surviving log-books date from the beginning of the 17th century. The information in them is tabulated in almost exactly the same form which present day entries take, with separate columns for time, date, course, variation, distance run, latitude, longitude, direction and force of wind, direction and strength of current and land in sight. Provided they knew these factors—true heading, current and run— navigators could plot their course on the chart.

The sea chart

The oldest known sea chart is what is known as the 'Pisan Chart' preserved in the Department of Maps and Plans in the Bibliothèque Nationale in Paris. It is a chart on vellum, $41\frac{1}{4}$ by $19\frac{3}{4}$ inches covering Europe from the Atlantic to Bruges in the north and Trebizond in the South. It dates from the 13th century. Although drawn to scale (for example a mile to the South of Sardinia is represented by the same distance as a mile in the North Sea) it is clearly not a geometric projection. If distances are respected, angles are distorted in the high latitudes, giving countries the most unexpected shapes.

This sheet of vellum shows all too clearly the appalling problems with which cartographers were faced once they tried to depict the world which lay beyond the Pillars of Hercules. Projecting a small portion of the curved surface of the globe— say Corsica—upon a flat sheet only slightly alters the outline of the coast. If however one takes an area as extensive, say, as France or England, those parts lying farthest from the centre of projection become completely unrecognisable. The 'Pisan Chart' seems to have been put together by some seaman from various separate portolans, using the method of continual approach. That is to say that if, for example, one set sail from a harbour on the west coast of Sardinia and ran a known number of miles on a given bearing, one knew one would make a landfall on the Spanish coast at, say, Valencia. Thus, apparently all the main points on the map were plotted by this rule of thumb method and linked together locally, as is evidenced by the two systems of rhumbs, one centred upon the Aegean Islands and the other to the west of Sardinia.

In the simplest terms, the system of rhumbs comprises a sixteen-point compass card with lines leading from the points to a series of secondary centres as can be seen on the opposite page in an example taken from a chart published by Blaeuw in 1636. While the plottings were clearly of use if one were setting a course in the Mediterranean, in broader seas the single-scale system, which shrank the poles, made the lines of longitude, which were parallel at the equator, come closer to one another the nearer they approached the pole, and meant that the north-south axis of the rhumb was totally meaningless when such a system was set, for example, in the upper left-hand corner of the map.

This was so clearly realised that in a chart dated 1500 by Pedro Reinel, which covers an area from the Mediterranean to Newfoundland and Cape Race, the north-south axis in these last named areas is represented by an oblique line of longitude.

What was required was a system of cartography which would always show the lines of longitude as vertical parallels and on which the compass course steered by the ship (its loxodrome which makes a constant angle with the longitude) could be shown as a straight line. This clearly meant that the higher the latitude, the greater the enlargement of the land masses on a scale which reached infinity since the poles—points—became straight lines at the top and bottom of the map of the world.

Shy attempts at expanding scales may be discerned in the maps of the Portuguese Nicolas de Caveiro in 1502 and of Lupo Homen in 1519. In 1537 Pedro Nuñes was to prove that loxodromes in plane cartography are not straight lines but curves spiralling towards the poles. Magellan's voyage in 1520 was the determining factor in directing

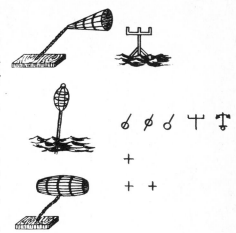

Earliest conventional signs in
The Mariner's Mirrour (1588!).

The principle of constructing rhumb-lines.

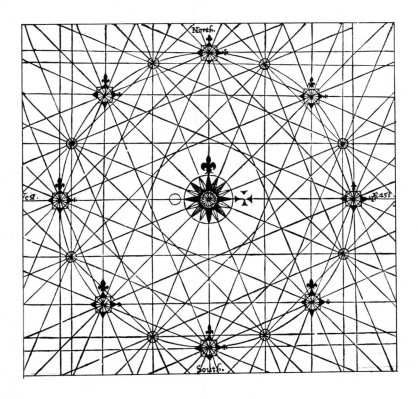

In *The Light of Navigation* (1612) Blaeuw gave the conventional signs on maps a graphic power which has remained unchanged until the present day.

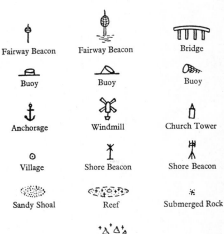

these discoveries to an outcome which would be really useful to seamen. The Flemish cosmographer Gerard Mercator ventured to include this outline upon his great planisphere of 1569 which was published in the year following in Ortelius's mighty atlas—the *Theatrum Orbis*—while the Englishman Thomas Wright set out in his celebrated *Certain Errors of Navigation Detected and Corrected* (1599) the principle of expanding latitudes in the construction of sea charts, without being able to prove it mathematically, for the formula could only be revealed by integral calculus as yet undiscovered.

However, although charts constructed on Mercator's system by men such as Thomas Hood (1592), Edward Wright (1599), Guillaume Le Vasseur of Dieppe (1601), Blaeuw (1630), Hakluyt and Gerritz now started to have a wide circulation, plane cartography, a hardy plant, lived on for another hundred years.

Marine charts were printed for the first time at the beginning of the 17th century and the conventional signs employed in Wagenaer's *Mariners Mirrour* were adopted and supplemented by Blaeuw. Until the rise of Naval Survey Departments among the sea-powers at the end of the 18th century, sea charts were published by independent cartographical publishers, always under the protection of a royal or princely warrant

Parallel rulers signed 'Hughes, 59 Fenchurch Street, London'. 18th century. English seamen ignored the protractor and remained faithful to this old-fashioned implement used to plot courses on sea-charts from one of the compass-cards printed on the chart itself.

and with that special status which, for example, Blaeuw enjoyed, being created official cartographer to the United Provinces in 1663.

The great voyages round the world in the 18th century were to bring these publishers a host of new plottings, and the map of the world has finally been filled in by the information which has been exchanged since the 19th century between the different naval surveys.

Plotting instruments and calculators

Plotting on a chart with the aid of parallel rules which had been carried on ships since the 16th century was done in this way. The bearing was traced by extending the appropriate point from one of the compass cards shown on the chart to the vessel's port of departure and then the run was marked off with that standby of the geometer, a pair of dividers. However, a slight calculation had to be made to convert miles measured on a longitudinal scale to the latitudinal scale which governed the actual distance run. This was where Gunter's Scales came in. These, the real forerunners of the slide-rule, were adjudged of such practical value that seamen continued to use them right down to the 19th century. Navigators have always had a certain preference for graphic systems, such as the abacus or diagrams rather than tables of figures. Admittedly, the fact that sailors were a trifle illiterate had something to do with it as

Above: Scandinavian traverse-board, 19th century. Equivalent to the landsman's abacus, this ancient seaman's memorandum pad, used aboard the windjammers, comprised a compass-card with holes punched along each of the 32 rhumb-lines at 11.25° intervals round the circumference in eight concentric circles each representing a 30-minute time-span. Every half-hour the officer of the watch would stick in a peg along the line of the ship's course which he had read from the compass. Every hour another peg was stuck into one of the holes in the horizontal lines drilled into the oblong board at the foot to show the speed in knots measured by the log. When his watch was over the officer was able to plot the track by the number of nautical miles run and the courses steered and plot the ship's position on the chart. Many a traverse-board was made by the ship's carpenter and more or less skilfully decorated. *Left:* Another 19th century Scandinavian traverse-board, painted black and white.

well. Gunter's Scales gave the logarithms as well as the natural values of trigonometrical lines then used in navigation. Such was the procedure until charts on Mercator's projection came into use, on which distances could be read directly on a latitudinal scale. To solve the problem of north-south and east-west courses (where there are differences both in longitude and latitude) use was made of whatever came to hand—the *quartier de reduction* or the *carré nautique* invented by Gemma Frisius in 1545, or even the *pieds de roi*, a draughtsman's tool from the 17th century onwards.

The Survey Department of the British Admiralty always remained faithful to the convention of printing compass cards on marine charts and hence parallel rules were ever the faithful companions of British seamen. Beautifully finished specimens survive of double or even triple rules, one interesting example incorporating a tubular roller with rubber tips. It suffices to roll the instrument on the chart for the flat rule to move parallel with itself. If they had no protractors or parallel rules coasters would use a traverse-board for rough plots.

The date when these traverse-boards were first used on board ship is not known. Time has taken its toll of them as it has of Jacob's Staff and Davis's Backstaff, despite their once widespread use. The traverse-board was a standard piece of equipment in the French Navy in the first half of the 19th century and the standard issue was a handsome brass affair mounted in wood.

Spheres and globes

From the 16th century onwards, terrestrial globes were relatively common. They were highly decorative and were part of the furniture of most libraries and 'cabinets of curiosities'. Their present-day value generally resides in the elaboration of engraver's, cabinet-maker's or metal-worker's skill which has gone into the mounting far more than in what is on the globe itself. Nonetheless, there are some globes which are prime sources of evidence for the geographical knowledge of the age in which they were constructed. Such, for example, are the globes which the Padre Vicenzo Coronelli produced to order and in limited numbers at the end of the 17th century. These globes were made to a standard diameter of about three feet six inches and generally come in pairs—a terrestrial and a celestial sphere—provided with an equatorial as well as a meridian ring, both made of copper and both marked off with scales. The meridian ring slots into the equatorial ring and allowed the poles to be tilted at any desired angle above the horizontal. Remember that latitude equals the angular distance along the earth's surface northward or southward of the equator measured in degrees along a meridian line. The globe rotates on its polar axis allowing one to set that part of the world where one presently is on the line of the meridian ring. With such devices, these globes became real instruments of mensuration and their large size enabled the user to ascertain with some accuracy local time, length of daylight and times of rising and setting of sun and moon for wherever he happened to be.

Another major producer of globes from 1622 onwards was the Dutchman, W. J. Blaeuw. His globes were made of papier-mâché covered by plaster-of-paris to which the cartographic segments, printed from copper-plate engravings, were pasted and then varnished over.

Celestial spheres showed the fixed stars—since the planets move they obviously could not be included—as well as the equator, as on terrestrial globes. The celestial sphere was provided with equatorial and meridian rings in which the vault of the heavens could rotate. All such astronomical problems as the rising and setting of particular stars or their passing through the meridian could be solved visually and without recourse to calculation. Obviously this type of mechanical abacus must have attracted seamen and, in fact, proof of the presence of globes on board ship is furnished by nautical instrument-makers' catalogues and by lists of individual ship's equipment. In 1576 Martin Frobisher ordered a marine globe and a plain metal globe doubtless so that he could plot his course on the latter. Less ornate, less precious and less bulky than the globes which were placed in libraries, these working tools enabled seamen to solve or at least to unravel a fair number of problems of marine astronomy. The particular advantage of the terrestrial globe was that on it the seaman could see the shortest course to follow. The tradition was perpetuated by those little travelling globes in their leather or shagreen cases.

Planetary and armillary spheres

Among the pieces of navigational equipment carried by ships in the 16th and 17th centuries were armillary spheres. Their name comes from the Latin word *armilla* meaning a bracelet or hoop. The purpose of these spheres was to realise the major co-ordinates of the solar system and hence to solve the major problems of marine astronomy.

The earth was placed in the centre of the sphere and the sphere itself realised by two horary rings set at right angles to the line of the poles. Another broad ring joined them in their midpoint. This represented the equator. Four other narrow rings represented the two tropics of Capricorn and Cancer and the Arctic and Antarctic Circles. One final broad ring cutting the narrow tropical rings at an angle realised the

Mid-18th century orrery with simple movement. Gilt on black lacquer.

Orrery constructed by Nicolas Fortin, *c.* 1750. Clockwork movement.

Travelling armillary sphere of the time of Louis XV. The case, gilt on black lacquer in a style which shows the influence of the French East India Company.

95

ecliptic or path of the sun. The ecliptic intersected the horary and equatorial rings and the point where it divided the last named was the point from which the right ascension of the stars was calculated trigonometrically, that is anti-clockwise on the equator.

As with terrestrial and celestial globes, the whole sphere was mounted in a meridian ring which was in turn set in an equatorial ring. The angle of the polar axis could be adjusted to set the latitude and the sphere could be rotated on this axis to take the time factor into account, the latter having been determined from the plots in relation to the meridian.

This ingenious device enabled equatorial co-ordinates to be transformed into horizontal and horary co-ordinates. It was the forerunner of the navisphere so widely used in sailing schools at the beginning of the 20th century. This was sometimes carried on board and was particularly useful for quick recognition of the stars.

Armillary spheres developed a wealth of complicated and useless attachments, and it is simple to distinguish between the more compact models used by seamen and those from gentlemen's cabinets of curiosities. Some spheres of wood or brass are of a very small size so as to be taken to sea, and these have cases which support the horizontal ring.

What might be termed the large, lecture-hall spheres have a whole series of other instruments to go with them to demonstrate the workings of the solar system. Although there is nothing specifically nautical about them, it is quite possible that they were used to teach naval surveying and this is particularly true of the planetary spheres. However these exceedingly beautiful and costly objects could not be used for calculation. They are in fact mere curiosities, especially the orrery, named after its inventor, a planetary sphere which mechanically represents the relative movements of the plants, Mercury, Venus, Earth, Moon, Mars and Saturn.

Time-keeping at sea: sand-glasses and sand-clocks

From the first moment that mankind put to sea, the reckoning of time became a major problem. By recording the passage of the sun through the meridian, a rough calculation of noon local time could be obtained. Local time, based upon the latitudes of the rising and setting of sun and moon was calculated and provided in the form of tables for seamen from the 17th century onwards. Until watches or marine time-keepers were invented, all the seaman had to reckon the time between the fixed points of the daily noon sight were sand-glasses and the dials which I shall describe later.

The time-keeper most commonly employed by Classical Antiquity was the water-clock. In the Middle Ages the sand-glass came into its own and, fragile though it was, this was the first clock which the men who made the great voyages of discovery took with them. The first care of the maker was to achieve exact calibration of the

Regulation ship's sand-clock of the 18th century. Half-hour glass.

Organ-pipe sand-clock, with glasses for the quarter-, half-, threequarter- and full hour. 16th century German with wooden mounts carved in the Gothic style.

17th century brass-mounted sand-clock with half-hour glass with 15-minute bubbles.

Small 18th century sand-clock with half- and full hour glasses. Mounted in wood and copper-gilt. Gilt-stamped morocco leather top.

Hour-glass. Each of the bubbles marks the quarter-hour. Brass mounting, 9.6 inches high. Sacred heart engraved on top.

Sand-clock with half- and full hour glasses. Brass mounting with Sacred Heart and Crown of Thorns engraved on top.

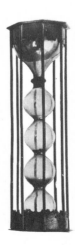

Large hour-glass (15.6 inches tall) used to callibrate smaller glasses. Each of the bubbles marks a quarter-hour. Iron mounting. From the Atelier des Boussoles, Brest. 18th century.

instrument with whatever in those days was the mean duration of an hour or part of an hour, and this, we must presume, varied from place to place. To achieve this calibration, the first concern was with the 'sand' itself which was either finely pounded eggshell or else black marble ground to powder and baked nine times. There were limits to the skill of the glass-blower so that when it came to the next step of calibrating the neck of the sand-glass, the favourite method was to use two separately blown bulbs and to insert between them a hard metal plate through which a narrow hole had been drilled. The amount of sand in the bulb and the precise size of the hole were calculated to allow the bulb to empty within a predetermined period. It was essential to preserve the sand from the humidity of salt air, and therefore the point at which the bulbs met the metal plate was sealed with wax and surrounded with a network of crossed threads. The instrument was then set in a stand comprising octagonal or circular head and base plates separated by thin bars or else within a leather, metal or cardboard tube.

Old sand-glasses were often measured against new ones to make sure they were not running too fast or 'eating the sand'. Such acceleration could be caused either by the refining process of the sand upon itself or by its wear increasing the size of the

18th century quarter-hour glass. The brass mount revolves and can close completely to protect the instrument. Embossed decorations include fleur-de-lys and two-headed eagle.

From left to right: 18th century chaplain's half-hour glass. The 5·5 inch brass mount turns so as to protect the instrument in transit. From Brest; small Japanese two-minute glass. The bronze mount is decorated with chrysanthemum flowers; small three-minute glass. Varnished wooden mount with twisted columns.

hole in the neck. Over the centuries sand-glasses for different lengths of time were adopted for sea-service. There were quarter- and half-minute glasses for log-timers, minute glasses and most commonly half-hour glasses known as 'clocks'. When the officer of the watch called the passage of the sun through the meridian, the helmsman would turn the glass. When he turned it once more after the first half-hour he would strike the ship's bell once, striking it twice after the second half-hour, three times after the third and so on. This is how the practice came about, which still survives, of giving a double ring at 1 p.m., two double rings at 2 p.m., and so on. If this method of measuring the time was to have any real value, the helmsman naturally had to refrain from turning the glass until the sand had run out of the bulb, but in practice he seldom waited so long, since he was anxious to cut short his watch.

Makers' imaginations ran riot with two-, three- and even four-glass models, the latter being known as 'organ-pipes'. This type of glass marked the quarters and the full hour. Large glasses in which the sands took four hours to run out and called 'battle glasses' remained in use aboard ship long after the introduction of watches

18th century graphometer signed by Langlois of Paris. A survey instrument known as a whole dial when the circle of 360° is complete, it was also an invaluable aid to naval cartographers. From the 18th century it became part of the standard equipment of survey-ships and it was to be found in dockside nautical instrument shops next to Davis's quadrants and octants. Leading makers—Langlois among them—added to the accuracy and fine decoration for which the instrument was prized.

99

and chronometers. They were used in exceptionally bad weather and when the ship went into action for fear that the ship's motion might jar and upset the delicate clockwork mechanism. In these conditions the 'battle glasses' were considered more accurate. Half-hour glasses remained in use on board ship until the middle of the 19th century, while the half-minute log-timers were retained as a standard piece of equipment on sailing ships until the early years of the present century, since the 'boat' type of log was kept as a stand-by in the event of the mechanical log breaking down. These short-timing glasses were always made in one piece without a metal plate between the bulbs since a slight error on the overall reckoning of the vessel's speed was in any case purely marginal.

Genuine ship's sand-glasses are much sought-after nowadays and hard to find. Although great care was taken of them at sea and they always stood in strong racks, it was different ashore where, being regarded merely as curios they were at the mercy of any clumsy pair of hands.

Time-keeping at sea: sun-dials and ring-dials

The increasing need for accurate timekeeping led to the development of sun- and moon-dials, of which there existed so many different models based on so many different principles that they alone would fill a book. We will restrict ourselves to four main types, two of them for use on land, which were eventually adapted for marine use.

The idea of determining the time by the position of the sun goes back to antiquity. Everyone knows that it is noon at the moment the sun crosses the observer's meridian (i.e. north-south axis), and that the sun rises and sets at a certain hour, which can be ascertained from the almanac for the year.

The shadow of a pole planted vertically into the ground describes an ellipse between sunrise and sunset. As the sun travels from east to west the shadow changes its position, and every position of that shadow corresponds to a certain hour. This principle, however, can only be applied for middle and high latitudes, where the sun is never very high in the sky and its azimuth changes constantly. On the equator, to take an extreme case, at the moment of the equinoxes (when the sun's declination is zero), an observer sees the sun rise bearing due east, where it remains until it passes the zenith and begins its descent bearing due west. In such a case it is not the direction of the shadow which changes but merely its length, and it alone indicates the hour. Thus, we have two basic types of sun-dial: altitude-measuring ones for regions and periods in which the sun is very high in the sky, and those which measure the angle of the shadow.

The altitude-measuring or seaman's quadrant was known to navigators in antiquity. It consists of a quadrant-shaped surface of wood or metal graduated along the arc from 0° to 90°. One radial edge is fitted with two pinnules or sights, and a plumb-line is suspended from the centre of arc. Sighting the zenith, the plumb-line indicates 90°, sighting the horizon 0°. Let us assume we are observing the sun at a time of the year when it is very high in the sky. The instrument then indicates, hour after hour, the increasing altitude of the sun as it rises, rapidly at first, more slowly towards noon. With the help of a half-hour glass, for example, a second arc graduated in hours and half-hours can be marked inside the quadrant's degree scale. 10° altitude might correspond to 6 a.m. local time, 25° to 7 a.m., and 70° to midday. Of course, a similar graduation has to be made for each month of the year. In practise, this means only for the first six, because the second six months are identical in reverse order. We end up with six concentric arcs graduated in half-hours. Between them, lines can be drawn joining points of equal time, and in this way the values for every day of the month can be ascertained with reasonable accuracy.

Of course, such a quadrant is only useful at the particular latitude for which it has been graduated, because the sun's altitude at midday is not the same at 20° as it is at 10°, for example. If it is to be used for other latitudes, an angle correction has to be applied.

The ring dial is based on the same principle as the seaman's quadrant.

Sun-dials which measure the direction of the cast shadow work on a different principle altogether, and they are used for times of the year and for regions where the sun reaches only modest altitudes. We have already said that the tip of the shadow cast by a pole planted vertically in the ground describes an ellipse. It is easy to

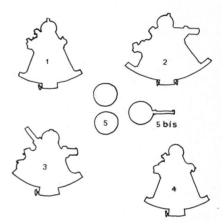

1. 19th century octant signed by Masselin of Nantes; 2. Early 20th century sextant signed by E. Lorieux of Paris; 3. Early 20th century sextant signed by F. M. Jones of London; 4. 19th century octant signed by Leroux of St-Malo; 5. English pocket-sextant signed by Cary of London; 5b. English pocket-sextant with telescope, signed 'Elliott Brothers, 56 Strand, London' with the owner's name, F. F. Barrington, additionally engraved.

On the right Bloud's sun-dial built at Dieppe in 1670. It is used by aligning the point marking 12 o'clock and the axis of the compass needle with the sun. The shadow of the compass needle on the graduated brass ellipse gives a direct reading. The ellipse can be moved according to the time of year to allow for the change in the sun's declination. Unfortunately, this instrument could only have been valid for a few years, while the magnetic variation at Dieppe was zero. On the left a Nuremberg Diptych. This consists of two leaves at right angles linked by a meridian thread, which has to be aligned to the north-south axis. This thread takes the place of a shadow pin or gnomon. The hour is read off by the shadow cast by the thread on the horizontal as well as the vertical leaf.

Both instruments could only be used for limited coastal navigation when there was no significant change in latitude, and in the case of Bloud's dial the magnetic variation had to be zero.

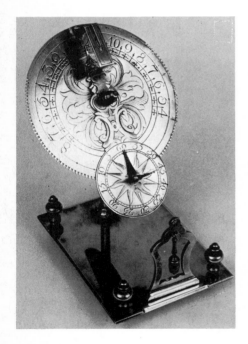

18th-century French equinoctial sun-dial. The pendulum is merely used to level the instrument. The large dial is revolved until the sun-light falls through the slit in the sight. The instrument is usable for a fixed latitude only but could be adapted for universal use if the plane of the dials could be inclined.

graduate this ellipse into hours, and one can immediately see the possibility of building a pocket sun-dial with a vertical pin, or gnomon, to cast the shadow. So that the axis of the ellipse can be aligned with the north-south axis a compass forms part of the instrument. To simplify the construction, the gnomon is mounted directly on the magnetic needle. Such a magnetic sun-dial is Bloud's instrument built at Dieppe in 1670. To compensate for the varying declination of the sun, the ellipse is adjustable, i.e. can be moved nearer to or further away from the gnomon according to the time of year. This sun-dial, too, is only usable for one fixed latitude and therefore unsuited for use at sea.

The sun-dial with axial gnomon, i.e. aligned to the polar axis, is based on the changing azimuth of the shadow cast. It is basically a ring, the plane of which can be angled to coincide with the latitude of the observer. The gnomon standing perpendicularly in the centre of the ring represents the polar axis. The sun's shadow travels with uniform speed round the ring, which is graduated in hours. This type of sun-dial is named Augsburg dial, after the town in Germany where it was built, and can be recognized by its hexagonal base-plate. Other instruments built on the same principle are the diptych-like Nuremberg sun-dial and the ring dial or Gemma's ring.

The ring dial, or Gemma's ring, was the mariner's first clock and was directly inspired by the Augsburg dial. It consists of three main parts: a ring representing the meridian, one quarter being graduated with a scale of latitude from 0° to 90°; another ring inside it and at right angles to its plane representing the equator, this being graduated in 24 hours; and an axis with a sliding sight, which is set to the angle of the sun's declination in the month of observation. The instrument is suspended from a ring, which slides on the outer rim of the meridian ring and which is set to coincide with the observer's latitude. The illustration on p. 103 will help to explain the construction and use of the ring dial. Some of these instruments were surprisingly small, no larger than 8–10 cm in diameter. Until the introduction of the chronometer they were widely used, chiefly by British navigators.

Another sun-dial based on the principle of the axial shadow pin is the Nuremberg Diptych. It consists of two hinged leaves which, when opened up, are at right angles to one another and are connected by a thread representing the axis. This is positioned in line with the meridian plane. The shadow cast indicates the hour on the vertical leaf as well as on the ring which surrounds the compass let into the horizontal leaf.

The ring dial (Annulus Astronomicus) is a more sophisticated version of the Augsburg dial. The instrument is suspended by the sliding ring, which is set on the scale of the meridian ring to coincide with the observer's latitude. The meridian ring is aligned to the meridian plane, when the central axis, which forms an integral part of it, represents the terrestrial polar axis and the hour ring, marked in Roman numerals, the equator. The sliding sight on the axis is set between 23.5° south south and 23.5° north depending on the month of the year. The sun-shine passing through a small hole in the sight indicates the hour on the hour ring. The instrument illustrated is set for latitude 57°, with the sun's declination at 2° south. The direction in which the sight points suggests that the hour might be around 1 o'clock.

The ring-dial is the mariner's sun clock and part of any inventory of navigational aids. With it, the hour can be determined for any given latitude and any number of navigation problems may be solved.

These Nuremberg Diptychs were made in large numbers. Made of fruit-wood, with glued-on paper dials, their exterior frequently decorated with compass cards and perpetual calendars, they were really bazaar curios rather than serious time-pieces. Lunar dials were made on the same principle. Both have the drawback of being usable only for one fixed latitude determined by the angle of the thread stretched between the two leaves.

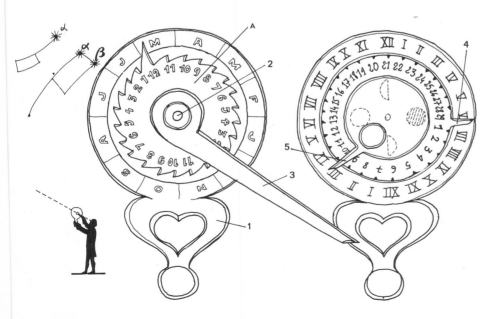

The nocturnal, which might be described as a 'star-dial', enables the mariner to determine the hour of night by observing the connecting line between stars α and β in Ursa Major (the Great Bear) in relation to the Pole Star, which is α in Ursa Minor. In the course of 24 hours this axis describes a full circle round the Pole Star. To take a sight, the inner, toothed disc (A) is turned until the projecting tooth coincides with the date on the outer disc, which is graduated anti-clockwise. In the illustration the date is approximately May 22. Then the instrument is held by the handle (1) at arm's length and moved until the Pole Star becomes visible through the central hole (2). Finally, the alidade (3) is rotated until its bevelled edge coincides with the line joining α and β in Ursa Major. The bevelled edge now indicates the hour on the toothed disc, in our case approximately 2 o'clock.

The reverse side of a nocturnal was frequently designed as tidal calculator. The outer disc is divided into twice twelve hours, the intermediate disc is graduated from 1 to 29.5, representing the lunar cycle of 29.5 days. The inner disc has an index spanning the intermediate and outer discs and some-times a window, through which the phases of the moon appear. To use the instrument, the tooth (4) on the intermediate disc is set to the establishment of the port (here 6 hours), while the index (5) on the inner disc is set to coincide with the age of the moon (here 10 days). The same index shows, on the outer disc, the time of High Water, which in the case illustrated is half past 3 o'clock.

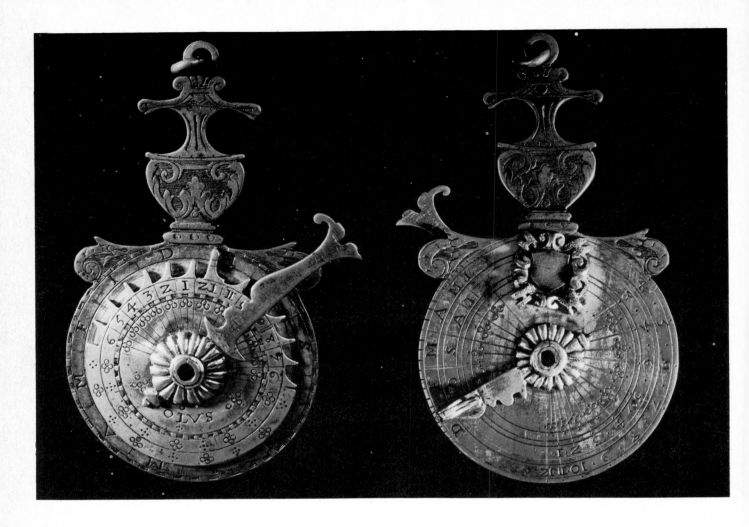

The nocturnal

Nocturnal, c. 1580, decorated in Renaissance style. On the right, the reverse side of the same instrument, showing a perpetual calendar and a sun-dial.

When observing the sky at night we notice that the stars in their relative movements (the earth being assumed as fixed) revolve round a celestial pole. The actual pole is not marked by a star, but Polaris, the Pole Star, is so close to it that it can be considered to *be* the pole for all practical purposes. The Pole Star, which is star α in Ursa Minor, the Little Bear, remains fixed, while in the course of the night the wheels of Charles's Wain in Ursa Major, the Great Bear, revolve round it. The line connecting the rear wheels of Charles's Wain (which are stars α and β in Ursa Major and are commonly known as the pointers) to the Pole Star moves as the hand of a clock and has been used by astronomers since the 15th century in connection with an instrument called a nocturnal. This was the mariner's clock at night.

Sometimes very small and made of metal, sometimes quite large and made of wood, the nocturnal consists basically of two round, concentric discs, the outer one incorporating a handle rather like that of a hand mirror. The larger, outer disc is graded in 12 months from January to December, in an anti-clockwise direction. The smaller circumference of the inner disc is divided into twenty-four equal parts, from 1 to 12 and again from 1 to 12, also in an anti-clockwise direction. A long index, or alidade, pivots round the centre of the discs. To use the instrument, a projecting tooth on the inner disc, marking 12 o'clock, is set to point to the date on the outer disc. The instrument is held at arm's length and moved until the Pole Star can be observed through the hole at the centre. Then the alidade is pivoted until its bevelled edge coincides with the line joining the pointers. The time can be read off the scale on the inner disc.

104

Whilst nocturnals were of little use for timekeeping at sea, many of them had a tidal calculator on the reverse side. In this, the outer plate circumference is divided into twice twelve hours, while the second plate is graduated from 1 to 29.5, representing the lunar cycle of 29.5 days. The inner plate has an index spanning the intermediate and outer plates. To use the calculator, the index on the intermediate plate is set to coincide with the 'establishment' of the port on the outer plate, the 'establishment' being the time which elapses between the time of meridian passage of the full moon or new moon and the time of the following High Water. Next, the index on the inner plate is set to indicate the age of the moon on the intermediate scale and it will, at the same time, indicate the time of High Water on the outer scale.

Clocks, timepieces, chronometers

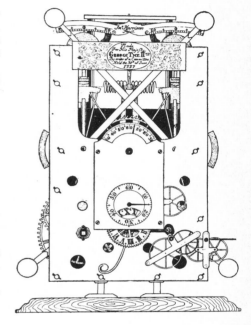

While the sand continued to trickle through hour-glasses and navigators calculated the time of day on their ring dials and the time of night on their nocturnals, countless learned men, pseudo-scientists, astrologers and magicians tried, each in his own way, to master the problem of time measurement at sea and with it the problem of determining longitude.

Longitude being the difference between different local times, the navigator had to know the time at his point of departure. Today, Greenwich Mean Time (GMT) is used instead. By comparing with it his own local time, easily determined at noon, when the sun crossed the meridian, he knew which longitude he had reached. The search for a reliable method of timekeeping led to quite a number of unrelated proposals.

One of them was to moor a chain of ships across the world's oceans, each of which would fire a cannon at a certain hour. In 1687 someone actually suggested making use of the old belief that a glass filled with water to the brim would overflow at the precise instant of a Full or New Moon. This would have provided an exact time-check, had it not been for the movement of the ship! In 1700 telepathy was brought into the picture. If a knife which had wounded a dog, so it was said, was dusted with certain powder, the dog, no matter how far away, would begin to howl at the same moment. All that was needed was a dog on board each ship and a knife at Greenwich, which had to be dusted with the powder at the moment of the sun's culmination.

That was all very well, but none of it worked. To overcome the lack of reliable marine clocks, Dr. Maskelyne, the Astronomer Royal, proposed a method of time calculation which dispensed with dogs and cannons. It was based on lunar distances, i.e. the angular distance between the moon and certain fixed stars. This method, which merely requires the use of a sextant and a reflecting circle, in conjunction with the current lunar tables, proved sufficiently reliable and was used until 1907, the year in which lunar tables were published for the last time. The valiant Captain Joshua Slocum, whose only timepiece on board was an old alarm clock, circumnavigated the earth by this method.

Unfortunately, the calculation of lunar distance was only possible at certain times, the procedure was highly complicated, and the results were not completely accurate. The attempts to develop a clock for use at sea continued.

Drawing on Galileo's observation, in 1616, of the isochronous oscillations of a pendulum, Huygens designed the first balance clock in 1657. In 1675 the spring was added. But the delicate mechanism did not stand up to the violent movements of a ship on a restless ocean. In an experiment conducted in 1669 by Captain Holmes over 3,000 miles of ocean, the error of longitude proved nearly 100 minutes of arc. To encourage research, the Board of Longitude was founded in Britain in 1713. It offered a spectacular reward to the inventor of a chronometer which would fulfill the following conditions: if a ship equipped with this chronometer could accomplish a voyage to the West Indies and back with an error of longitude of less than 1°, the inventor would receive £10,000; if the error was less than 40′ he would get £15,000; if it was less than 30′ the reward was to be £20,000!

The prize money was to go to John Harrison in 1768. In France, the Académie des Sciences in Paris offered a similar prize, which went to the Basle mathematician Daniel Bernoulli in 1747.

The Englishman John Harrison was the son of a carpenter and made clocks as a hobby. The first timepiece he ever built was all wood. But the first clock intended

Harrison's second chronometer, inscribed 'Made for His Majesty George the IInd, by order of a committee, held the 30th of June 1737.'

for use at sea and finished after 8 years' work was all metal and weighed 100 lb. It was presented to the Board in 1736 and tested at sea in 1737 but did not fulfill the conditions. The second clock was finished in 1739, the third, which still weighed 30 kilos, 18 years later. All three are today in the National Maritime Museum at Greenwich, where they cannot only be seen but actually heard ticking, for after 200 years they are still in working order. Harrison's clock No. 4, finally, was the size of a pocket watch. Completed in 1759 it was successfully tested in 1762 by John Harrison's son during a voyage to Jamaica. After five months at sea it furnished a longitude to the last degree: it was only 1′54″ out! After 36 years' intensive effort Harrison at last got his prize of £20,000.

Two copies of Harrison's clock were made by the clockmaker Larcum Kendall by commission of the Board of Longitude. One of them accompanied Captain Cook on his voyages of 1772 and 1776, the other went on board the *Bounty* and after having spent some time with the mutineers on Pitcairn eventually returned to London.

Berthoud's third chronometer, dated 1775, which Borda used during his circumnavigation in 1776. The hours, minutes and seconds are shown on three separate dials.

Despite Harrison's success, many problems concerning the balance and the escapement remained to be solved, and innumerable ingenious proposals were made. One need only look at the mechanisms on show in clock museums attributed to English watchmakers like Larcum Kendall, Thomas Judge, John Arnold, Thomas Earnshaw, William Forsham, Edward John Dent, James Fergusson Cole, Aaron L. Denisson, to the Swiss Berthoud, Bulle, Grandjean, Jürgensen, Dubois, Richard, Ulysse Nardin, and the Frenchmen Le Roy, Brequet, Motel, Winnerl, O. Dumas, Vissiére, Jacob, Rodanet, to name but the most important ones.

The inventor of the word 'chronometer', Pierre Le Roy (1717–1785), describes in his book *La meilleure maniére de mesurer le temps en mer* a longitude clock presented to the King of France in 1766 and already names all the principles of modern chronometry: reduction of friction, perfect isochronism of the balance unaffected by the escapement system, temperature compensation of the balance, removal of the residual effects of temperature fluctuations and insensitivity of the

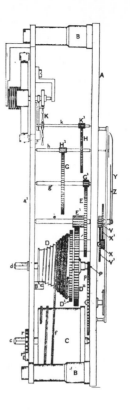

Chronometer signed by
Josiah Emery, London, late 18th
century. This is already very close
to the accepted classical pattern.

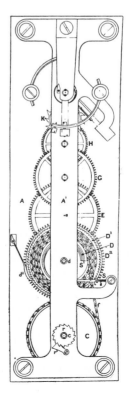

Exploded diagram (for demonstration purposes) of a modern chronometer. Top: side elevation. Bottom: ground plan. We can distinguish the mainspring barrel and fusee linked with a chain wound up in a spiral, which gives a constant turning moment, independent of the spring tension, and a perfectly regular clock. We can also see the bi-metallic balance, which compensates for temperature fluctuations.

mechanism against shocks and ships' movements.

To attain the aims he had set himself, Le Roy used a balance of 108 mm in diameter and weighing 153 g, the pivots of which rested in four rollers, while the axle was carried by a torsion bar. Two bent glass tubes filled with mercury compensated for temperature fluctuations. Later this compensation was achieved by the bi-metallic balance (steel-and-brass).

Ferdinand Berthoud (1727–1807) was granted a license as clockmaker to the French King and Navy. After his first (1760) and second clocks (1763), which were enormous, heavy and cumbersome machines because of the weights, later to be replaced by the mainspring, he finally produced his clock No. 3, not much larger than an ordinary saloon clock. His model 52 has ruby bearings and resembles a modern chronometer quite closely. His nephew, Louis Berthoud (1750–1813) took over from him.

Around 1870 the chronometer arrived at its present-day mechanical concept: mainspring with barrel, fusee, free moving escapement, bi-metallic (steel-and-brass) balance, cylindrical spring, ruby bearings. The instrument is housed in a brass drum with screw-on glass lid. The base of the drum is weighted with lead and has a sprung lid covering the wind-up hole to keep out dust and moisture. The drum is hung in gimbals inside a tight-fitting mahogany box with an inner glass lid. The box, which

Clock by Jules Callame inscribed 'Marine Impériale Sémaphores'. c. 1860.

itself is a handsome piece of cabinet work, has copper corners, angle pieces and a copper handle. For transport there is a padded box with a leather strap.

Chronometers are wound every 24 hours, at the same fixed time, with a special key. A complete winding takes eight to ten turns, an indicator on the face showing the state of winding. A chronometer is never reset by physically moving the hands but left to run down and re-started at the exact moment when the time it shows coincides with G.M.T.

As a rule, ships used to be equipped with two or even three chronometers in case one of them was irregular. Besides, all three could be checked against each other,

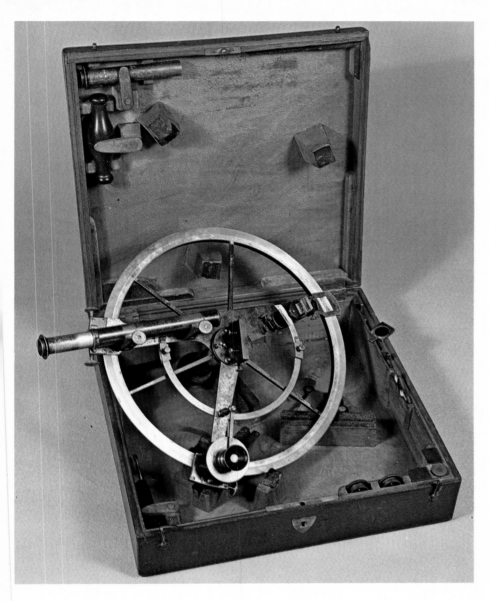

Borda's reflecting circle in mahogany box. The arc and vernier are made of silver, the frame of blackened copper. French model signed by Jecker, Paris. Late 18th century.

Method of holding the reflecting circle for taking sights.

Left: Early 20th-century box-sextant with leather case and screw-on Galilean telescope, signed Elliott Brothers, 56 Strand, London and bearing the owner's name: J. F. Barrington. The diameter of the instrument is a mere 7.5 cm. In the middle a similar model without telescope, signed Barton Linnard Ltd., 1918, No. 5369 and bearing the owner's name: Folliard. On the right, to illustrate the scale, an ivory folding rule, each section of which is 5 cm.

Mid 19th-century English-made pocket sextant, 10 cm high. The rack on the arc is 50 years ahead of its time. Normal-size sextants did not yet have one.

A very valuable English sextant in a mahogany box with brass corners and fittings. Amongst the numerous accessories are coloured shades, a prismatic telescope and tools for adjusting and cleaning. The arc is made of platinum, the vernier of massive gold. The signature on the arc reads: Heath & Co. Ltd., Crayford, London. No. 8853, Patent No. 17840. On the inside of the lid the Certificate of Examination by the National Physical Laboratory, 1909.

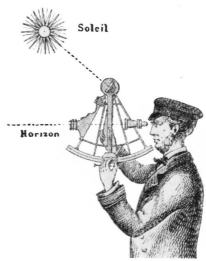

Soleil

Horizon

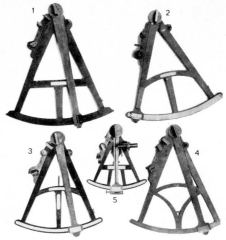

Stages in the development of Hadley's octant: 1. ebony model without vernier scale, wooden arc with diagonal divisions, two horizon glasses for taking sights, either with the observer facing the observed object or with his back turned, according to the object's altitude above the horizon. 2., 3., 4. similar models improved by the addition of a graduated ivory arc and a vernier on the index bar. 5. perfected octant with brass index bar and a telescope replacing the sight. The second horizon glass has been dispensed with, coloured shades for direct observation of the horizon have been added, as has a handle by which to hold the instrument. We notice that in octant No. 3 there is a small ivory pin attached to the crossbar of the frame. This was designed to hold the pencil with which the observer jotted down the sight taken on the small ivory plate below it. More frequently this was let into the reverse side of the frame. Once the altitude was noted, the observer could complete the latitude calculations in the comfort of the cabin below.

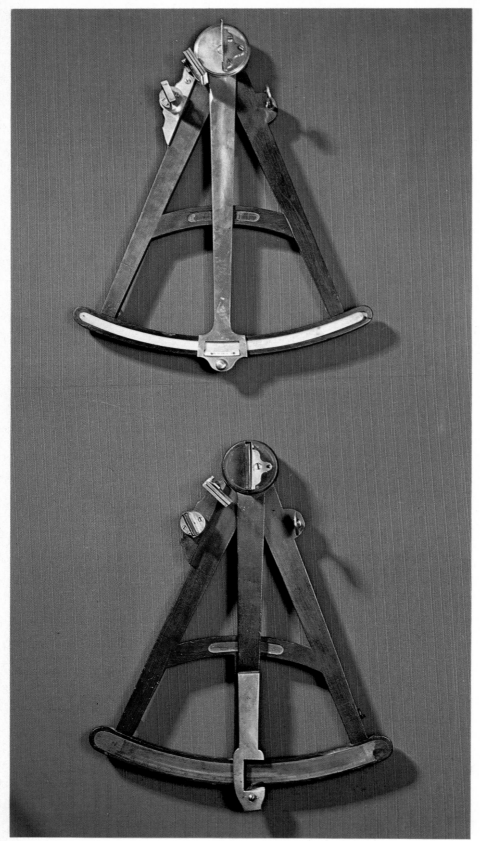

Two late 18th-century English octants. *Top:* ebony model with copper index bar, ivory arc and vernier, simple sight. Index mirror and maker's ivory name plate are missing. *Bottom:* model with wooden, copper-reinforced index bar, wooden arc with diagonal divisions, no vernier.

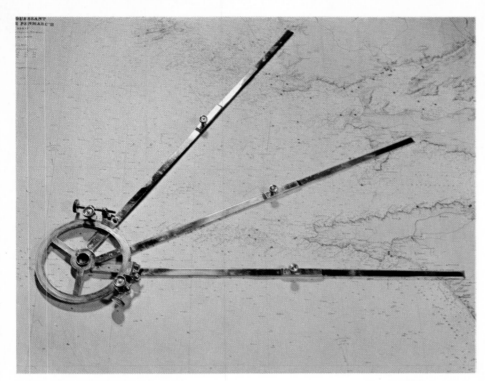

Station pointers as used for hydrographic survey. After the angles between three prominent points along the coastline have been measured by sextant or reflecting circle, the surveyor can fix his precise position on the chart, which is of great importance especially when making soundings. Late 19th century.

17th-century Augsburg dial signed 'A. Vogler', with its original box and an instruction sheet in German and French. This instrument had an advantage over the Nuremberg Diptych in that it was usable for all latitudes, but on the other hand it was never as accurate as the ring-dial. Even in its day it could have been no more than an amusing gadget.

113

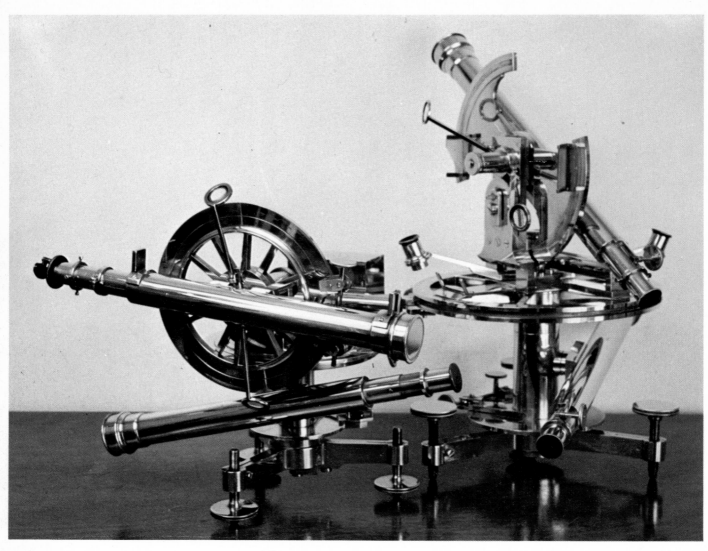

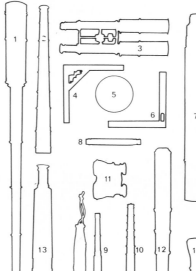

Two 19th-century theodolites. The one on the left is inscribed 'Dépôt de la Marine'. A survey instrument of extreme precision, it was used by hydrographers for terrestial surveys. By comparison with the graphometer and circumferentor, whose successor it is, the theodolite has gained in precision but lost in ornamentation. Nevertheless, it remains a particularly handsome scientific instrument.

1. Telescope with five extensions. Unsigned English model, 19th century. 2. Traveller's telescope with seven extensions. Unsigned French model, 19th century. 3. Rare type of binoculars with dual controls, i.e. focussing and adjustable eyepieces. Signed 'Dollond, London', 19th century. 4. Square for work on sea-charts, similar to Gunter scales. 18th century. Signed 'Delure, Paris'. 5. Dry compass with copper-engraved card. Spain, 18th century. 6. Square by Langlois, Paris, 18th century. 7. Ship's telescope with lens-hood. Unsigned English model, 19th century. 8., 9., 10. Small Victorian traveller's telescopes, one in its leather pouch. 11. French pilot's binoculars, 19th century. 12. Venetian telescope by Leonardo Semitecolo, 17th century. Tubes of cardboard and leather, eyepiece frame and tube rings of ebony. 13. Ship's telescope with lens-hood, covered with shagreen. Signed 'Husband & Clarke, Denmark St., Bristol'. Late 19th century. 14. Rare type of telescope with twin eyepieces. Unsigned English model, 19th century.

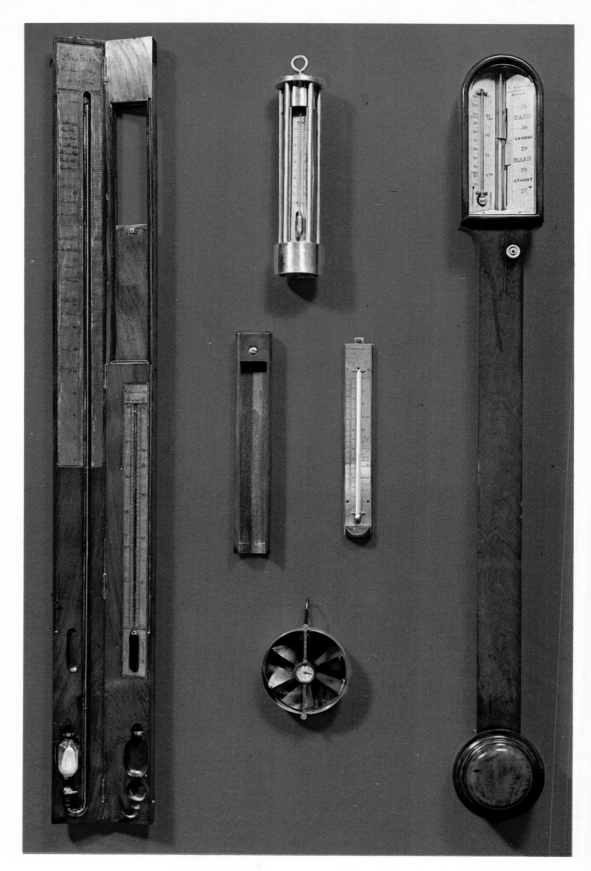

which was an important safeguard at a period when radio time checks were not yet available. The daily rate of variation of a good chronometer should be no more than one to three seconds. It is rare for such an instrument to go wrong except, perhaps, as a result of exceptionally violent shocks.

Since chronometers are subjected to very little wear and tear and last practically forever, they are handed from one ship to another with some cleaning and oiling in between. This explains why chronometers appear so rarely on the market and why, if they do, they fetch such high prices.

Astro-navigation: from astrolabe to sextant

Even before it was established that the earth is a globe, the ancient astronomers observed that the angle which the celestial pole (roughly marked by the Pole Star) made with the horizon, i.e. its altitude, was not the same in different places on earth. From this observation of altitude grew the first inklings of the concept of latitude. Once the spherical shape of the earth had been proved, it could be established that the latitude of a place was equal to the altitude of the celestial pole above the horizon.

Soon the astronomers found that there was a fundamental equation which could be applied at the moment of culmination of a heavenly body: the latitude of an observer is equal to the zenith distance (which is the complement to altitude) of the heavenly body plus its declination. The declination could be found in the tables for the particular day, which left the zenith distance to be measured.

The first instrument to be used for this purpose was the mariner's astrolabe. Its graduated metal ring represented the meridian; the instrument's gravity, when suspended by a metal ring, provided the axis zenith-nadir. Two sights were lined up with the observed body to give a reading which was the altitude (or zenith distance).

The oldest known descriptions of an astrolabe go back to the 12th century, but this was the type used by astronomers on land. It was an ornate and elaborate instrument, which on one side had the usual graduated disc and an alidade, on the other a plan projection of horary and equatorial co-ordinates (similar to those found in the modern Star Finder). The marine version of the instrument dates no further back than the end of the 15th century, the period of great voyages of discovery, when important navigation instruments were developed and the principles of astro-navigation established.

The two oldest mariners' astrolabes which we have come across are in the Dundee Museum (dated 1555 and of Portuguese origin) and the National Maritime Museum at Greenwich (dated 1585). The latter was found at Valentia in Ireland in the wreck of one of the ships of the Spanish Armada. While astronomers' astrolabes for use on land were still made in the late 18th century, and there are quite a few of them about even today, mariners' astrolabes are now extremely rare. In fact, there are no more than some fifteen in the whole world. Many of them went down with their ships, and when, in the 17th century, the cross-staff came into use, they were no longer made.

Around the middle of the 15th century the seaman's or Gunter's quadrant, which was somewhat lighter than the astrolabe but also based on gravity, was used at sea for measuring altitude. We have already met it in the section on sun-dials. Today it is as rare as the astrolabe.

All these instruments, while satisfactory for measuring latitude, were insufficiently accurate for longitude calculations, even lunar distances. What was needed was an instrument which could measure minutes of arc with precision.

In 1730 John Hadley proposed his reflecting quadrant, which was principally an octant and, in fact, very similar in principle to an octant previously designed by Sir Isaac Newton. In modified form it was presented to the Admiralty in 1731, tested, approved and commercialized as Hadley's quadrant. Hadley's 1730 model did not yet have glass mirrors but speculums of polished metal, nor did it have coloured shades. In fact, at that time a reliable technique for grinding surfaces of glass absolutely parallel had not yet been found. Another thing which was still lacking was the vernier scale; instead, the diagonal scale was used to divide the arc. The first octants were made rather large, up to 50 cm in radius, in an effort to make the scale legible down to one minute of arc. Once a vernier scale came into use in 1758, angles to the nearest $\frac{1}{2}$ minute of arc could be measured.

While initially the octant was considered a costly luxury, by the end of the 18th

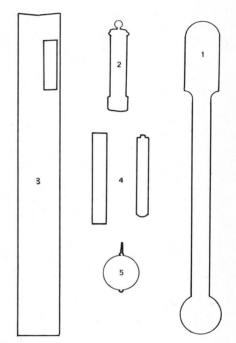

1. Ship's barometer-thermometer with adjusting screw in polished mahogany case. Signed 'H. Blackwood, Glasgow'. 18th century. 2. Caged depth-thermometer used in hydrographic work for measuring the water temperature. Signed 'Lehalle, Paris' and marked 'Marine A.G.'. 19th century.
3. Traveller's barometer-thermometer in mahogany case, hand-written graduations on lemon-wood scales. Early 19th century. By Mercier, Paris. 4. Deck thermometer with its mahogany case. Signed 'Vv. Chevalier, Paris'. 19th century. 5. Small ship's anemometer signed 'Biram's patent, Winter, Newcastle.' 19th century.

117

The seaman's astrolabe measured 15 to 30 cm in diameter. It was made of a 15 to 20 mm thick bronze ring with large openings cut into the top half to reduce wind resistance but almost solid at the bottom to provide the necessary weight (total weight appr. 2 kilos) which made the instrument hang perfectly vertically. The alidade B has two pinnules D and D′, through which sights are taken. The instrument is hand-held, freely suspended by the ring A. Since direct observation of the sun (1) would have been blinding, method (2) was preferred. Maximum accuracy in fine weather with a calm sea was to 1° of arc, which corresponds to a possible latitude error of 100 km!

Spanish seaman's astrolabe, 16th century.

Gunter's quadrant has two sights v and v′ and a plumb-line p. Sights were taken directly (1) or by cast shadow (2), the observer pressing the plumb-line against the graduated arc. Angle N is the zenith distance. Maximum accuracy to 1°.

118

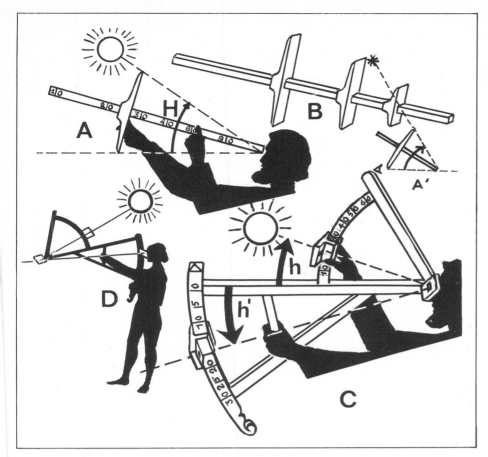

The cross-staff, which was frequently made of pear wood, consisted of a square-sectioned staff 3 to 4 feet long (100 to 130 cm), with a sliding bevelled vane. Vanes of different length could be used depending on the altitude measured. The four sides of the staff had different scales, each corresponding to one of the vanes. In taking a direct sight (A) the lower and upper edges of the vane were aligned with the horizon and the centre of the sun respectively and the altitude (H) read off on the staff. For great altitudes a back sight (A') was preferred.

Davis's quadrant (C), also made of wood, consists of two arcs of 30° and 60° resp., each with a sliding sight. The sum of angles h and h' gives the altitude of the observed object above the horizon. It was common for sights to be taken with the observer's back to the sun (D), which was more convenient and did not require him to keep an eye on two sights at once. Under optimum conditions the instrument's accuracy was to 1/10°. In late 18th-century models the upper sight sometimes incorporates a lens.

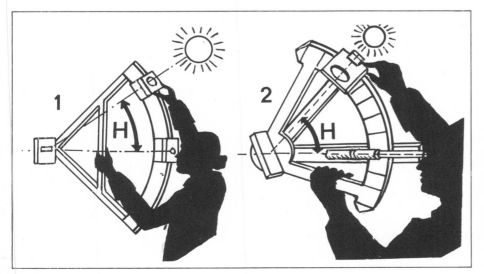

About 1730 the French astronomer Pierre Bouguer modified Davis's quadrant by combining the two arcs in a single one (1). Altitude H of the observed object is now the difference between the two sight angles. One sight has a lens. Models with pivoted index bar and telescope (2) were the forerunners of those with movable index mirror. Diagonal divisions on the arc gave an accuracy to 5 minutes of arc. For maximum accuracy the quadrant's radius was often as much as 1 metre.

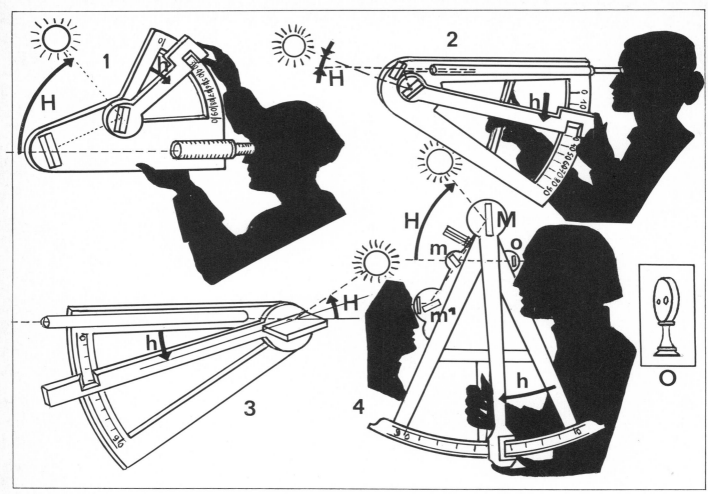

Ancestor to our sextant, Hadley's prototype (1) incorporated a fixed mirror and a movable index mirror. When the twice reflected image of the observed object and the direct image of the horizon are coincident as seen through the telescope, the altitude can be read off the arc. Very similar is Newton's quadrant (2), which was merely an experimental instrument, while Hadley's quadrant was already designed for use at sea. The experimental quadrant by Robert Hooke (3) was first described in 1666. Hadley's octant ($\frac{1}{8}$ of a full circle = 45°) in its final version (4) has a sight (o) sometimes with two holes to cope with a very bright horizon, coloured shades and a second horizon glass m for taking back sights. The arc has diagonal divisions, the vernier was not added until 1760. The instrument's accuracy is to 1 minute of arc.

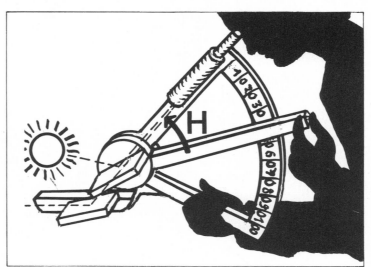

century it was to be found on every ship. Hadley's quadrant (or octant) was designed for measuring angles between 0° and 90°, which made it unsuitable for measuring lunar distances in excess of 90°. This became possible when, in 1757, Captain Campbell of the Royal Navy introduced the nautical sextant, which was capable of measuring angles up to 120°.

Amongst the first makers of sextants in the 18th and 19th centuries we must name Mégnié, Lenoir, Jecker, Le Maire, Fortin, Ponthus Lepetit and Lorieux in France, Dollond, Nairne, Troughton, Ramsden, Adams, Bird and Spencer Browning & Co. in England, Carl Bamberg in Germany, John Bliss & Co., Edmund & George Blunt, Edmund Brown & Son, John Dupee, Henry Glover, Thomas Greenough, William W. Hagger, Benjamin King Hagger, James Halsey, John Payne, John Kehew, the King family, Frederick W. Lincoln (later the famous firm of Hutchinson), Richard Patten, Edward Samuel Ritchie and Samuel Thaxter in the U.S.A.

Many 19th-century sextants and octants bore the name of whoever sold them in this or that port after having assembled them from mechanical and optical parts bought separately. A large number of old ebony octants were modernized and equipped with telescopes (in place of the older sight vanes), coloured shades and handles. The wooden, quadrant-shaped carrying cases were usually painted and decorated with colourful vignettes. Those of the earliest octants without handles, both English and American, were extremely flat with a bulge for the two mirrors. All these cases are in demand by collectors. Those which contain tools for dismantling the instrument and adjusting the mirrors are particularly rare.

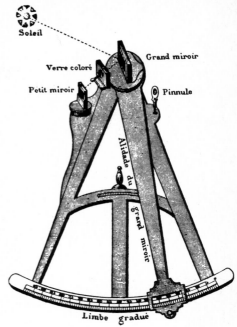

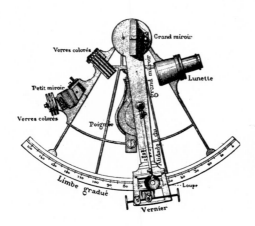

Quadrant designed by the American Thomas Godfrey in 1732. Drawing on the work done by Caleb Smith, this instrument has little in common with Hadley's quadrant.

All-metal oxtants and sextants

The need for measuring angles to 1/10 minute of arc soon led to the introduction of all-metal frames for sextants, which were unaffected by wet conditions and temperature fluctuations. From 1760, brass index bars with clamp blocks came into use, and in 1776 the first metal frames and arcs appeared. At that time James Cook took one of Ramsden's new-type sextants with him on his voyages. By 1757 the sight vane had been replaced by an achromatic telescope by Dolland. The vernier scale[1], although described by the French mathematician Pierre Vernier as early as 1631, was not applied to the sextant until the end of the 18th century. Although perfect in principle, the vernier scale became of true benefit to sextants only after a perfect arc graduation was achieved with Ramsden's ingenious dividing engine. Around 1810 a small magnifying glass for the vernier scale was added. The first double frames, which overcame the problem of frame distortion by heat, appeared in 1830. Later

[1]Although the invention of the vernier scale is usually ascribed to Pierre Vernier, it appears that the German Christoph Clavius explained the method in a treatise on astrolabes as early as 1611. Occasionally, the scale is referred to as Nonius scale after Pedro Nunez (lat. Petrus Nonius) the Portuguese mathematician, who described a dividing scale similar in principle but different in application.

the use of precious metals, i.e. silver and platinum for the arc and vernier scale became common. After 1850 any further improvements of the sextant were aimed at aesthetic perfection and small details such as the precise adjustment of the mirrors, reduction of error of eccentricity, further strengthening of the metal frame, addition of the Wollaston prism between the index mirror and horizon glass, and the use of all sorts of telescopes. The last improvements to the sextant were the clamping mechanism and the tangent screw in 1905 and finally the micrometer drum in 1926, which enables an angle to be measured to the last 1/20 minute of arc without magnification.

Sextant boxes, from 1850 onwards, were square, and a complete example contained, apart from the instrument itself, at least two squares for squaring the mirrors, a screwdriver, a spanner or key, a magnifying glass and different telescopes

Only through being constantly tested in practice could navigation instruments be perfected for use in all weather conditions. This picture of a Biscay crossing on board a P & O liner illustrates that sextants frequently got as wet as the men who used them.

with lens caps. Different methods were used for wedging the sextant in its box by the handle to protect it against shock. The manufacturer's label inside the lid also lists the error of eccentricity for different angles.

Box sextants and pocket sextants

The box sextant illustrated on p. 110 was invented by William Jones in the late 18th century and measures angles up to 150°. Most surviving models of this compact yet surprisingly robust and accurate type of sextant are late 19th century. The cover can be unscrewed and screwed on the other side to form a handle. Two coloured shades, a telescope and lens cap are part of the instrument. Angles are read off a graduated arc and a silver vernier scale with an integral magnifying glass. Angles can be measured to the nearest minute of arc. The instrument was mainly intended for terrestial observation with an artificial horizon and was very popular with surveyors, but it was also successfully used on board small ships, above all by the Frenchman Jean Lacombe during his single-handed Atlantic crossing.

The pocket sextant, on the other hand, is no more than a smaller version of the normal sextant and mesures angles up to 120°. Mostly of English manufacture, this instrument was never more than 10 cm high. Two interesting examples can be seen at the National Maritime Museum at Greenwich: the smaller, made by Sir Allen

Young and used by Captain MacLintock on board the *Fox* in 1857 to 1859, the other used by Captain Richard on board the *Assistance* between 1852 and 1854.

The reflecting circle

It was the German astronomer Tobias Mayer who, in 1752, invented the reflecting circle and produced the first experimental model in an effort to find an instrument in which the main shortcoming of the octant, namely errors of graduation and of eccentricity, would be absent. The idea was taken up and improved on by the French Naval officer Borda, who built his first reflecting circle in 1772 and tested it successfully on board *La Boussole*.

The instrument's circular limb is graduated in 720°, which, as in the sextant, is twice the actual angle. The angular distance of two observed objects is obtained by taking the mean of two readings of two opposed verniers. The reflecting circle completely eliminates error of eccentricity and significantly diminishes errors of graduation and reading. Besides, the possibility of measuring angles up to 180° made it suitable for tackling all navigational and hydrographic problems. The instrument is held by a handle, with the plane of the limb in line with the two observed objects, which could be in a vertical or a horizontal plane. Thus, it was used not only for altitude observations but, above all, for measuring lunar i.e. horizontal distances in longitude calculations, for which it was ideally suited.

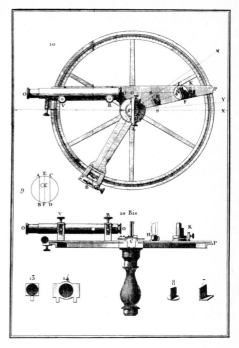

Parts of Borda's reflecting circle.

Early 19th-century English bubble sextant. This type of sextant did not become popular for use at sea because it is difficult to use in a seaway and gives inaccurate results.

Variations on the theme of sextants with artificial horizon: here a model by R. Rust, which is levelled with the help of a balanced pendulum.

Borda's reflecting circle was first built in France by Lenoir from 1777 onwards. It measured 26 cm in diameter. In England a slightly different version was built by James Troughton under the name 'full circle'. Used widely during the great voyages of discovery, the reflecting circle continued to be used as navigation instrument as well as for hydrographic purposes by the ships of the French Navy until 1914. After that date it was only used as survey instrument on hydrographic vessels.

Inclinometer by Lenoir, c. 1820. This extremely sensitive instrument was used in ocean surveys to measure the vertical component of the earth's magnetic field. The results were drawn up in variation charts, which were indispensable to navigators in the days when the magnetic compass was the main navigational aid during long sea voyages.

Hydrographic and oceanographic instruments

In as far as many of the concerns of hydrography are in the service of navigation, the problems of hydrography have always occupied the mariner, and a number of instruments are common to both. Having already dealt with these, we shall now take a brief look at instruments which are purely hydrographic. A knowledge of the earth's magnetism is essential to navigation, since the navigator has to allow for the difference between true and magnetic north when steering a compass course. This difference, known as 'variation' is different for different parts of the world and changes yearly. On ocean charts it is indicated by isogonic lines, i.e. lines joining places of equal variation, on coastal charts of larger scale it is shown inside the compass rose. Measurement of the earth's magnetic field was one of the most important tasks accomplished by the great exploratory voyages of the 18th and 19th centuries. The inclinometer, an instrument of extreme accuracy, which measures the vertical component of the magnetic field, was employed for the purpose. A very handsome example of an inclinometer made by Nairne of Holborn to the plans of The Rev. W. Mitchell and used by Captain Cook on his voyages can be seen in the National Maritime Museum at Greenwich.

Two other instruments, though hardly usable on board because of the ship's movement, were part of the inventory: the circumferentor and the graphometer, which are surveying instruments. Made of non-magnetic brass they consisted of a graduated circle or semi-circle respectively spanned by a diametric bar with sighting holes at opposite ends, which were aligned to magnetic north as indicated by a built-in compass. A second alidade with sights at opposite ends and pivoting round the centre of the circle was aligned to take a bearing. These very handsomely engraved

Graphometer by Nicolas Bion, complete with its shaped box. 18th century.

Two artificial horizons for use in taking hydrographic sights on land or on a mooring in calm weather. *Left:* mercury horizon complete with trough, case and filler bottle. *Right:* mirror horizon with adjustable legs and level.

and ornamented instruments were used by surveyors on land to chart the coastline. They were normal items in the catalogues of scientific and navigational instrument makers in the 17th and 18th centuries.

Circumferentors and graphometers were superseded at the beginning of the 19th century by the reflecting circle, which measured angles not only in the horizontal but also in the vertical plane. Eventually the theodolite took over, which is today the principal surveyor's instrument in general and is found on board all hydrographic survey vessels.

For plotting the obtained bearings on a chart it was necessary to develop a special instrument. Ordinary dividers, which gave only moderately accurate results, were good enough for the everyday requirements of navigation, but when it came to preparing hydrographic charts, a rather more precise instrument was needed. Thus, in 1750, the station pointer with its three arms came into use. If preceded by a

Sampling bottle, type Richard, as used on hydrographic vessels for taking water samples and measuring water temperatures at great depths. Early 20th century.

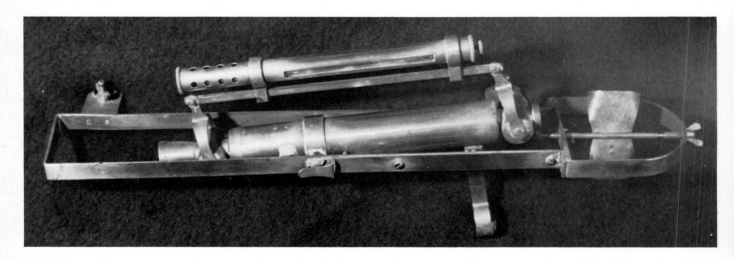

triangulation measurement by sextant or reflecting circle it gives an accuracy to the nearest 1/20°.

Oceanography, a comparatively recent science, had its true beginnings at the end of the 19th century and was greatly furthered by Prince Albert of Monaco, who undertook many deep-sea expeditions. Oceanography, apart from the classical instruments of navigation and hydrography, uses very specialized equipment frequently built to the plans of researchers. Hundreds of instruments, some of them very complicated, like various sounders and probes, sampling bottles and diving equipment, have been developed over the years.

Meteorological observation and forecasting. Instruments used in marine meteorology.

When, in 1850, Matthew Fontaine Maury's *Sailing Directions* and *Pilot Charts* were published in the United States, marine meteorology was still in its infancy. Maury's charts were based on the evaluation of innumerable entries in the logs of merchant ships. His statistical deductions were definitely useful but had very little to do with meteorology. The basic laws of meteorology concerning the interaction of pressure and temperature had not yet been discovered. Nevertheless, we must do justice to the observation instruments of that period, especially since they were far ahead of their time.

The barometer was by then well known to mariners. Torricelli (1643), Pascal (1648) and Otto von Guericke (1654) with their research had laid the basis for the development of the open-tube mercury barometer, which was subsequently built in large numbers. From it Hooke developed the first barometer with dial and needle

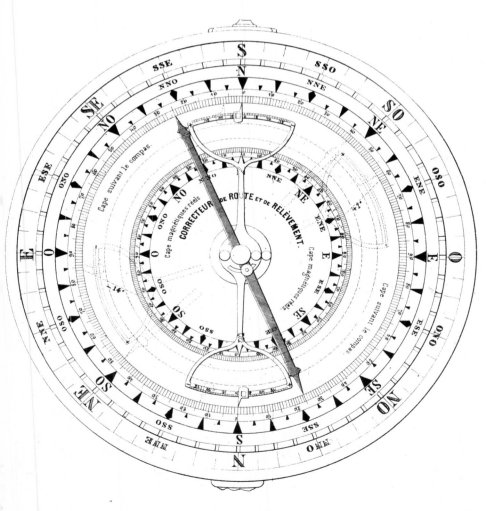

Part of a strange instrument built on the principle of hurricane dials, which were supposed to be useful in calculating the strength and track of approaching hurricanes.

indicator, and this served as a model for all the 18th-century drawing-room barometers. Whether they were of the column or the dial type, until the end of the 18th century all barometers only bore the most summary of information like 'fair' and 'rain'.

Marine barometers, which were hung in gimbals, were remarkable above all for their ornateness. They were frequently combined with thermometers and hair-hygrometers, as the one illustrated on p. 128. The accuracy of these instruments left much to be desired, partly because the glass tubes were not of uniform section and partly because a method of desiccating the mercury completely had not yet been found. Instead of a complete vacuum there was a small quantity of water vapour in the upper part of the tube which expanded as the temperature rose and falsified the reading.

The first really reliable thermometers date from the beginning of the 19th century. There were two types. In one, the open end of the glass tube containing the mercury rests in a cup of mercury of a diameter 100 times that of the tube. It is read by means of a vernier moved by a toothed wheel and is suspended by a simple ring at the top of the copper tube, which houses the instrument.

In the second type, invented by Fortin, the mercury in the cup rests on a piece of chamois leather, which can be pushed up by a screw to zero the instrument. The level in the tube is once again read with the help of a vernier graduated in millimeters, or in 1/20 inch in England.

For use at sea the mercury barometer did not prove very satisfactory except in fine weather. As the ship moved violently, it often happened that the mercury was flung to the top end of the tube and burst it. The author knows of several cases where members of the hydrographic service spent the best part of their time on trains between Paris and Toulon or Brest carrying barometers as though they were holy relics.

Aneroid barometers are of two types: the Bourdon type consists of a vacuum tube of elliptical section, which is bent in a circle. Changes in pressure change the section of the tube and thereby increase or reduce the diameter of the circle. This change is amplified and recorded on a dial by a needle, or on a drum by a stylus.

Vidi's barometer, on the other hand, uses a number of metal vacuum boxes with a spring inside to prevent them being crushed, which are more or less compressed by changes in atmospheric pressure. The more vacuum boxes an instrument contains, the more sensitive it is.

The first barograph, still on the mercurial principles, dates from 1780.

The first thermometer was made in Florence in 1641 and contained alcohol. Its imaginative graduation quite properly equalled zero to the temperature of ice, but 'hot' was taken to be the temperature at which butter melts! It had a spiral-shaped tube, possibly to speed the flow of the liquid!

Precision thermometers first appeared in the 18th century. They had neither zero point nor graduation, but seamen used them to detect the approach of what we now call a warm or a cold front.

More frequently used than commonly realized was the oceanographer's depth-thermometer. It was actually used daily by deep-sea fishermen to determine at which depth of water the temperature would be right for certain species of fish. An easy way to ensure a good catch.

Wind speed and direction could be measured as early as 1734 by a type of hair anemometer which is on show at the Conservatoire National des Arts et Métiers in Paris.

Before it became common to install semi-spherical anemometers with electronic transmission at mastheads, wind speeds were measured quite accurately with hand-held rotary anemometers together with a fifteen- or thirty-second hour-glass. The dial was graduated in meters per second or from 1 to 12 Beaufort Scale.

Other interesting relics of marine meteorlogy as practised in bygone ages are those curious compass roses called 'hurricane dials', which were used to determine graphically the route a ship had to take to avoid the eye of an approaching hurricane. The readings of a number of scales and indicators had to be combined in a complicated way. The more costly instruments were made of brass, the simpler ones of horn.

Gimballed ship's barometer with combined thermometer and hair hygrometer. Signed 'J. Sewill, Liverpool'. 18th century.

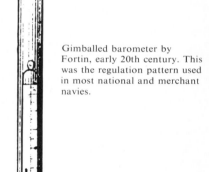

Two late 19th-century rotary anemometers. The instrument on the left, (signed 'Stutz, Lille') measures 13 cm in diameter, that on the right (signed 'Casatelli, Manchester') 10 cm in diameter.

Optical instruments on board

From the very moment of their appearance, telescopes played an immensely important role on board ships, for the ability to see further than the naked eye not only meant better recognition of signals but enabled the navigator to spot cliffs, rocks, enemy ships or any other danger in time to take avoiding action, which might otherwise have been impossible.

The principle of the telescope has been known since Galileo, and although the great scholar pronounced quite a few erroneous principles, that of his telescope served at least as a starting basis. There remained, above all, the practical problem of making good lenses. The art of cutting glass had its beginnings in Italy in 1623, but the quality of optical lenses remained mediocre for a long time, and until 1800 a telescope was hardly more than a pretext for superb ornamentation.

The first telescopes were made of cardboard tubes covered with copper sheet and with a lens panel and eye-piece of wood or horn. Sometimes the tube itself was made

Gimballed barometer by Fortin, early 20th century. This was the regulation pattern used in most national and merchant navies.

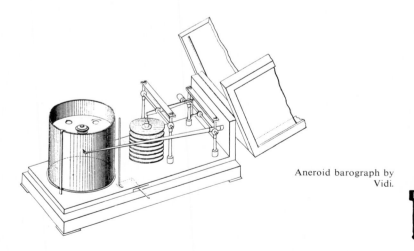

Aneroid barograph by Vidi.

of wood, in which case it was assembled of glued laths of trapezoidal section, the section of the tube being octagonal, hexagonal or square.

Since lenses with short focus suffer considerably from aberration (a phenomenon which causes distortion), long-focus lenses had to be used for telescopes until the end of the 18th century. Besides, since the field gets smaller as the magnification increases, the magnification was uniformly limited to three to four times in order to get field large enough to absorb the ship's movements. If one wanted more, one had to extend the tubes enormously. Many telescopes in those days had eight to ten tubes extending to 1.5 m or more.

Until the 18th century, the technique of extruding metal tubes was unknown, but subsequently telescopes were made of extruded copper tube. A further improvement were two erecting lenses to reverse the image, which had so far been upside-down.

The discovery of the achromaticity of dioptric systems by John Dollond in 1757 meant a considerable step forward in the sciece of optics. Chromatic and spheric aberration were overcome by two types of glass of different refractive indices, crown glass and flint glass, being coupled in one lens system. From then onwards lenses of short focal length could be used and telescopes with greater magnification built, yet the field had to remain sufficiently wide for the instrument to remain useful on a rolling ship. A compromise was therefore accepted by all 19th-century telescope makers to build marine telescopes with one extension tube only. Made of extruded brass tube of maximum lightness, such an instrument measured about 50 cm closed and had a diameter of about 7.5 cm. The outer tube was covered with leather or leather braid-work and frequently decorated with signal-tables. Lens attachments included a hood against the sun and a lens cover for protection. The eyepiece was covered, when not in use, by a pivoted disc. On the ocular tube of old ship's telescopes one can normally distinguish a number of rings scratched with a sharp tool. These are a kind of distance scale and facilitate focussing prior to observation. There did exist, in the 19th century, instruments with a larger number of extension tubes which took up less space, but these were mainly used by travellers.

Y-shaped telescopes with one lens and two eyepieces were invented in 1677 but never became popular. The first known example bears the signature of the famous Père Chérubin.

The first known model of binoculars was designed by Père Rheita in 1643 and made of two cardboard-telescopes side by side. Prismatic binoculars appeared at the end of the 19th century, and this principle permitted a reduction of the bulk of the instrument and yet a simultaneous increase of field and magnification. Binoculars gradually replaced telescopes on board ships, but the conservative mariner, who valued the great magnifying power of his telescope, remained true to it for a long time. Meanwhile, the art of using a telescope on a rolling ship, which largely depends on the helmsman's skill, has become lost.

Catalogues of nautical instruments

Catalogues published by makers and dealers of nautical instruments are of great value to collectors for identifying and dating pieces of their collection, although precise descriptions are frequently lacking.

From the 17th century onwards, such catalogues were common. Here, for example, is one which tells us what was offered by John Seller 'either at his house by the Hermitage Stairs at Wapping or at his city shop by the Royal Exchange'[1]:

Azimuth and meridian compasses
Hanging and pocket compasses
Brass compasses (i.e. dividers) for Platts and Charts
Steel-pointed compasses (i.e. dividers) for scales

Cross Staves	Nocturnals
Gunter's Scales	Plain Scales
Sinical Quadrants	Almicanter Staves
Astrolabes	Height Rules
Sliding Gunters	Davis's Quadrants

[1]From *The Geometric Seaman* by E. G. R. Taylor and M. W. Richey (Hollis & Carter).

| Gunter's Quadrants | Tide Tables |
| All sorts of Running-glasses | One, two, three and four Hour-Glasses |

One minute, Half minute and Quarter minute Glasses
Logs, Log-boards, Log lines, Sounding Leads

The following is an excerpt from the list of the younger Benjamin Cole, at the Sign of the Orrery, 136 Fleet Street. It is dated 1768:[1]

Pocket cases of drawing instruments in silver and brass
Plain and plotting scales in brass, ivory and wood
Gunter's 2 foot and 1 foot scales in brass and wood
Protractors
Parallel Rules 6 inches to 36 inches
Sectors in brass, ivory or wood
Theodolites with vertical arcs, spirit levels, telescopes etc. (10 gns to 20 gns)
Circumferentors, the principal instruments for surveying in the West Indies
    (£1.16s to 3½ gns)
Hadley's Quadrant with Diagonal Divisions (£1.14s)
Hadley's Quadrant with a nonius (2 gns to 3½ gns)
Davis's Quadrant (12s to 1 gn)
Cole's Quadrant
Sutton's Quadrant
Gunter's Quadrant
Azimuth Compasses
Amplitude Compasses
Mariner's Compasses either for the Cabin or for the Binnacle
Pocket Compasses
Armillary Spheres (£12 to £50)
17 inch, 15 inch, 12 inch, 9 inch, 6 inch and 3 inch Globes (10s to 6 gns)
Reflecting Telescopes (£1.16s to £50)
Achromatic Telescope of any length (1 gn each foot)

More recent catalogues, like the one of the famous instrument maker Plath, should not be neglected either. They may be less picturesque but contain much more precise descriptions.

Another source of information are contemporary accounts of voyages. The following are some of the items contained in a list of nautical instruments for Frobisher's voyage in 1576:[2]

> A greate globe of metal in blanke in a case, a greate instrument of brasse named Armilla Tolomei or Hemisperium, an instrument of brasse named Sphera Nautica, a greate instrument of brasse named Compassum Meirianum, a greate instrument of brasse named Holometrum Geometricum, a ring of brasse named Annulus Astronomicus, a little standing level of brasse, an instrument of wood a stafe named Balestella, one very greate carte of navigation, a greate mappe universall of Mercator in prente, 6 cartes of navigation written in blanke parchment whereof 4 ruled playne & 2 rounde, 29 compasses of divers sorts, 18 hower glasses, a astrolabium . . .

Sometimes, rather than using trade cards or catalogues, navigational instrument makers spread their reputation by sticking labels inside their instrument boxes. For example, we find one inside a sextant box which reads: 'Joseph Roux Fils aîné & Co., hydrographic instrument makers near the port of St. Jean, make and sell all sorts of compasses, steering, azimuth and others, hour-glasses of many qualities, sextants, octants, cross-bars, telescopes, achromatic telescopes of different lengths, night telescopes, opera glasses, dividers, scales, instrument cases. They keep a stock of linen, wool and cotton cloth for the making of flags, as well as portolanos (pilot guides), harbour plans and hydrographic charts by all the cartographers at Marseilles.'

[1] From *The Geometric Seaman* by E. G. R. Taylor and M. W. Richey (Hollis & Carter).

[2] From *The Art of Navigation in England in Elizabethan and Early Stuart Times* by Lieut. Cdr. R. N. David W. Waters (Hollis & Carter).

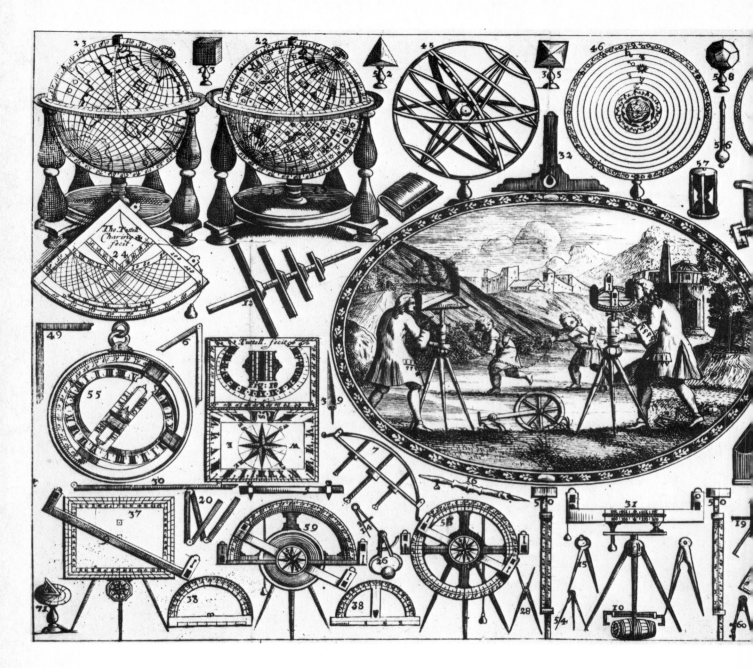

Trade card by T. Tuttell (early 18th century), maker of astronomical navigational and surveying instruments. We recognize a number of familiar instruments: graphometer (59), ring dial (55), astrolabe (1), Azimuth compass (3), Davis's quadrant (41), nocturnal (34), cross-staff (12), armillary sphere (45).

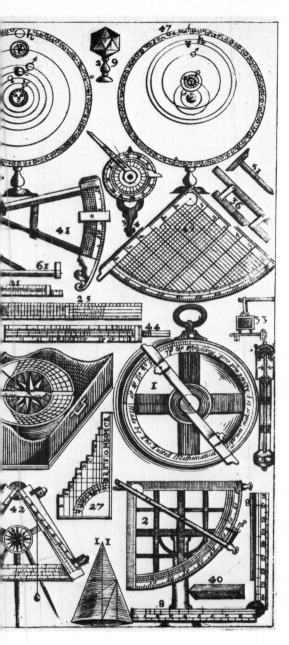

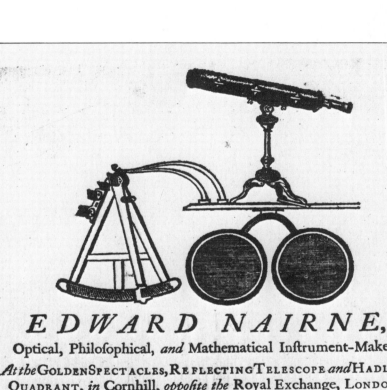

EDWARD NAIRNE,

Optical, Philosophical, *and* Mathematical Inftrument-Maker,

At the GOLDEN SPECTACLES, REFLECTING TELESCOPE *and* HADLEY'S QUADRANT, *in* Cornhill, *oppofite the* Royal Exchange, LONDON;

MAKES and Sells Spectacles, either of GLASS or BRAZIL PEBBLE, set in neat and commodious Frames, some of which neither prefs the Nofe nor Temples.

CONCAVES for Short-Sighted Perfons; READING, BURNING and MAGNIFYING-GLASSES.

Newtonian and *Gregorian* REFLECTING TELESCOPES; alfo EQUATORIAL TELESCOPES, or PORTABLE OBSERVATORIES.

REFRACTING TELESCOPES of all Sorts; particularly one of a new CONSTRUCTION (which may be ufed either at Land or Sea) that will ftand all Kinds of Weather without warping, and is allowed by thofe efteemed the beft JUDGES, who have made feveral late Trials of them at Sea, to exceed all others yet made in *England*; alfo a peculiar Sort to be ufed at Sea in the Night.

MICROSCOPES, either DOUBLE, SINGLE, AQUATICK, SOLAR, or OPAKE; likewife a new-invented POCKET MICROSCOPE, that may be ufed with the SOLAR, and anfwers the Purpofes of all the other Sorts.

CAMERA OBSCURAS for delineating Landfkips and Profpects (and which ferve to view Perfpective Prints) made with truly Parallel Planes; SKY-OPTIC BALLS; PRISMS for demonftrating the Theory of Light and Colours; CONCAVE, CONVEX, and CYLINDRICAL SPECULUMS; MAGICK LANTERNS; OPERA GLASSES; OPTICAL MACHINES for Perfpective Prints; ·CYLINDERS and CYLINDRICAL PICTURES.

AIR PUMPS, particularly a fmall Sort that ferves for Condenfing; AIR FOUNTAINS of various Kinds; GLASS PUMPS; WIND GUNS; PAPIN'S DIGESTORS; alfo a PORTABLE APPARATUS for ELECTRICAL EXPERIMENTS, which is allowed by the CURIOUS to exceed any of the Kind.

BAROMETERS, DIAGONAL, STANDARD, or PORTABLE.

THERMOMETERS, whofe Scales are adjufted to the Bores of their refpective Tubes; HYGROMETERS; HYDROSTATICAL BALANCES, and HYDROMETERS.

HADLEY'S QUADRANTS, after the moft exact Method, with Glaffes, whofe Planes are truly parellel; DAVIS'S QUADRANTS; GLOBES of all Sizes; AZIMUTH and other Sea Compaffes; LOAD-STONES; NOCTURNALS; SUN-DIALS of all Sorts; Cafes of DRAWING INSTRUMENTS; SCALES; PARALLEL RULERS; PROPORTIONAL COMPASSES and DRAWING PENS.

THEODOLITES, SEMICIRCLES, CIRCUMFERENTERS, PLAIN TABLES, DRAWING BOARDS, MEASURING WHEELS, SPIRIT LEVELS, RULES, PENCILS, and all other Sorts of OPTICAL, PHILOSOPHICAL, and MATHEMATICAL INSTRUMENTS, of the neweft and moft approved Inventions, are made and fold by the abovefaid *EDWARD NAIRNE.*

Advertisement by Edward Nairne, a famous 18th-century English supplier of 'optical, philosophical and mathematical' instruments.

V

Naval small-arms, flags and uniforms

Naval boarding pike.

Trying to compress a subject as extensive as that of naval small-arms into a few pages is fraught with dangers when one considers that experts and historians have dedicated numerous very detailed works to the subject of side-arms and firearms. Arms collectors attach great importance to even the smallest detail, and it is to them, above all others, that Bottet's remark applies that 'the collector gets no pleasure from the things he collects unless he can identify them accurately'. Indeed, arms collectors go to extreme lengths in this pursuit of precise identification, to the point where they can recognize a piece infallibly by the tiniest detail, especially if it is regulation issue.

Besides, one might argue, a subject should be dealt with in depth or not at all. On the other hand, no collector of items of style and quality can escape the fascination of weapons. This is, no doubt, due to their evocative powers: the mere feel of a hatchet or sabre in our hand turns us into pirates. Thus, any collector of marine objects, even without specializing in arms, has at least a pair of pistols or a sabre with an anchor engraved on the blade in his collection. Even if the provenance of such a sabre is hardly in question, there still remains the date and country of origin to be established. In the case of pistols there is the added question of whether they actually were used for Sea Service, to use the contemporary term.

I have, therefore, decided to present the subject in just its basic essentials and to give, at the end of this book, a list of reliable sources to which the novice can turn for further information.

Certain accepted ideas about the weapons that seamen are supposed to have carried still flourish widely. People love to pronounce resounding words like cutlass and blunderbuss. But this is only a very small facet of a subject which has a much more serious and complex side to it, namely that of regulation weapons used by the navy. It is these pieces, often of outstanding quality and now exceedingly rare, that form the backbone of a good collection. And here it must be said again that quality, of course, is far more important than quantity.

If this book succeeds in giving the collector a basic survey of naval weapons, in pointing out certain common errors and generally introducing him to the world of arms then it will have achieved its object.

Naval small-arms

In trying to understand the diversity of arms used by different individuals we have to go right back to the early days of military history. Until the middle of the 18th century no country had an established navy. When the king called his nobles to arms, they rallied to defend their country. Regiments were formed in all the provinces, and the men wore uniforms in the colours of their commanders. Their armament was the same only within their own regiment and certainly differed from that of other regiments in other provinces. For warfare at sea no special warships but converted merchant vessels were used. Thus Francis I completely failed to appreciate the importance of a national navy when he fought Charles V, and when Andrea Doria, to whom he had initially appealed for help in defending France, went over to the enemy, he had to turn to the Turks for protection at sea. It was only under Richelieu that a royal fleet began to be formed, made up partly of ships bought abroad and partly of vessels built in France by Dutch shipwrights, who were the only ones with the necessary know-how. In 1642 France had a fleet of sixty-three ships and twenty-three galleys at Toulon. That was the first national or rather royal navy.

Only towards the end of the 17th century did ships have regular crews of seamen, both regulars and conscripts. In times of war their rather scanty numbers were swelled by soldiers. Fusiliers became temporary ship's gunners, and if all the ship's guns had at least the same bore that was already an achievement. The individual soldiers, of course, were armed differently according to regiment.

What sort of times were these? Spain had no longer a navy. At Lepanto her fast galleys had gained a victory over the Turks, but this was not only the first but the last victory of the first Spanish navy. The defeat of the Armada in 1588 and the wars against the Netherlands, Britain and France, lost Spain 280 ships between 1548 and 1621. After the battle of the Dunes in 1639 Spain decided not to rebuild her fleet. In the short time that it existed its organisation had only been very basic and certainly never extended to 'regulation' weapons.

There remained three maritime nations who had the means to descend on the vast and fast disintegrating Spanish Empire: France, Britain and the Netherlands.

Regulation issue

The successful revolt of the Netherlands gave a decisive impetus to the Dutch navy. In 1602 the Dutch East Indies Company was founded. At first the Dutch navy was made up of vessels of that company (which was organised very much along military lines) and of armed vessels of the Dutch merchant navy. A proper national navy, which could challenge the mighty fleets of Britain and France, did not evolve until much later, towards the end of the 18th century under Admiral Ruyter. Until then the exploits of Heemskerk, Heim and Tromp were no more than acts of audacity against the decadent Spanish fleet, which demanded no great effort.

Britain, originally a purely agricultural country, came by her role as a maritime power almost by chance. It was, in fact, through Queen Elizabeth's pirates Hawkins, Drake, Lancaster and Cavendish, who returned from plundering Philip II's colonies with their holds filled with booty, that Britain acquired a taste for seeking her fortune at sea, or rather across the seas. In 1599 the Company of London Merchants was founded which traded with the East Indies. The Admiralty and the Navy Boards date from the reign of Henry VIII.

Big regular navies, as mentioned earlier, did not come about until the 17th century. The main problems that had to be tackled were the organization of the fleet, the armament of vessels, their repair and maintenance, the building of naval dockyards and the recruitment and organization of ships' complements. The 'naval' armament consisted of bronze field guns mounted on wheeled carriages, while the equipment of individual members of the crew resembled closely that of land soldiers and was obviously a fairly incongruous medley despite an order in 1674 and again in 1689, which attempted to define weapons for Sea Service.

Regulation boarding dirk of the French Navy, mid 19th century, with triangular blade, hardwood grip and leather scabbard with metal chape.

Britain was the first country to define positively a firearms model specifically for Sea Service, as we can see from a Board of Ordance order dating from 1704. In France, the first naval hand-gun dates from 1777. One might, therefore, assume that from that date onwards the collector could rely on accurate models and documents by which to follow the history of 'official' naval weapons. Far from it. Not only have certain models completely disappeared, but there are neither written specifications nor drawings to go by. This is the fault of the method by which these weapons were ordered from the contractor.

In France, in the 18th century, a model of a particular regulation issue was made by a Paris gunsmith and, stamped with the seal of the War Ministry, was sent to the contractor together with a copy of the *Règlement*, which gave a number of specifications for its manufacture. Sometimes there was no order, though, in which case the deal was negotiated directly with the contractor. It was not until the early 19th century that it became customary to draw up agreements, lists and drawings. This illustrates the difficulties with which anyone is faced who wants to do research on regulation weapons in archives. The bibliography at the end of this book lists a number of works on naval arms, which are essential for identification purposes to any collector.

The first French firearms order dates from 1717 and concerns two muskets: one a hand-gun carried by soldiers, the other a wall-piece. This represents an effort to put an end to the eternal arguments between the royal administration and the regimental commanders about the poorly armed state of the troops hired by the king. In this way, the 'regulation' arms, which were the property of the king, became binding for both parties. They were kept in the royal stores to be issued to the troops only in case of war.

The navy was not faced with the same urgency in this matter and retained the privilege to choose its equipment and buy its arms as it saw fit. In fact, the personal armament of individual sailors was altogether less important. A foot-soldier without a gun was worthless. The crew of a ship, however, had their cannon to fight with and, if the worst came to the worst, their sails to escape with. It was by no means inevitable for a vessel to be boarded and for hand-to-hand fighting to break out. The British

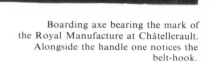

Boarding axe bearing the mark of the Royal Manufacture at Châtellerault. Alongside the handle one notices the belt-hook.

Board of Ordnance was so convinced that hand weapons were only a minor detail that, instead of equipping sailors with the best possible weapons, it stipulated, on the contrary, that they should be simple and robust but as cheap as possible. It subsequently became apparent that eventually the cheapest had to be paid for dearly, for in those days, when technical progress was so slow, a model might have to remain in service for 50 years without ever being taken apart, as long as the material stood up to it.

What, then, were the specifications for these weapons issued specifically for Sea Service, or rather what exactly distinguished them from similar weapons used by the Army?

Characteristics of naval weapons

Naval small-arms comprise side arms, i.e. pikes, axes, cutlasses, swords and dirks on the one hand, and firearms, i.e. muskets, rifles and pistols on the other. At first sight there seems nothing particularly naval about any of these, since they are almost all equally used by land soldiers.

Those who absolutely insist that there are certain characteristics by which to recognize weapons used for Sea Service like to say that pistols with bronze barrels are all Sea Service pistols, because bronze does not rust. To this it must be said that the bronze barrel was by no means exclusive to Sea Service pistols. In England, up till the 19th century, it was used on a large number of non-regulation pistols, which sailors might have carried when going ashore in ports where they had need to defend themselves.

These small British and Belgian pistols were often fitted with a dagger-blade or bayonet that folded back against the barrel for use when the pistol had been discharged. They really rank as shock weapons rather than naval arms, much like the bayonetted blunderbusses and the 'duck's foot' pistols. The latter had five to seven barrels arranged fanwise, and although they may have rendered useful service to a ship's captain trying to quell a mutiny, it is difficult to imagine an officer of a royal navy using such an undignified instrument.

The blunderbuss was introduced on board British ships in the second half of the 17th century. First-rate vessels carried ten of them, but they were never fitted with bayonets.

The volley gun, a seven-barrelled carbine, appeared in the (British) Royal Navy around 1870. It was so heavy that it was fired only from the tops, and it disappeared again during Nelson's time, because he objected strongly to the tactical use of firearms from high up in the rigging. Paradoxically, he himself was killed by one of them at Trafalgar.

In France, the blunderbuss was most often used as wall-piece, and although it did crop up on some vessels, it was not a regulation issue.

The belt-hook, with which pistols were fitted on the side opposite to the lockplate, is not an exclusively naval feature either. If it is handy for a seaman to carry his pistol in his belt while using both hands to climb up the ratlines, it is equally useful to a cavalryman or to mounted police. Thus, the belt-hook cannot be called a typically naval accessory.

We could say the same of the ramrod-swivel on some cavalry pistols, which secured the ramrod against loss when loading on horseback.

As for the cutlass, this is perhaps more easily identified as a naval weapon from the time it appears as a regulation issue, thanks to the anchor which was nearly always engraved on the blade. The fact that the anchor is sometimes missing complicates matters, and the 'soup ladle', the black iron basket hilt is equally found in some countries on the sabres of the marines, the artillery and the pioneers.

Sea Service muskets are different from others only in that they have a bit more copper on them. The upper and middle bands were made of brass, whereas in Army muskets they were made of iron. But this, again, is not infallibly so, and there is not really any typical feature by which a gun can be identified as a Sea Service weapon. One has to refer to recently published catalogues by experts and compare the general appearance of the weapon as well as the various marks or stamps on it.

Early 19th-century flintlock blunderbuss used by the British Navy. On top of the bronze barrel a long bayonet of triangular section, which can be folded back and locked against the stock.

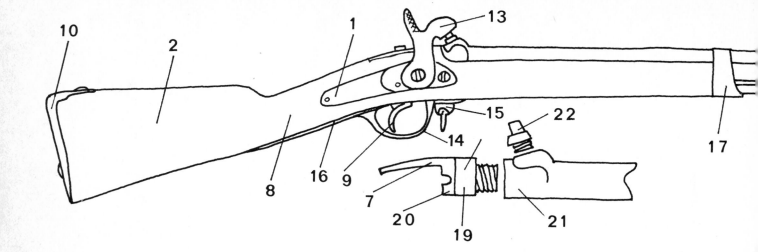

The identification of firearms

Before discussing the different identification marks, we will spend a moment on looking at some of the basic parts of the flintlock and percussion gun.

The forbears of these two systems were, successively, the matchlock (in which the burning match was lowered into the pan to ignite the priming powder by a simple mechanism like a 'serpentine'), the wheel-lock (in which a serrated iron wheel, released by a trigger, rasped against a piece of pyrites or flint releasing a shower of sparks), and the snaphaunce (in which the cock holding the flint was released by a spring to strike a serrated piece of steel). The snaphaunce system was improved and developed into the flintlock, which was in use until the invention in 1820 of the detonating cap and the perfection of the percussion lock around 1830 to 1840.

In a musket or pistol all the mechanical parts like steel, cock etc., are mounted on the lockplate. The details are shown in the drawings on this and the following pages. The lockplate is a completely separate unit fixed to the stock by screws and a counter-plate. The barrel is another separate part, which is fastened to the stock either by means of pins and studs or by bands (upper, lower band etc.).

Sea Service percussion musket, model Kropatschek (1878).

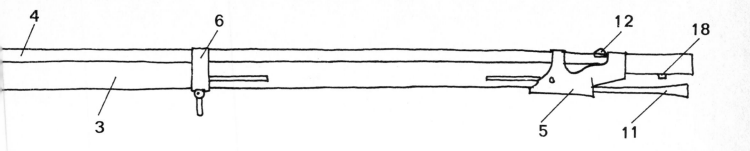

Parts of a Sea Service percussion musket: 1. lockplate, 2. butt, 3. stock, 4. barrel, 5. upper band, 6. mid-band, 7. top strap, 8. grip, 9. trigger, 10. butt plate, 11. ramrod, 12. foresight, 13. hammer, 14. trigger guard, 15. swivel, 16. tang, 17. lower band, 18. bayonet socket, 19. screw-in breech block, 20. tang, 21. breech end, 22. nipple.

The wooden parts (stock, butt) are reinforced with metal mounts (butt plate, trigger guard etc.). The terminology is sensibly the same for comparable parts of a musket and a pistol.

The adoption of the percussion lock to replace the flintlock around 1830–1840 was not, strictly speaking, a revolution but only a logical development and in some cases merely involved some re-tooling. The interior mechanism remained the same. Where formerly the cock had had jaws to hold the flint it now had a hammer which struck the percussion cap. The pan, the steel and its spring were removed and in place of the pan an iron plate was fitted. The three screw holes thus exposed were plugged up. The barrel was tapped to hold the nipple. It was mainly obsolete but still serviceable regulation weapons which were adapted in this way. New regulation percussion models were, of course, designed with a new lock and a nipple from the start.

It is usual for firearms to bear a number of marks or signatures, which are those of the persons who built them and put them together. Not only can a piece be identified with their help but also its completeness and uniformity ascertained. They show, for example, whether a gun has been regularly modified or re-tooled or whether it has been tinkered with, i.e. has had bits and pieces added to it over the years. Marks (or their absence) trace the *curriculum vitae* of a weapon. They are mostly found on the barrel, the lockplate, the butt and the ramrod.

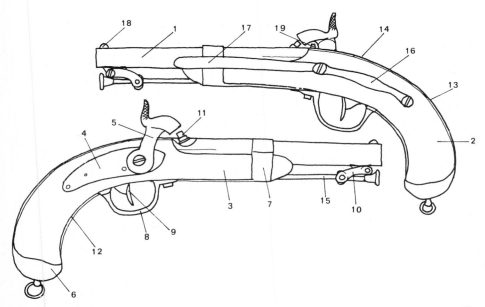

Parts of a Sea Service percussion pistol (model 1837–1842): 1. barrel, 2. grip, 3. fore end, 4. lockplate, 5. hammer, 6. butt cap, 7. band, 8. trigger guard, 9. trigger, 10. swivel lug, 11. nipple, 12. trigger-guard tang, 13. grip plate, 14. top strap, 15. ramrod, 16. counter-plate, 17. belt-hook, 18. foresight, 19. backsight.

Chronological outline of firearms used by the British Navy with some comparative French models:

Muskets

France		Britain
	c. 1680	Small arms of ships of the line include flintlock muskets, brass-barrelled musketoons and blunderbusses with iron furniture.
1689 Two naval muskets		
	c. 1715	Special Sea Service muskets with 42 in. barrels and flat locks. Heavy brass furniture with flat buttplates introduced.
	c. 1745	Barrels of Sea Service muskets reduced to 36–40 in.
	1752	Sea Service muskets made with bright and black barrels, all to be fitted with bayonets.
	1757–1758	Muskets for the Marine Marine Corps to be similar to the Short Land Pattern with 42 in. barrels but with flat sideplates and no escutcheon plates.
Système 1763–1766		
	1771	Rounded locks to be fitted to Sea Service muskets.
Système 1777		
	1780–1787	Seven-barrelled guns issued to men in the fighting tops, all made by Henry Nock.
1793 Rifled carbine for fightine tops		
	c. 1800	India Pattern muskets shortened for use as Sea Service muskets.
Système 1816		
	c. 1820	Two categories of Sea Service musket—Short with 26 in. barrels; Long with 37 in. barrels. Made with a mixture of old and new patterns of furniture.
	Patt. 1839	First percussion Sea Service muskets made from converted flintlock parts in 1836, but Land Patt. 1839 musket then adopted for the Navy with the barrel reduced to 30 in. Standard bore of 0.753 in. introduced.
	1840	Trial issue of Heavy Navy Rifle modelled on the 2-grooved Brunswick Rifle but with a 33 in. barrel of 0.796 in. calibre.
1841–1842 Muskets of Système 1822 and 1840 converted to percussion		
	Patt. 1842	Land Pattern 1842 musket similarly shortened for Sea Service.

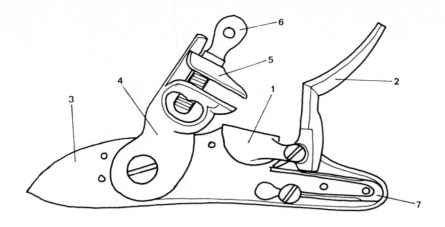

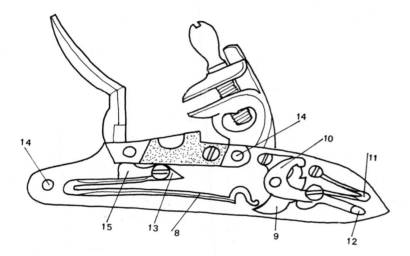

Parts of a flintlock: 1. priming pan, 2. frizzen or steel, 3. lockplate, 4. cock, 5. upper jaw, 6. jaw screw, 7. frizzen spring, 8. mainspring, 9. tumbler, 10. bridle, 11. scear spring, 12. scear, 13. mainspring tail, 14. screw hole, 15. mainspring claw.

France		Britain
	1852	Patt. 1842 muskets bored out to 0.758 in. cal., and rifled with 3 or 4 grooves for Marines. Converted Sea Service muskets similarly rifled. The Minié expanding bullet used in both rifles.
Système 1857 New Rifling		
	Patt. 1858	As part of a series of Enfield rifles special Navy rifle constructed with 33 in. barrel of 0.577 cal., rifled with 5 grooves. Later fitted with cutlass sword bayonet.
1866 Chassepot rifle		
	1867	Navy rifles converted to Snider breechloading action.
	1871	Adoption of Martini Henry rifle for Navy. Calibre reduced to 0.45., 7 groove rifling.
Système 1874 Gras rifle		

141

ENGAGED 16 MAY 1843.

Engraving on the cylinder of a Sea Service revolver. The scene shows the victory of the Texas Navy over the Mexican Navy on 16 May 1843. Engraving by W. L. Ormsby, N.Y.

Three revolvers. *Top:* Model Lefaucheux using pin-fire metal cartridges (1858). *Centre:* American Colt percussion pistol presumably used for Sea Service on account of the scene engraved on the cylinder which depicts a naval battle (1851). *Bottom:* French regulation naval revolver with percussion lock using metal cartridges (1870).

France	Britain
1878 Kropatschek magazine rifle	
1889	Introduction of the first magazine rifle, the Lee Metford with 0.303 cal., 7 groove rifling; the box magazine holding eight cartridges.

Throughout the 17th, 18th and first quarter of the 19th centuries British naval firearms were of inferior quality to those of the army. Some 19th century Sea Service muskets, in fact, have furniture of early 18th-century type. It may be, however, that this type of furniture, outdated on other military firearms, was retained by the Navy deliberately because it was of strong construction.

Pistols

France		England
	c. 1680	Flintlock pistols issued to ships of the line (40 to a first rate).
	c. 1715	Sea Service pistols with flat locks, 12 in. barrels and belt hooks introduced. The rounded butt cap with short ears; no bridle to the frizzle.
Système 1763–1766 Dragoon pistol in use by Navy	**1764**	Locks cease to be dated. The Crown and word Tower only engraved on the plate.
	c. 1780	New-style flat lock for naval pistols. The 12 in. barrels of 0.56 in. cal. Wooden rammers retained.
Système 1786		
	c. 1810	Sea Service pistol barrel reduced to 9 in. Modified rammer pipe holding a steel rammer.
Système 1816		
	1820	Pocket flintlock pistol for the Coastguard with 4½ in. barrel and swivel rammer. Safety catch to the lock.
	c. 1830	Last flintlock pattern made with a 9 in. barrel and swivel rammer. Locks normally bear cypher of William IV.
	1832	First percussion pistols set up for the Coastguard from converted flintlock parts.
Modèle 1837–1842 Percussion pistols, some converted from Système An IX, An XIII, 1806, 1822		
	c. 1840	Two patterns of Sea Service/Coastguard pistols on issue—one with lanyard swivel on butt, the other with lanyard ring. Both models with 6 in. barrels, swivel rammers and belt hooks. Various percussion locks used, some converted from flintlocks.
Modèle 1849		
	1854	Admiralty order first supplies of Colt's Navy percussion revolver. Model 1851, 0. 36 in. cal.

A Buccaneer musket.

Dutch cutlass with scabbard, c. 1830.

Modèle 1858
Le Faucheux pin-fire
revolver

1860   Deane & Adams' double-action percussion revolvers of 54 bore preferred to the Colt.

Modèle 1870
Centre-fire revolver

1870–1880   Centre-fire cartridge revolver by John Adams (Mks. II & III with interchangeable parts) with 6 in. varrel, 0.45 cal. issued to Navy.

Modèle 1873–1874
11 mm. cal.

1880   First model of Enfield revolver, 0.476 cal.

Modèle 1892 8 mm. cal.

1893   Navy re-armed with the Webley revolver first approved as a government revolver in 1887. Made in 0.442 in., 0.476 in., and 0.455 in. calibres. Naval models distinguished by letter 'N' stamped on frame.

The following are the marks which a piece might receive in the course of its manufacture:
A On the barrel:
    1. Initials of the works proof-master
    2. Initials of the senior controller
    3. Initials of the barrel controller
    4. In France the initials M.R. (Manufacture Royale), E.F. (Empire Frrnçaise) R.F. (Republique Française) in front of the touch hole
    5. Year of manufacture next to the touch hole or facing it
    6. Denomination of model on the trigger guard tang
B On the lock:
    1. Maker's name
    2. Initials of locksmith
C On the butt:
    On the dowel-plug of (French) shoulder-held guns the initials R.F., E.F. or M.R. (see A4), the month or year of manufacture and initials of inspector or senior controller. Since pistols have no plug these marks are on the grip itself.
D Sights and ramrod:
    Initials of accepting inspector
The names of inspectors, controllers and examiners were entered in the records of the artillery corps.

The buccaneer musket and the trade musket

Before concluding this section on naval firearms we will take a quick look at a type of musket which is commonly associated with seafaring although it was never really used on board and certainly not as a regulation weapon. It is the Buccaneer musket, which was popular in the Caribbean from 1680 to 1750 and even 1770. With a barrel of 0.708 in. calibre it had the exceptional length of 5 ft. 6 in., the barrel itself measuring no less then 4 ft. 4 in.

This gun, to which the pirates had become as accustomed as the bison hunters of the far North to theirs, was the only one for which there was any demand in Santo Domingo and Louisiana, and consequently the French government could hardly ignore this opportunity to seize the distribution monopoly. All vessels bound for the Carribean were ordered to deliver a certain number of these muskets to the Royal Colonial Magazines, which were the sole authorized distributors. The price for a musket varied between £20 and £30 depending on whether the furniture was of iron or copper.

There were a number of different versions of this musket. For example, there was the *demi-boucanier*, which weighed only 12 lbs (as compared with 14 lbs for the *boucanier*) and had a barrel of 4 ft. In Canada the Royal Magazines sold a version called *Grand Tulle*.

Hilts of swords worn by naval officers, c. 1840.

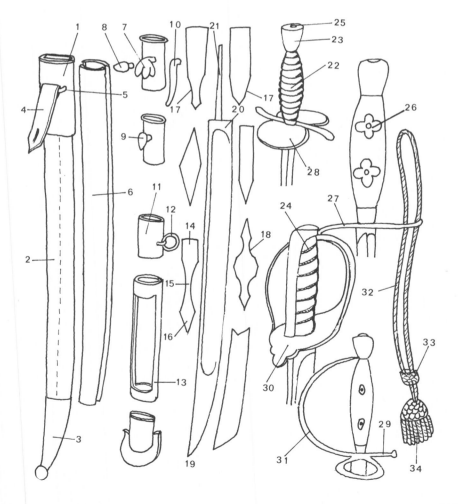

Parts of swords, cutlasses and dirks:
1. top locket, 2. sheath, 3. chape, 4. sling, 5. catch, 6. wooden lining, 7., 8., 9., 10. frog hooks, 11. mid-locket, 12. ring, 13. locket, 14. back of blade, 15. hollow ground blade, 16. edge, 17. false edge, 18. groove, 19. point, 20. shoulder, 21. tang, 22. grip, 23. pommel, 24. filigree inlay, 25. tang button, 26. rosette rivet, 27. crossbar, 28. shell guard, 29. quillon, 30. half-basket hilt, 31. knuckle guard, 32. cord, 33. slide, 34. tassel.

The Buccaneer muskets were by no means shoddy ware. Their purchasers, even if they were rough and ready hunters, demanded high quality in what were, after all, the tools of their trade. The muskets made for trading purposes were not, though, of the same high quality, and their price varied from one make to another. But of course they were not the subject of government deals. The merchants on the African coast and in the East Indies ordered these guns from independent manufacturers at Saint-Etienne or Liège. In a deal made in 1751 between the East Indies Company and a gun manufacturer at Saint-Etienne the following specification was made for a trade gun: '... 0.63 in. calibre, length of barrel at least 3 ft. 6 in., copper furniture, round lockplates with two screw holes, wooden ramrod, walnut stock in one piece ...'.

Obviously, this left quite some scope for the manufacturer, especially when it came to the quality of metal used for the barrel. According to one anecdote of the day the suspicious African chiefs, after a few 'explosive' experiences, insisted that the traders demonstrate their guns before concluding the deal. The risk was small, though, because the powder used was as poor as the guns.

These two types of gun, the Buccaneer Musket and the Trade Musket, are now very rare and much in demand, and numerous so-called authentic pieces are, in fact, nothing but poor copies.

This necessarily very incomplete survey of naval firearms owes much to the research of M. J. Boudriot. We can only regret that there is not yet an equally extensive documentation on naval firearms in other countries. Perhaps his work will inspire others.

Naval side-arms

Until not so many years ago very little had been done in the way of classification of naval arms. Today this has been remedied, as can been seen from the bibliography at the end of this book. The purpose of this short survey is merely to give a general introduction to the rich documentation on the subject of naval side-arms.

Naval side-arms can be divided into three categories: 1. pikes or thrusting weapons, 2. boarding axes, 3. swords, cutlasses and dirks. Among the latter we distinguish between those used in action and those used for ceremonial or duelling purposes.

Thrusting weapons have been used in the navy from very early days. They were useful, for example, for repelling a boarding attempt. The oldest description of this kind of weapon can be found in an ordinance by Louis XIV of 1689: 'Halberds and partizans mounted on ash handles, stronger than those used on land'. Not only were sailors equipped with them, but petty-officers and cadets, too, had spontoons and boarding pikes up to 8 ft. long. In common with the halberds these were no longer used after 1758. The last pike model was of 1833, a relatively short weapon only 5 ft. long and terminating in a very simple triangular steel tip just under 1 ft. long.

The boarding axe seems to have been left to the sailors' own initiative until 1833 when a regulation defined it as a hand weapon with a cutting edge on one side of a T-shaped blade and a point on the other, the blade being riveted to a blackened ash handle fitted with a belt hook.

Cutlasses, swords and dirks have in common the same principal parts: blade, hilt and scabbard. The blade is characterized by its length and whether it is straight or curved. The extremity opposite the hilt is the point (even if it happens to be the broadest part of the blade as in a scimitar); the thickest part near the hilt is the shoulder. This tapers to the tang, which is either forged in one piece with the blade or is soldered on. On this the grip is mounted. The steel blade may be polished or damascened, engraved, blued, or wholly or partly gilded.

The blade is also characterized by its section. It may be triangular and hollow ground as in a sword, or lozenge-shaped if it is a double-edged blade, grooved over part of its length in a cutlass (this makes it lighter and more supple), or simply quite flat.

The cutting part of the blade is the edge, opposite which is the back of the blade, which can be flat, rounded or convex in section. Marks such as the manufacturer's name and the date are most frequently found on the back of the blade near the shoulder. On the flat of the blade, near the shoulder, one normally finds an anchor engraved.

Regulation epaulettes of naval officers, early 20th century. Unmarked midshipman's dirk from the time of the Restoration.

146

The hilt, in the sabre, starts with the guard, in the sword with one or two quillon(s) and two shell guards, one of which folds back when the sword is carried in the sheath. In naval swords the shell guards are frequently decorated with anchors. A plain, black basket guard which envelopes the hand is typical of naval cutlasses. Opposite the quillon emerges the knuckle-guard, into which the hand fits. Then comes the grip, made of wood, horn, ivory or metal, which is riveted to the tang. If the grip is wood, it may be covered with leather or shagreen (green-dyed sharkskin) to give a better grip. The grooves of the grip are sometimes inlaid with gold wire. The grip terminates in the pommel, into which the tang is riveted (with a button-head or screw).

Dirks have only the most elementary of guard: a straight crossbar or two straight or inverted quillons with an escutcheon in the middle.

The sword knot which hangs from the hilt originally served to secure the weapon to the wrist. For this purpose it has a slide. Since it has become a military insignia it is only found on officer's swords and terminates in a tassel, which varies in design and makes it possible, within limits, to date the weapon.

The scabbard consists, externally, of a shaft which may be of iron (black, nickel-plated or polished), of brass (plain or nickel-plated) or of leather. If it is made of leather and not stiffened it is relatively flexible when the weapon is not inside. On the other hand it may have a wooden lining, made of two half-sections, which stiffens the scabbard and protects the blade. The pointed end of the scabbard terminates in a metal chape, the open end in a locket which, for the purpose of attaching it to the belt or sling, incorporates a frog-hook (olive, demi-olive or shell-shaped) or a ring, or even a leather loop or strap. There may be one or several more lockets, with or without rings, on the shaft of the scabbard. Swords, cutlasses and dirks worn up-and-down have one locket with a ring on either side.

Dirks worn by officers until 1860 were never regulation issue. There is no agreement on whether those worn by French midshipmen under the Restoration were. Theirs was a small sabre with a curved blade and mother-of-pearl grip, sheathed in an engraved copper scabbard. The supposition that in the Royal Navy only midshipmen wore dirks is, according to May and Kennard, erroneous. From 1780 till 1820 they were worn even by senior officers. In 1827 midshipmen were forbidden dirks, but in 1856 they were ordered to wear them again. A new design was introduced in 1878 and again in 1891. These were very handsome weapons indeed with the typical lion's head pommel and blued and gilt blade. Before 1856 officers' dirks in the Royal Navy, and in most other navies for that matter, were very varied in shape, with either straight or curved blades, ivory grip, langets engraved with a crown-and-anchor, blued and engraved blade, but always, whatever their shape, with a lion's head pommel.

Royal Navy cutlasses

The first regulation cutlass of the Royal Navy appeared towards the beginning of the 19th century, around 1804. It had a long, straight, flat blade and the well-known black iron hilt with a circular shell and another disc the same size as the knuckle guard.

In the 18th century naval officers preferred a small-sword of the hunting-sword type. A very popular small-sword was the 5-ball type, so called because both the guard and knuckle-guard were ornamented with five balls. This ornamentation was also used on dirks.

The order of 1800 put an end to this variety by prescribing two patterns of uniform sword: the ornamented sword for Flag Officers, Captains and Commanders, the plain sword for Lieutenants and Midshipmen. They were straight swords with lion's head pommels and langets engraved with an anchor. There followed a short-lived attempt by high-ranking officers to revert to greater originality by adopting the 'Mameluke sword', which had a very curved blade and grip, straight quillons and no knuckle guard.

In 1856, when all the midshipmen had their uniform dirks, the officers uniformly wore swords with lightly curved Wilkinson blades. Later there was a fashion for swords with 'claymore' blades, which were straight with two grooves. These swords had a white fish-skin grip, lion's head pommel and half-basket ornamented with a crown-and-anchor badge.

Scabbards followed the shape of blades, and they were fitted either with two lockets and rings on the same side if the sword was worn by two slings from a waist belt, or one locket with a ring on either side if the sword was worn up-and-down.

Presentation swords and firearms

The long-established custom to present swords to senior officers who had distinguished themselves in service has provided us with a number of splendid weapons. In contrast with the relatively sober and functional regulation weapons, these are outstanding in the lavishness and originality of their ornamentation and design. Of course, the armourer, unrestrained by uniform regulations, could give his imagination full reign. Presentation swords make wonderful and fascinating presents for appreciative collectors. Not only are they interesting for their personal associations, recalled by the engraved date of presentation, name of recipient and mention of his merits, but also for the fact that they represent all that is technically most beautiful in this type of weapon, even though one might critisize the extravagance of their ornamentation.

In Britain the best-known presentation swords are those which were awarded by the Patriotic Fund at Lloyds between 1803 and 1820. These fall into four categories graduated by value: the £30 sword, the £50 sword, the £100 sword and the most valuable, the Trafalgar sword.

The heavy, curved blades of these swords are blued and gilt, the grip is ivory and the guard gilt. The scabbard is of gilt metal with panels of leather or embossed velvet. Although they were not of uniform pattern, these swords were worn by their recipients with full dress.

The extravagant finish of the blades, hilts and scabbards with gold, ivory and precious stones is frequently matched by that of presentation firearms: carbines. muskets and especially pistols. The latter were frequently presented as pairs in a box together with all the necessary accessories. These weapons were so beautifully finished and so precious that they hardly ever left their case, and whoever is fortunate enough to come across any of these will find that even today they look as though they had only just left the gunsmith's workshop.

Naval flags

Regulation weapons are not only instruments of combat but also distinction marks of particular corps or branches of the Army or Navy. Equally, uniforms serve not merely to clothe men but also to group and grade them. For this reason it seems justified to include flags in the section on uniforms and insignia.

Flags and signals have always been of great importance to any navy. Since they are used to communicate from a distance, they must be simple in shape and pattern. For a seaman the colours and designs of flags are as easy to read as the alphabet is for a schoolboy. Modern flags are made of a coarse wool cloth called bunting. they are bound by a hem along one edge (the hoist), and sewn into this hem is a short length of line the upper end of which terminates in a wooden toggle to be made fast to the halliard shackle, the lower end in an eyelet to be made fast to the other end of the halliard with a sheet bend. As we will see, a number of different types of flag are used by the Navy.

The national ensign, or ensign for short, indicates the nationality of a vessel. Since ancient times the ensign has been the subject of detailed legislation and has

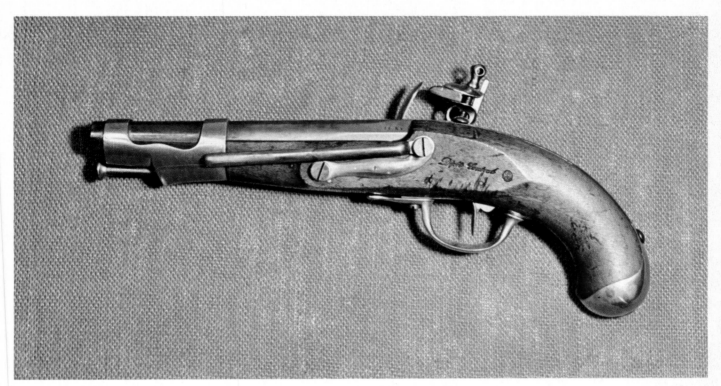

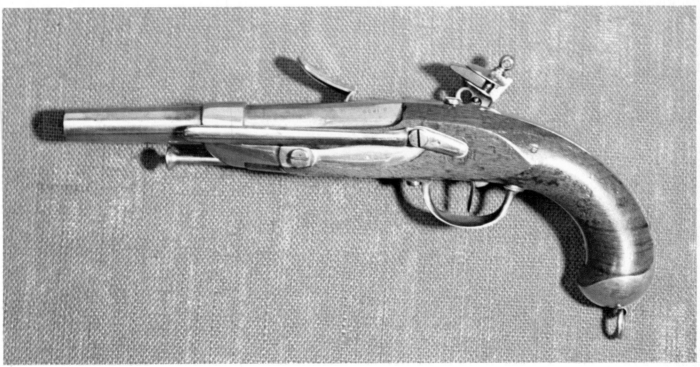

19th-century naval pistol marked
'Manufacture Libreville' (Charleville).

Naval pistol of 1816, marked
'Manufacture Tulle', with belt-hook and
characteristically shaped band.

149

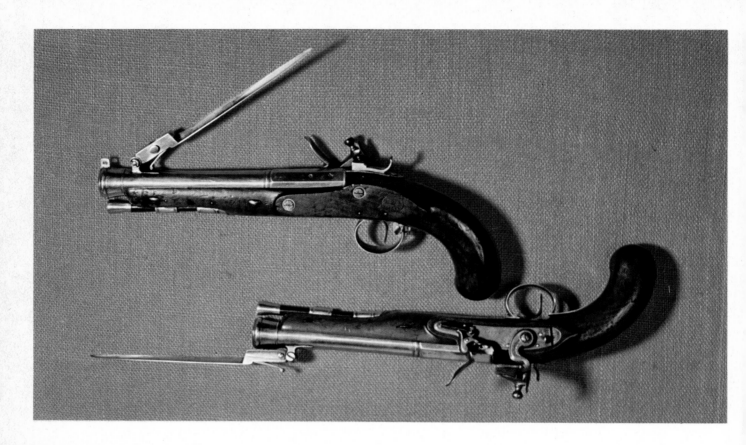

Pair of English Sea Service pistols
signed by Clarke of London, with bronze
barrels and folding bayonets.

Cutlasses from (*top to bottom*)
France, Germany, Russia, America and
once again Russia, all 19th century.

Heavy sword of the type worn by a
French Admiral in the First Empire,
decorated in the style of the swords worn
by Officers of the Guard. Blued and
gilded blade, tortoiseshell scabbard with
gilded locket and chape.

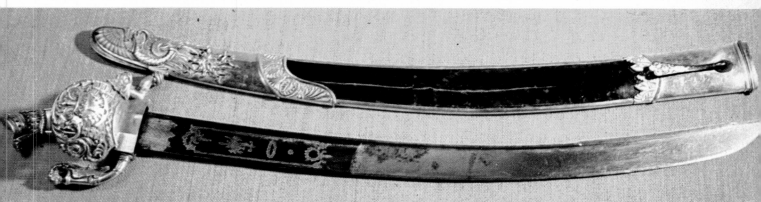

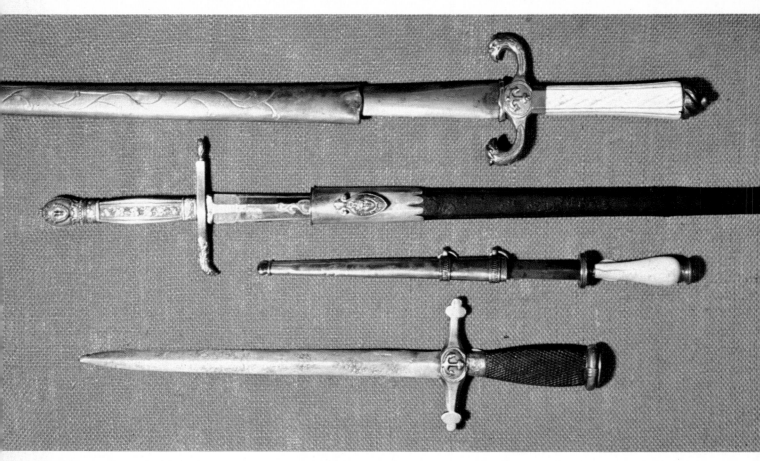

Four dirks worn by French naval
officers during the Second Empire and
Third Republic.

French naval officers' swords.
Top: Third Republic, *bottom:* two
swords of the Second Empire.

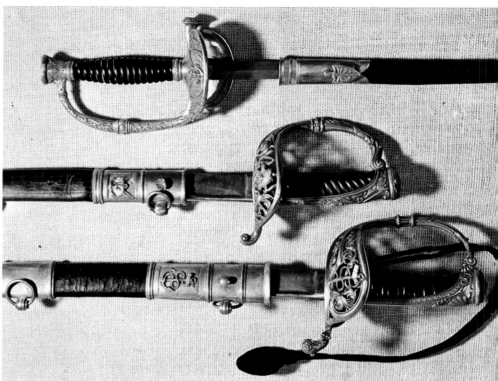

always been the most important outward proof of a vessel's lawfully registered nationality. It confers rights and imposes obligations. A vessel without an ensign, i.e. without nationality, is a pirate ship.

National ensigns appear to be as old as the history of navigation itself. At a time when fighting navies did not yet exist, armed merchant vessels hoisted the flags of their kingdom or principality in combat. Not until a national navy was established did merchant vessels fly the national ensign, which was, however, frequently different from that flown by naval vessels. The tradition has survived in Britain, where the Royal Navy flies the White Ensign, which shows the red Cross of St. George on a white ground with the union in the upper corner near the hoist, whereas the Merchant Navy flies the Red Ensign with the union in the same place, the Royal Naval Reserve the Blue Ensign.

In France under the Old Regime (before 1789) the national ensign was white with fleurs-de-lis and the French arms on it, but galleys and merchant vessels had separate flags. In 1790 the ensign flown by the French Navy and Merchant Navy was made uniform: white with a blue-white-and-red union in the upper corner, with the red nearest the hoist. In 1794 the Tricolour became the national ensign.

Obviously the collector can hardly hope to find anywhere a complete national ensign which has once flown on a ship. If he is lucky he may come across a fragment, a piously guarded relic of an ancient naval battle. Battered by the wind and the spray these flags were mostly torn to shreds and finally reduced to dust in some store room. Even if they still existed, their sheer size would be unmanageable, for by order the width of certain flags from staff to end had to be equal to the maximum beam of the ship. Also, it was the custom to increase the length of the action pennant by a metre for every month spent in service. Since some ships spent as much as three years at sea one can imagine the length of their pennants!

There are, however, numerous collections of model flags. With a bit of dexterity anyone can draw a flag which is missing in his collection. For identification purposes, marine paintings are a valuable help. Good marine painters have never failed to depict flags with great accuracy, not least because they are picturesque in their colours. A universal history of naval flags is yet to be written, and this would obviously be welcomed by all shiplovers.

Besides the national ensign, which is flown from a flagstaff at the stern, or at the gaff peak or mizzen masthead, or on warships at the bow and on square-riggers over the bowsprit, a number of other flags are flown from halliards. Above all, on warships, there are the command pennants. These distinguish the ships of certain high-ranking naval officers or indicate their presence aboard a vessel. Thus, special pennants are flown for the Commodore of a Squadron, a Commander in Chief, an Admiral or a Head of State visiting on board. Every navy has its own flag etiquette.

One flag particular to French shipping has now disappeared: the *arondissement* flag, which French coasters and fishing vessels had to fly for recognition and customs purposes and which enabled the authorities to keep a tighter control over tax fraud and smuggling.

Signalling flags have always been of great value for the transmission of signals over a distance. A look at some 17th and 18th century signalling tables reveals a multitude of combinations used by navies in action. But not until the 19th century was the first international flag signalling code drawn up, using flags of different shapes: rectangular, rectangular swallowtailed, trapezoidal and triangular. Different shapes, colours and patterns made up the letters of the alphabet and the numbers 0–9. Besides, there were substitutes for letters already used if only one set of flags was available. This first system gave frequent rise to confusion and so, in the 20th century, all maritime nations eventually agreed on a new International Flag Code, which is in use today. Each code flag hoisted singly has a complete meaning, (e.g. H = I have a pilot on board, P = I require a pilot, B = I have a dangerous load, Q = I require health clearance), or they can be flown in pairs (e.g. N.C. = distress signal), in threes or fours. The message can be decoded with the help of the International Signalling Code. Publications of older systems of flag signalling make fascinating collector's pieces.

A completely different type of flag and one which is rather more difficult to identify is the house flag, flown from the mainmast of sailing ships and the foremast of steamships. Sometimes one is lucky enough to come across one of these huge rectangles of bunting, its colours bleached by wind and weather during countless

Two sailors' leather hats, c. 1860.

voyages across the oceans, but it is bound to be difficult to identify. There have been countless different shipping lines in the course of the centuries. Some are still in existence, but many have ceased to exist or changed their names. Research in archives does not always help, because some shipping lines were extremely short-lived, having invested their capital in a single ship the loss of which meant bankruptcy. Nowadays house flags have to be registered, but that was not the case in those days. Despite these difficulties, dedicated collectors are not put off. Some concentrate on a particular theme, for example, the flags of all those companies which inaugurated the North Atlantic route, above all the famous Black Ball Line. Or those of the companies whose sailing ships, in the 19th and 20th century, did the long haul to Australia and Chile round Cape Horn, among them A. D. Bordes, Laiesz and Erikson. And more recently, there are the steamship companies. Who still remembers the house flags of the first paddle-steamer companies on the Far East route? Considerable research remains to be done in this field, coupled, perhaps, with research into funnel colours.

Some help can be got from the archives of Lloyds, Veritas and the American Bureau, but real finds are more likely to be made by searching through old leaflets, brochures and newspapers in libraries.

Another different type of flag, though basically related in its use, is the Club Burgee. The ancient tradition of yacht club members to fly the flag of their club has, over the decades, provided us with a large number of club burgees, among the most famous of which are those of the R.O.R.C. (Royal Ocean Racing Club), R.Y.Sq. (Royal Yacht Squadron), N.Y.Y.C. (New York Yacht Club), C.C.A. (Cruising Club of America), Y.C.F. (Yacht Club de France) . . . .

We have left till last a flag which would be the crowning glory of any collection, if someone could find it: the celebrated black pirates' flag, the 'Jolly Roger', depicting the skull and crossbones. Many old etchings show it, but probably no-one who ever really saw it lived to tell the tale!

154

Naval uniforms

If the collector of flags is likely to be discouraged by the lack of authentic material and frequently has to be content with facsimile models, the collector of uniforms will be luckier. Even if he cannot always lay his hands on a complete uniform, he will, at least, find one or other piece belonging to it. When it comes to exhibiting his treasures, however, he has, to be content with small model figures, unless he has the means and facilities of certain museums.

Uniforms in the true sense of the word, both for naval officers and sailors, are comparatively recent. The first attempt at an uniform regulation for the navy was made between 1820 and 1830. Until then everybody wore more or less what they liked. Officers were dressed like fashionable noblemen of their time, sailors according to their means and the work they had to do. The uniform which was introduced in the 19th century did not spring from a whim of fashion (as did, to some extent, the uniforms of land soldiers, who were dressed according to the caprices of princes, e.g. in white, with jabots, etc.), but was really the official recognition of what sailors had been wearing through the centuries: practical and comfortable clothes, light or heavy according to the climate, made of linen, oilskin and wool.

Long before the introduction of uniforms, sailors wore trousers with wide legs and narrow waist, undervests, shirts, wool or linen smocks, oilskin jackets, sou'westers and sailors' caps. Ship-chandlers knew so well what was wanted that for centuries they never tried to offer anything different. Sailors' chests invariably contained the same pieces. Those of the Newfoundland fishermen wooden clogs, oilskins and sou'westers, those of the coastal fisherman blue or red linen smocks and trousers, those of deep-sea sailors high leather seaboots and red, knee-length pants. All over the world one finds the same with slight variations. It is the tradition, the custom, and what the sea demands. However fiercely independent in his spirit the sailor may be, in his dress he is surprisingly conventional.

Legend has it that in 1748, when the officers of the Royal Navy did not yet have a uniform, King George II gave them one in blue with white braid, because he loved the colours of the Duchess of Bedford. But uniforms did not become the rule for officers until 1820. They could wear what they chose, except if their commander imposed a uniform on them, as was the case on board *H.M.S. Blazer*, where sailors had to wear blue-and-white striped jackets, which later became fashionable in cricket clubs under the name of 'blazer'.

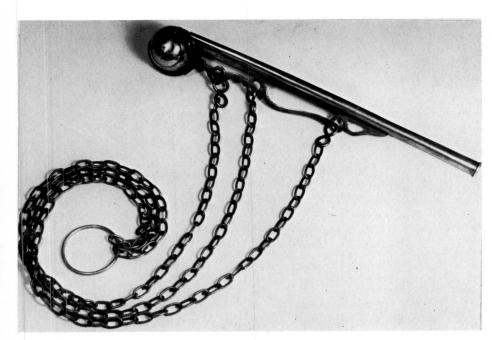

Bosun's silver whistle, 19th century. This is a handsome officers' model, bosuns had rather more modest whistles made of chrome- or nickle-plated brass, sometimes decorated by their owners with engravings.

In 1840 the French Admiral Casy complained about the lack of a uniform for sailors. Their stiff leather hats were by no means all cut alike, they just reflected the common taste of sailors in those days. As for the sailor's collar, its origin is a purely practical one. Towards the end of the 18th century, sailors had adopted the fashion of gathering their long hair at the nape and holding it together by a mixture of grease and pitch. This kept the hair out of their eyes when they worked in the tops, but it made their clothes dirty, which is why they took to wearing a neckerchief knotted in front. Doubtless this was the forerunner of the sailor's collar. The three white stripes according to British authors, symbolize Nelson's three victories at Aboukir, Copenhagen and Trafalgar, but it is doubtful that in other countries, especially France, they had the same glorious meaning. A universal history of marine uniforms ought to be written to answer this and similar questions.

Collectors of uniforms can choose from a multitude of items: Sailors' hats of hardened leather, buffalo skin, oilcloth or straw, plain or varnished; caps with or without pompom, sometimes with a black ribbon on which the name of the ship is printed in gold letters. Other coveted pieces are cocked hats and other officers' headgear. Not only are these very handsome objects to collect (gilt, with braids, feathers and escutcheons), but they are not as anonymous as are sailors' hats. Frequently the name of their ex-owner is written on the inside of the leather band, and this is what gives them their value, at least if the owner was a known, high-ranking officer. The dome-shaped, tinplate hat-boxes in which cocked hats used to be kept also make interesting collector's pieces, as do officers' uniform chests. The latter are made of wood and linen, or tinplate, and are veritable coffins with compartments for every part of an officer's regulation equipment. Sailors, too, had sea-chests or sea-sacks, which were often magnificently decorated with paintings or embroideries by artistic sailors themselves.

Amongst the uniform pieces there are furthermore remarkable shoulder pieces and epaulettes, belts with buckles or plaques, beautifully engraved, and the gilt copper gorgets worn by officers of the naval artillery.

Rather less costly but quite difficult to come by are the rank badges, which appeared in most navies at the end of the 19th century. These and similar objects would form a suitable start to a young beginner's collection.

Reaching beyond the confines of the Navy proper we come to the uniform buttons of specialized services and of civil shipping lines. The choice here is immense, and their interest, as with medals, lies in the inscriptions, which are veritable mines of historical information.

Gorget worn by men of the naval artillery in the First Empire.

Two belt-buckles. *Left:* seaman
of the guard, *right:* naval officer.

French naval uniform buttons, from
top to bottom and *left to right:* port
officer, harbourmaster, royal corps of
naval construction, corps of signals,
disciplinary company, naval prison
officers, engineers and stokers, staff of
ships of the line, Imperial Shipping Line,
Compagnie des Chargeurs Réunis,
Compagnie Maritime Franco-Russe,
Canal, du Midi, Sea Service, Royal Mail
Steam Packet Company, Compagnie
Franco-Américaine.

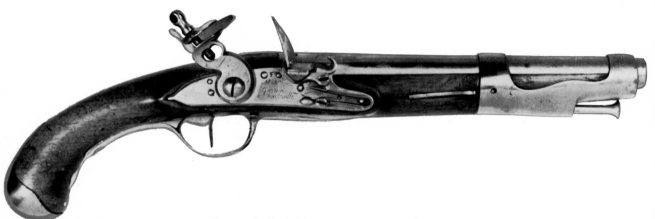

In concluding this survey we must take a quick look at the bosun's whistle and the instruction handkerchief.

The bosun's whistle, which is a ball-whistle with a long pipe, often made of silver, is characteristic of the navy, where all orders are 'piped' according to a laid-down pattern. Although not a regulation issue, the bosun's whistle is a fixed part of the bosun's equipment, as well as that of certain officers. Officers' whistles are frequently little masterpieces of the silversmith's art.

Instruction handkerchiefs, which appeared towards the middle of the 19th century, were not as frequent in the navy as they were in the army. They were large squares of fine cotton fabric, usually in two colours: black design on red background. Whilst for army soldiers the subject matter was normally theoretical weapons or cavalry instruction, for sailors there was a line drawing of a warship with a copious descriptive legend underneath. Sailors used these handkerchiefs to wrap up some small items which they carried in their pockets. Never did they use them as neckerchiefs and even less as pocket handkerchiefs, for fear that the design might suffer in the wash.

VI

The equipment and ornamentation of ships

A ship is a world in itself. More than any other, the single-handed sailor, who sets out on a long voyage, quickly realizes this. Once at sea, he has no choice but to rely on himself and on the gear and provisions with which he has equipped his boat. The technical knowledge and human qualities of the sailor, together with the reliability of the ship in all weathers are one thing. Another is the need to have the ship equipped with all the everyday things that are needed under all conditions and without which the ship might never reach its port of destination. An inventory for ocean-going ships makes anyone who is not in the trade feel giddy. For the professional it is just routine. More than thirty centuries of navigation on the open sea have taught seafarers to equip themselves in readiness for anything, and each generation brings some new indispensable things while throwing overboard the superfluous and antiquated.

Hence it is the whole of the ship's equipment that we intend to survey in this chapter. But since, for the reader, it is only a question of collector's pieces, we shall spare him all that weighs about a ton or measures more than three or four metres. Of what remains we shall retain only that which is curious, unusual, of historic interest or simply beautiful in form and material. Concerning this latter point let us say from the outset that, contrary to the assertions of people who don't know any better, the sailor is not just an ignorant chap who lives on rum and tobacco. We are dealing here with orderly, civilized people who, by a sort of grace of Neptune, are artistically gifted and have beautified and dignified all the implements of their daily life. The man who, today, piously gathers together these relics of a by-gone age, is not making a mistake.

Gear and fittings, furniture and ornamentation

Everything is different on board a ship to what it is on land. Everything here is designed especially for use at sea, based on daily experience. We have already taken a look at the artillery, the propulsion engines, the navigation instruments and the small-arms and shall now concentrate solely on
—instruments and gear not used for navigation
—furniture and furnishings
—ship's ornamentation

159

Let us go on board our ship and live the life of a sailor for twenty-four hours. In this way we shall discover hundreds of things which we would like to have in our collection. In our thoughts we shall move from a warship to a fishing vessel, from a windjammer to a modern liner. It will be a trip through the universe of things connected with ships and the sea.

From the forecastle to the poop

Here we are on our sailing ship. The breeze is filling the sails, and in the wake the sea-gulls are screeching, searching for some piece of waste food that the cook might well throw them. He is busy in the galley, where the stove is beginning to rumble. The coffee-pot is steaming away: a vast conically-shaped pot made of tin-plated sheet-metal, topped by a cylindrical filter. It is held in place on the stove by a grid of iron bars, adjustable on two notched rails which are firmly fixed to the stove. The galley equipment is sparse. On a bulkhead there hangs a cylindrical container made of sheet-metal, with a tap, which holds the galley's daily water ration: about 50 litres (11 gallons) to prepare the crew's meals. Athwartships, a table made of thick deal planks occupies the total width of the little den. There is a special block for chopping well-scraped and washed meat, with a groove for kitchen knives. Under the table there is a shelf with a retaining ledge for stowing pots and pans, all of them strictly functional in galvanized metal. In one corner we find a kneading trough in which the ship's bread is prepared. An oil-burning storm lantern provides the only lighting.

A cabin-boy comes to fetch the morning coffee. Let us follow him to the sailors' quarters: a rectangular deck-house built forward between the forecastle and the mainmast. It is divided in two fore and aft, so that in turn each watch of eight to ten men can get a rest while the other watch is on duty. There is no luxury here, either: a big deal or oak table framed by two benches worn smooth, the whole thing screwed to the deck by long bronze bolts. Above the table hangs a large, lyre-shaped paraffin lamp made of copper with a conical black iron shade. From the deck-head, suspended by ropes, there hangs a sort of tray which is divided into compartments to take the forks and spoons. No knives, because every sailor has his own knife with a short, strong blade, made fast to a long lanyard for securing it round the waist when working up aloft. A framework of whitewood fiddles, which stop the plates and mugs on the table from sliding, is also pulled up against the deck-head when not in use. Every sailor has his plate and tin or enamelled mug, usually dented and showing by its red and brown stains that it is used for wine, coffee and tea. The mugs are kept in narrow personal lockers at the entrance to the crew's quarters. In them are kept heavy-weather clothing: oilskins, trousers, sou'westers and sea-boots. The lockers are wooden, with a door and padlock. At the far end of the crew's quarters we find a round cast-iron stove, a kind of shipyard stove, which burns anything, especially bad, smoky coal. Around the table, along the central bulkhead and the fore-and-aft bulkhead which separates the two watches, two-storey bunks are aligned, one after another, the lower rows 50 to 60 cm (20 in. to 2 ft) from the deck, the upper ones 1.60 to 1.70 metres (5 ft. 3 in. to 5 ft. 7 in.) above the deck, so that both those in the upper and lower bunks have sitting headroom and also so that those in the upper bunks can climb up using the lower ones as a foot-hold. These bunks are fitted out simply. A deal-plank frame with an oak lee-board, often painted to avoid upkeep, bears a strong canvas mattress stuffed with oat-husk or seaweed, and a cotton blanket. Here and there, attached to the partitions by bits of line, there hangs a ship model, or a ship in a bottle on which the owner is still working, some poor souvenir, a fan, a walking stick, a whalebone, a little canvas bag, tied at the top, containing a sail-maker's kit, or some half-finished sailcloth cap. At the foot of the bunks and often underneath the bottom bunks are the sailors' sea-chests, which contain all their personal belongings. They are rough wooden chests, about 1 metre × 50 cm × 50 cm (3 ft × 18 in × 18 in) in size. They are slightly wider at the base for stability, and have short feet to keep them off the floor and out of the wet, from which the crew's quarters are not always sheltered. The handles are rope-work, made by each sailor himself, often in the shape of a ring going through a wooden bracket screwed to the sides of the chest. The lid has rims along the sides but not, generally, along the front. An iron-hinged clasp caps a ring, into which a padlock fits. The chest shows

Preceding page and above: 18th-century stern lanterns of ships. As Fresnel lenses were not yet invented, the light produced by a paraffin lamp inside the lantern was intensified by panels of convex or bull's-eye glass, which acted as magnifying glasses.

Log-line on reel, stowed in its wooden tub, which catches the water after the line has been hauled out of the sea.

vague signs of having been painted. The owner has cut his name on the lid with a knife or has painted it on 'artistically'.

In fine weather the chest is taken out on deck to make an inventory of its contents and to get the linen dry, for, washed in sea-water, it never dries completely and develops mildew. Inside, the lid is decorated with one of those naive paintings of ships which we have already seen. The chest itself always contains one or two little drawers in its top part, in which small objects are stored. In the remainder of the chest the sailor, as in a field wardrobe, stores his changes of clothing, all in perfect order and neatly folded. The most refined put in some 'scent', a few sprigs of lavender, rosemary or laurel. For the most part, the sea-chest will accompany the seaman during the whole of his career at sea. Sea-chests are not sold at ship-chandlers but are made by sailors themselves, and rarely do their fittings contain the slightest scrap of brass, which would be too expensive. The deep-sea fishermen also have their chests, even less elaborate, with a curved lid, often longer and higher and used as a bench, for cod-fishing vessels rarely have benches, nor tables, and the men eat off their knees.

A ship's carpenter's chest, in which he kept his 'ritual' tools.

On board cod-fishing vessels and wooden merchant sailing ships the crew's quarters are forward, between the cable-locker and the hold. It is a black, foggy, smoky and foul-smelling hole. The sailors' bunks are no more than dog-kennels. On each side, plain openings about 1.20 metres × 60 cm (4 ft. × 2 ft.) in size have been cut in the wooden bulkhead—unadorned and worn by the rubbing of oilskins—through which the sailor makes his way into his narrow hut. In it are a board and a seaweed mattress. Sometimes a sailcloth curtain cuts out the light and noise, which is very necessary, since the two watches, port and starboard, share quarters. A companionway made of solid oak, worn by boots, leads up from the crew's quarters to the companion hatch, a solid wooden structure with two doors or simply planks slid in grooves. Sometimes the top of the companion hatch can be slid back to let in a little air and light.

Sea-chest of a Danish sailor, W. Petersen of Elsinor. Late 19th century.

161

Caulking tools.

Let us not leave the foreship yet. On the last iron sailing ships there is an impressive anchor windlass situated centrally beneath the fo'c'sle. It is worked from the top of the forecastle by men walking round the capstan pushing the bars. Nearby we find a well-polished bell, which is sounded rapidly to inform the captain that the anchor is aweigh or sounded once for every 'shackle' (= 15 fathoms) of chain paid out or hauled in. It is also used in fog or at anchor for giving the statutory number of clangs to indicate the ship's presence. On the very old wooden ships, the bell-mount was a sort of little belfry with carved sides and a roof in the shape of a pagoda, and the bell hung by a wooden beam in the manner of church bells. On the later sailing ships the bell is hung from a simple, curved iron stirrup. There is invariably a short bell-pull on the clapper, artistically plaited and knotted, which is an example of the sailors' talent for 'fancywork'. The bell itself bears the vessel's name, its port of registration and sometimes the date of construction. That is how a curious visitor rediscovered the name of a famous ship anchored in the Mississippi at New Orleans, which could not be identified by its delapidated rigging. On scratching the bell's paint-work with a knife, he discovered, to his great surprise, the renowned name of *Cutty Sark*.

Beneath the forecastle there are the animal pens. A cow chews the cud, a pig grunts noisily. Right opposite are the hen coops and rabbit hutches, firmly fastened and padlocked, for this choice food is reserved for the officers 'aft'. In fine weather the cages are moved out into the open, so that the poultry may 'thrive'.

Aft of the latrines, which are primitive installations, no more than a hole in the floor washed by the sea, we find the workshop of 'Chips', the carpenter and the boatswain's stores. There is nothing particularly nautical to be found in the carpenter's shop except several adzes. A pile of timber for running repairs is lashed on deck. In the bosun's stores we find innumerable pots of paint, mostly white and black, of red lead and varnish, paint brushes and tar brushes and a whole assortment of flat and triangular scrapers as well as scaling hammers against invading rust. There are also

The perplexing variety of ship's blocks in this table illustrates why it took sailors years of practise to become thoroughly familiar with all the fittings used in a ship's rigging.

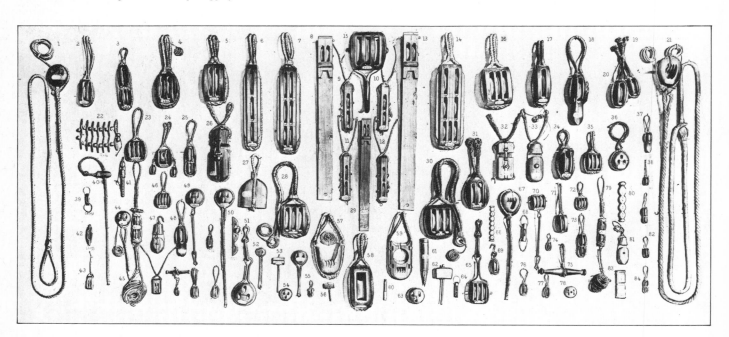

stones for holystoning the brass and the deck. They are white bricks, which crumble away, elbow grease serving as binding material. In the rigging store we find real treasures: shackles, all sizes from 8 to 100 mm (which weighs 10 kilos = 22 lbs), mooring swivels, chain links, cable clamps, rigging screws as tall as a man. All this is obviously well looked after and smells of good grease and tar. Above all, there is the most spectacular stock of blocks imaginable: blocks with wooden shells, iron blocks, snatch blocks, fiddle blocks, swivel blocks . . ., anything from the tiniest flag-halyard block to enormous, three- or four-sheaved purchase blocks for hoisting the yards. In the glorious days of the windjammers it was not uncommon for 100 different blocks to be used in a ship's standing and running rigging. The chart from the Musée de la Marine (Paris) illustrated below gives an idea of the diversity.

For working on steel cable, there is an impressive assortment of enormous iron marline-spikes 30 to 50 cm (12 in. to 18 in.) long, as well as chisels and hammers of comparable proportions. In the third store, marked by a small bronze-plate which says 'lamp-locker', we are confronted with a whole stock of lanterns stored in racks. (These door plates, variously inscribed 'Engines', 'Captain', 'Officers' Mess' etc., are sought-after collectors' pieces and can still occasionally be found in breakers' yards). There are galvanized lamps, copper and brass lamps (but mostly painted to avoid oxidation), red and green side lights, stern lights with clear glass showing a light to half the horizon, anchor lights with all-round illumination, red lights which signal 'Unable to manoeuvre', storm lanterns, oil-lamps for lighting the cabins and alleyways, wick compass-lamps in narrow china tubes, even candle-sticks in gimbals. There are also some signal lamps, including some powerful carbide ones. Then there are spare lantern glasses, round ones, flat ones, Fresnel lenses. In the lamp-locker of a warship we would also find stern lights of the 'rat-trap' type, which give out a narrow pencil of light and are used for sailing in line formation.

Back on the sailing-ship's deck, we notice, along the bulwarks, rows of belaying pins for belaying the running rigging. There are more belaying pins on the U-shaped 'fife rails' at the foot of the masts. These are made of strong oak beams supported by handsomely made balusters. At the foot of the mainmast we also find the crank-pump with a cast-iron hand wheel, a beautiful machine though clumsy and heavy, driving long crank-shafts which descend to the bottom of the hold, to the pump well.

Between the mainmast and the poop rises the deck-house where the boatswain and the carpenter live, as well as the apprentices, when there are some on board.

The poop bulkhead is the vertical wall which marks the fore part of the poop. Two strong steel or wooden doors protect the two alleyways against the seas which sweep across the well-deck. The wooden doors are magnificent objects, made of heavy planks of tongued and grooved teak, 6 cm to 9 cm (2½ in. to 3½ in.) thick, bound by steel brace-rods, with screw-bolts sunk into the wood and the holes dowelled at the ends. In the top of the door there is generally a thick glass port-hole circled with copper. The hinges of the door are made of bronze of standard pattern, so is the lock with its ring-shaped handle. Bolted to the poop bulkhead we notice a bronze plate giving the name of the shipyard that built the vessel, the gross and net tonnage, and the date of launching. These plates, the largest of which reach a size of 30 cm × 50 cm (12 in. × 18 in.) are handsome objects to collect.

To get to the poop, we have to go up companionways (never called 'stairs' on board). Usually these are straight, but occasionally they turn at right angles so that we start our ascent facing aft but arrive facing athwartships. As we go up we notice that the handrails are made of polished teak or mahogany and possibly have carved lions' or other masks at the ends. The hard-wood treads may have scalloped brass strips along their edges.

Here we are on the poop. All around runs a protective balustrade made of mahogany. At the forepart of the poop there are two casks made of varnished wood, hooped with well-polished copper and closed by a wooden lid. They are the drinking-water tanks, on which the helmsman keeps a watchful eye. Everyone can come with a bowl and get a drink, but no-one is ever allowed to take the smallest drop of it away. These very handsome pieces of deck equipment have today become great rarities.

In the middle of the poop a deck-house shelters the chart-room. This austere steel construction, riveted to the poop deck, replaces the original wooden deck-house of the early windjammers. Theirs was a superb hardwood structure with moulded and varnished mahogany panels and port-holes to admit the light. Let us go into the

From top to bottom: Wick holder and four types of navigation lights in use on ships during the 19th century.

163

Wheel of the American sailing ship *Three Brothers* built in 1856 at Greenpoint, L.I. for Commodore Van der Bilt.

Mahogany saloon bench with pivoting back-rest.

sanctuary of the ship's master, which even the officers only enter briefly to prick the chart or enter up their watch in the ship's log.

Inside, the walls and deck-head are panelled with mahogany. In the forward part, the chart table takes up most of the room. It is about 90 cm to 1 metre (3 ft. to 3 ft. 4 in.) high and with a sizeable table-top, big enough to spread out large sea charts. Underneath are large, self-locking chart drawers, which contain sea-charts of the world's oceans, for the big clippers, on their voyages round the world, would navigate in the most distant corners of the seven seas. The drawer handles are made of copper, or they may be simple wooden knobs. On the chart table a groove holds the pencils, rubbers, magnifying glasses, protractor, dividers etc. for the chart work. An oil lamp sways overhead with the movements of the ship. Along the side of the chart-house a narrow bench covered with dark leather gives the captain a chance to take a moment's rest during his long watches on the poop in difficult navigational situations, which demand his presence on the poop. For, although sailing ships move relatively slowly, they take quite some time to change course, and the decision to tack to avoid imminent danger cannot wait until the captain has made his way up from his cabin to the poop.

Continuing our inspection of the chart-house we discover an aneroid barometer, some pigeon-holes containing navigation handbooks, pilot guides, light lists and various tables. A set of shelves hold the sextant boxes. In some low lockers along the bulkheads there are stored the distress flares, the loud-hailers, the signal lamps and the pneumatic fog-horn, a long copper cylinder attached to a horn which bellows when activated by a piston. When there is fog, the instrument is taken out on deck. We also find spare log-lines and -rotators and a spare recorder, as well as leads and tubes for sounding the bottom. From the chart-house an artistically worked companionway leads down into the starboard alleyway, the captain's, where we shall go in a moment.

On the poop, aft of the deck-house, we come across the saloon deck-light, which admits daylight to the after saloon. Frequently this is a very fine piece of cabinet-making with moulded timber frames fitted with copper bars to protect the glass panes against knocks or falling rigging. Frequently there are wooden benches with arm-rests built along the long sides of the deck-light. When the fronts of these seats are not fitted with glass panes to admit additional light, the benches are used as roomy chests, in which are stored some much-used items of gear such as flags, especially if there is no flag locker in the chart-house. Of course, on these deck-light benches no sailor or officer would ever dare to sit, not even in port or at anchor. They are strictly reserved for the captain and his guests. When the weather is bad and the deck covered with spray, a big sailcloth cover is fitted over the deck-light and its benches. A number of British and German sailing ships had just a very simple deck-light and no deck-house, in which case the captain went on to the poop by a companionway similar to the one in the forward quarters when they were still below decks. The poop companionway, that of the 'Old Man', was of varnished mahogany, rather high and equipped with two moulded doors shutting with a handsome brass lock.

Aft of the deck-light, the helmsman has before him the steering compass in its binnacle, well braced on all sides. The wheel, as high as a man, cannot be handled comfortably except when the helmsman is raised slightly so that he can reach the upper spokes. Hence on each side of the wheel a grating on four feet has been screwed to the deck. On his perch, which also keeps his feet out of the seas that sweep the poop, the helsman can control the wheel easily and at the same time keep an eye on the compass and on the sails. A brass ring in the centre of the wheel bears the name of the ship and her port of registration. One of the spokes of the wheel is capped with bronze (or brass). When this is uppermost, the helmsman knows that the helm is centred. Aft of the helmsman is the mechanism which transfers the motion of the wheel to the rudder plate. It is essentially an enormous screw with coupling rods, the whole thing being enclosed in a long wooden wheel box on four high, lathe-turned feet, which is familiarly known as 'the tortoise'. On the sides of the wheel box the name of the vessel is frequently carved, the lettering picked out in gold and white.

Having finished this tour of the poop, let us go down below by the 'Old Man's' companionway. The after accommodation on board sailing ships differs greatly from one vessel to another. On some ships the long poop houses not only the officers' quarters but also those of the crew, and on the remainder of the deck there is no other deck-house. On sailing ships like the *Cutty Sark* the poop is encumbered with a very low deck-house, the purpose of which is to give headroom in the officers'

164

quarters, which are sunk into the poop deck. This only leaves a small deck space free aft for the helmsman and the officer of the watch. A large stern saloon is, nevertheless, the most common arrangement. It is divided into 'the cabin', two alleyways, two rows of side cabins from poop bulkhead to stern and, between the alleyways, a large rectangular room containing the sail-loft forward and the saloon pantry aft.

Here we are in the cabin, which is lit by daylight coming through the deck-light. The furnishings are dark, tidy: beautifully grained woods, mahogany panels, mouldings, top-class cabinet work. Along the sides, doors give access to the cabins or the store housing valuable provisions such as alcohol and tobacco. At the after end of the cabin there is a bench covered with studded leather cushions, in the fashion of the period. In the fore part of the cabin we find a sideboard housing crockery and glassware, all carefully stowed to stay in place in a sea-way. In the middle of the cabin the table presides, massive, made of polished mahogany, with its feet fixed to the deck with bronze screws. Between meals, at sea or in port, a ritual dark green or red felt cloth covers this immaculate table-top. Flanking the table, two cane-seated or leather-cushioned benches receive the saloon guests, usually officers who take their meals with the captain. These very special benches are only seen at sea. They have a pivoting back-rest bar, as illustrated on page 164, which can be adjusted to make the seat into one facing the table, or one facing the other way, without the bench having to be turned round.

Saloon of the English wool and tea clipper *Cutty Sark*. A remarkable example of cabinet-maker's work, it illustrates the clever use made of the small space left for the officers in the stern sections of the ship.

165

Toilet cabinet on a passenger ship around 1880. Mahogany and brass, about 1.70 metres (5 ft. 7 in.) high.

At the head of the table the captain's armchair often presides. The three-footed, cast-iron pedestal is, of course, screwed to the deck. It supports a shell-shaped, pivoting seat, which allows the occupant to seat himself without acrobatics. These very nautical seats are found just about everywhere in officers' cabins and, on mail and passenger steamers, in the dining rooms and the passengers' cabins. When night has come, the cabin-boy lights the oil-lamps on the bulkheads, in the alleyways and in the cabins, and the polished copper gleams. The very handsome saloon lamps have a diffusion globe of frosted glass and a brightly polished brass shade, which reflects the light downwards onto the saloon table. Sometimes one or two polished mahogany glass trays with recesses to take the feet of crystal glasses are hung from the beams in the captain's cabin.

The saloons of some English sailing ships depart from the Spartan severity of the classic furnishings and reflect some of the Englishman's traditional comforts. A beautiful Delft tiled fireplace is often found in the saloons with a bright wood fire burning in it. There may be a big built-in looking glass over the sideboard, and a decorated pendulum clock. Or there may be a rocking chair, which the user has no need to set in motion, as the sea attends to that. There may also be a rattan or willow chair bought at Bombay or Karachi for a few shillings. Carpets are not forgotten, but they are rolled up in bad weather when people move about the saloon in boots. Some extraordinary mats, which fall into the category of sailors' 'fancywork' but attain the size of real carpets, are occasionally seen on the floor of captains' cabins. They are made of interlaced and plaited ends of old rope no longer safe to be left in the running rigging but still solid enough to be walked on.

What has become of all this glowing harmony of tawny woods and flashing copper, caressed by the gentle light of oil lamps? Certain saloons of sumptuous style have been transported just as they were from the breakers' yards to the offices of some shipping company, as was the case in Chile, Germany and Italy. Men of taste and feeling could not bear to see these treasurers demolished. The original saloon of the *Herzogin Cecilie,* for example, can now be seen at the Åland Museum at Mariehamn. These rescues were rare. The rest went on their way to cabinet makers who used the materials to patch-up middle-class furniture or make into rather more 'conservative' pieces. However, very occasionally, we come across something at sales which betrays its origins on board a ship: a bench with a pivoting back-rest, a table with holes in its feet, a dresser with fiddles, or a sideboard which the casual viewer criticizes as 'lopsided'. Its shape can be justified solely by the receding lines of a ship's stern, and the suspicion that we are dealing with a piece of ship's furniture is confirmed by the fact that all hinges and locks are made of bronze and the drawers, shelves and compartments are clearly equipped to stop things from sliding about.

But these exceptional treasures must not make us despise the humbler accommodation of other ships such as trawlers and coasters. There, we find the moving beauty of well-worn implements of practical use. The cupboards, tables, benches, chests and lockers which we find in the quarters of the Great Banks fishing schooners are made of strong oak and deal. Everything is built around the ship. The enormous hole in the table that turns up at some dealer's once accommodated the mizzen mast. The prism-shaped locker which was once fitted into the side of a ship can clearly only recover its justification for existence on board a ship. An accustomed eye does not miss these things.

Tiller of a 19th-century sailing ship. The tiller was often the only decorated and carved part of fishing vessels. This one, made of oak, is 3 metres long. Such great lengths were necessary to give the helmsman the maximum leverage in his considerable efforts to keep the ship on course when sailing close-hauled.

Mess-room sideboard on a big mid-19th-century sailing ship with typical stowage for plates. The upper doors are on slides, and all the inside ledges and shelves have fiddles to keep things in place. A certain dissymmetry is apparent between the two sides of this piece of furniture made of fine, solid mahogany, and this was caused by the need to fit it into a particular space, in the poop.

But let us go back on board our sailing ship. We still have to visit the officers' cabins. A landlubber is always surprised to see seamen living in rooms like kennels, but, frankly, they only spend very little time there, since most of their duty hours are spent on deck in the strong sea wind. Perhaps there is a certain secret pleasure in finding oneself once more in the confined space of a cabin after having been surrounded by miles and miles of heaving, inhospitable salt water. The bunk is aloft, mounted on a four-drawer chest of drawers. The front of the bunk is mahogany, the handles are brass. There is also a couch, the officer's traditional article of furniture, on which he stretches out, fully dressed, while waiting to be called on the poop. The front is mahogany, there are two drawers underneath, and the rest is deal, with a horsehair mattress covered with imitation leather. There is, furthermore, a drop-leaf with an inset square of copper or wood, and a locker with shelves, of which the only luxury is the bronze lock.

Where then is the so-called 'ship's furniture' with its brass corners, flush handles, flashy copper-work? Is it in the captain's quarters? We shall go there in a moment but not find it, either. This furniture of British origin, some of which is authentic, has indeed sailed the seas at times, but on the whole it was found in the luxury cabins of passengers bound for India or Australia. These luxury cabins were relatively spacious, and it was pleasant to put into them a trunk with drawers, immediately usable, or a travelling bureau full of readily accessible documents. What's more, the sea journey was only a stage. Afterwards might come garrison duties of several weeks, in the course of which these pieces of 'trunk furniture' would come into their own. The very handsome camphor-wood trunks with copper corners and escutcheons, popularly supposed to be seamen's luggage, are in fact the exotic purchases of long-distance sea travellers, although some people even go so far as to allege that camphor-scented linen has a comforting effect on the poor, lone sailor and that it was he who bought this luggage.

There is no point in inspecting any more officers' cabins on sailing ships like ours; they are all alike. Let us instead, in our mind, board a first-rate ship of Nelson's time. Even the admiral is lying in a simple wooden frame suspended by tackles in the manner of hammocks. His total furniture is a few lockers with a small stock of clothing. Everything is transportable and can be dismantled in a few seconds when the fighting starts. What about officers in general? Like their commanding officer, they have the minimum of furniture and luggage. Their 'cabins' are, as in hospitals, simple sailcloth compartments. Sometimes a monstrous 36-pound cannon takes up three quarters of the space. On warships it is very much later, towards the middle of the 19th century, when the artillery begins to leave the batteries and move into gun turrets, that a few things appear which deserve the name of furniture. The decks no longer have to be cleared for action and one tries to settle in to live on board. There is no luxury about navy regulation furniture, neither in the crew's quarters nor in the officers' mess and cabins. Only for top-ranking officers, above all the Admiral of the Fleet, the navy does things in grand style aboard the warships of the Edwardian era.[1]

On the mail and passenger steamers, at the turn of the century, everything is done to make passengers forget that they are at sea. The first-class cabins are palatial. Only the port-holes and the leeboards to the beds are nautical features. The dining rooms offer all the comfort and pomp of a large international hotel, except that we meet again the well-known swivel seats on their cast-iron bases, screwed to the deck.

The emigrants live in their parts of the boat, which are the darkest and least ventilated. More like stable-boxes than cabins, the wooden compartments of their quarters have nothing particularly maritime about them any more than their refectory, where the white wood and the tin cans are worthy of barracks. In the third class, where there are sometimes six to a cabin, the requirements of the situation enforce some sea-orientated fittings. There the double- or treble-decker bunks are fitted with leeboards, and there are extra-flat wash stands, sometimes with self-emptying wash basins. No running water, of course. No table or desk, either, but simply a plain board and an office chair.

19th-century ship's candle-stick in gimbals. A round glass shielded the flame from air-currents.

[1] A number of these fine furnishings were removed at the moment the ship was put in reserve. A number can be seen at the National Maritime Museum at Greenwich. The Navy Memorial Museum in Washington possesses a mahogany sofa in the French Empire-style, with legs in the shape of dolphins, which was one of the furnishings on board the frigate *Constitution*.

Figurehead of 19th-century American merchant ship: 'Guiding the vessel in its flight, by a path, none other knows aright'. (Longfellow: *The Building of a Ship*.)

Figurehead of an
unknown German
merchant-ship.

Rudder-head from a
18th-century Flemish yacht.
The innumerable coats of
paint have weakened the
carver's chisel cuts and have
given the face that
indefinable, fixed, rather
haunting expression found
in all nautical carvings
which have known the wind
and spray of the open sea.

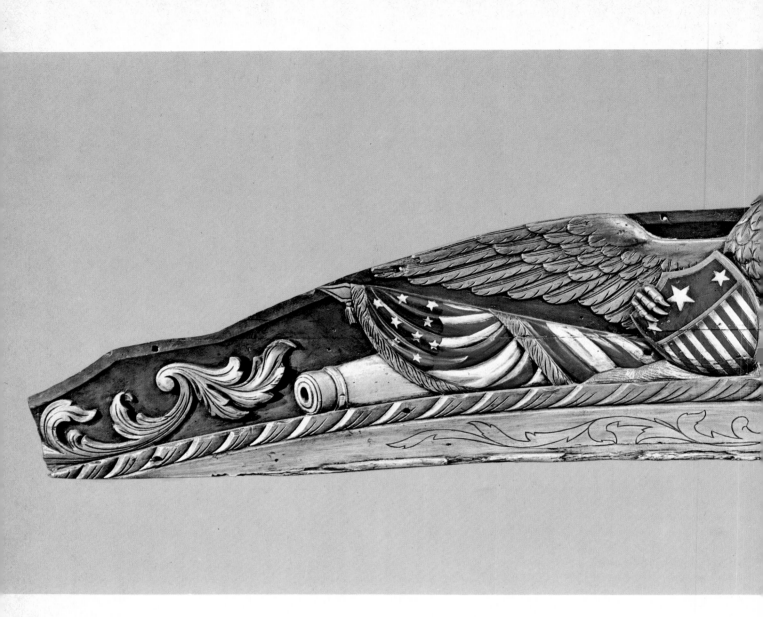

172

Stern board of the Yankee whaler *America*. Apart from figureheads, these boards were the only decorative elements allowed on their ships by the austere Quaker ship-owners. Local history has it, that despite the ingrained superstitions of the sailors the Society of Friends had the figurehead for the whaler *Rebecca*, which was considered too flashy, removed and burnt on the beach. The same respect for Quaker philosophy had them remove the figurehead of the *Rousseau*, in fact a statue of J. J. Rousseau himself, and replace it with a simple carved motif called a billet head.

As for the eagle, a popular theme in the United States and frequently represented as figurehead, it continued to be popular with steamers, where it was displayed on the wheelhouse or the paddle-boxes of paddle-steamers. Bellamy carved hundreds of flat eagles for steamships, known as 'Bellamy Eagles', which were sold all over New England.

Stern-board of an English sailing ship.

The captain's cabin on board the American whaler *Charles W. Morgan*, shows how simply 19th century captains lived on board: a shelf with a few navigation books and the Bible in a prominent position, an overhead compass to keep an eye on the helmsman and—the only luxury in the midst of this austerity—a solid bed mounted on pivots to protect the occupant from the ill-effects of rolling.

A figurehead representing the Prince of Joinville, in the company of a 17th-century 'treasure' chest, a spy-glass, a sailor's hat and a cutlass.

The inside of a gun-battery aboard a Swedish vessel, about 1800. For taking their meals, the men had a few pieces of light, movable furniture, which could be quickly dismantled. Priority was indeed given to the cannon, the lord and master on board.

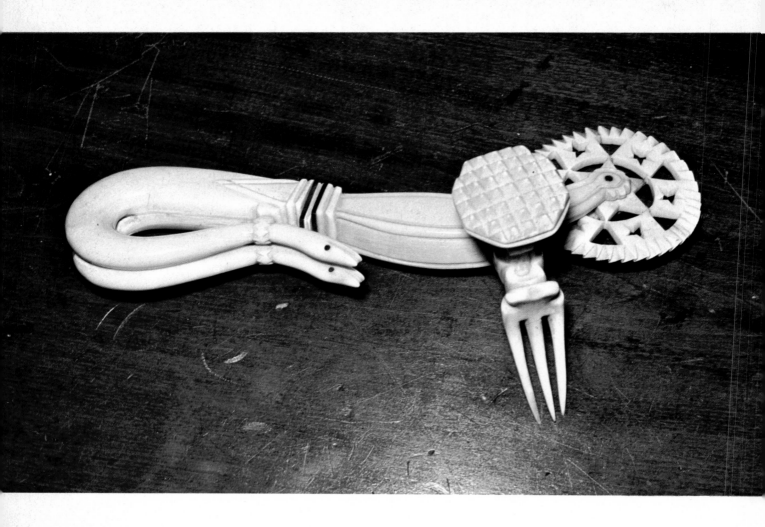

Pastry wheel, or pie crimper, made by an American whaler. No Nantucket or New Bedford housewife would have wanted to be without this useful instrument. It was obviously to a large extent homesickness which prompted the sailors to make domestic implements of this nature. In the midst of the hardships of their life at sea these evocative objects transported them to the warmth and comfort of their homes ashore.

Before leaving the passenger ships let us take a quick look at the splendid cane-seated, solid mahogany 'deck-chairs' or 'rest-chairs' on the first-class deck, where it is pleasant to sit, covered by a blanket, and watch the sea slip past. Indispensable accessories to these deck-chairs are the oval or rectangular 'butler's trays' which are placed on scissor-legged stand to form little tables. Used ashore by butlers to serve tea to guests 'on the lawn', they have quickly been appreciated by stewards on board passenger ships and have become a ritual accessory to cruises.

On board steam and sailing yachts around 1900 the luxury and quality of furniture and furnishings seem to have found their absolute peak. The materials used and the finish of cabinet work attain perfection. We meet again all the elements of furniture which we have seen on large sailing ships, but modified for the sole pleasure of the owner and his guests.

After this long diversion to the realm of ship's furnishings, let us return to the captain's quarters on board our sailing ship. The captain's suite, always situated on the starboard side of the poop, starboard being the 'privileged' side of the ship, comprises an office, a sleeping cabin and a bathroom. Although the captain does not often receive visitors in his quarters but preferably in the saloon, the office has a large couch against one wall, which serves to seat chance guests in port and at sea is used by the captain for taking an after-dinner nap in fine weather and for resting fully clothed when he is expecting to get a call on the poop. A writing desk with drop-leaf or roller, fixed to the bulkhead, is used for the daily paper-work during the voyage. On the bulkheads we find also a long mercury barometer, a round aneroid barometer, a rifle, a spy-glass and framed photographs. In a big cupboard are stowed the ship's

documents, all the ship's logs, duplicates of letters and voyage reports since the ship was launched. In a corner of the office there is the chronometer locker with two or even three chronometers, rewound each day at the same time by the captain and kept like holy relics in this sheltered room away from jolts and variations of temperature. As to the ship's money, it is kept in a safe bolted to some strong portion of the timbering. It is a little chest, smaller than the famous iron treasure chests with which privateers' vessels and the King of Spain's galleons used to be equipped. These iron treasure chests were mostly, but not exclusively, built at Nuremberg or Toledo. It is customary to say that the two or four holes drilled in the bottom were for bolting the chest to the cabin floor, but could they not equally well have been used for bolting it to the floor-beams of a castle? As they are secret chests, the key-hole is not always where it seems to be. It has to be found by pulling a number of metal tongues and slides. The locksmith's work on the inside of the lid is not only mechanically impressive but also very decorative.

In the captain's sleeping cabin we find the same sobriety as in the office. The bed, covered by a quilt, contains, of course, four drawers. There are one or two oil-lamps in gimbals, fitted with a smoke-shield if they are too near the deck-head. The bathroom has nothing very interesting for us. It is fitted out as anywhere else, except that it has no taps. In fact, since water is so scarce on board, the bath only comes into use in port, when it has to be filled, by the pot-full, with warm water from the galley.

Let us cross the alleyway. In the space contained by the two alleyways, the fore-part of the saloon and the forward bulkhead of the poop, there are the pantry, aft, and the sail-loft, forward. The pantry allows access to the lower provisions store containing all the ship's communal provisions. In the pantry itself, apart from a tin sink, a small fresh-water cask and a little oil-stove, there are only a number of beech or deal pantry cupboards. Let us go to the sail-loft. There, in sturdy compartments, all the ship's spare sails are stored, dry, neatly folded and marked for immediate recognition. After all, a three-master has no less than fifteen square sails, eight stay-sails, four triangular fore-sails, a mizzen sail and, possibly, twelve studding sails. Sometimes, there are even two or three spare suits of sails, the oldest being set in fine weather and the new, strong ones in the howling gales of the Roaring Forties. Since we have no intention of collecting these huge sails with their heavy boltropes or even steel-wire luffs, weighing sometimes more than a ton, we shall cast an interested glance at all the sailmaker's equipment kept in this room. Not only are necessary repairs done on board, but new sails are also made, as much as an economy

The third-class dining room on board the passenger ship *Champollion*, early 20th century. The chair-backs are in the twisted style popular at that period, while the tripod pedestals of these typical swivel chairs are screwed firmly to the deck.

A rope-cradle in which 200 metres of Manilla rope can be coiled, drained, dried and aired between uses.

177

A 17th-century treasure chest made in Nuremberg.

measure as to keep people busy. Making a new sail is a formidable task which takes weeks and thousands of stitches by hand. It is not done by the sailmaker alone, but six to eight of the most qualified men are appointed to help him. For a sailor on board a big sailing ship it is an honour to be chosen for this task. Each sailor has his own little sail-cloth bag in which he keeps his personal implements: various sizes of triangular needles, greatly treasured and kept in tallow inside a bullock's horn, often engraved with a ship or some other nautical motif, two palms, one for sewing, the other for roping the sail, scissors, and a sailmaker's hook for pulling the cloth while stitching it. The bulky equipment is provided by the shipping company. There is the sailmaker's bench, worn smooth by the rubbing of coarse canvas trousers. In it are a number of holes to take various sizes of box-wood fids, serving mallets, prickers and marlinspikes, all simple tools with which the sailor produces strong yet elegant results.

Sometimes the bosun stores the caulking gear in the sail-loft. This consists mainly of a long, round mallet with iron hoops, caulking irons for driving the caulking cotton into the seams and rave hooks or ripping irons for cleaning the old caulking out of the seams. These tools are put in typical low boxes, on which the caulker sits when working on deck.

So we have finished our tour of the ship, but let us not leave the sailing ships yet. We still have to visit a cod-fishing vessel, a tunny-fishing vessel, a whaler and a slave-ship before going aboard a steamer.

Cod-fishing vessels, which were three-masted sailing ships at the beginning of the nineteenth century, became topsail schooners towards 1870. This rig, made up entirely of fore-and-aft sails, facilitated manoeuvring, since there was no longer any need to send men aloft as there was with square-rigged ships. There is no luxury on these fishing vessels, all is solid and practical. Most of the arrangements which we have seen on board the large sailing ships are repeated here, and in addition there is the fishing gear. This is efficient yet rudimentary, the art not being in the gear itself but rather in the way of using it. The deck work with cod is done in five stages. The cod, head down in an iron cask, has its entrails removed with a gutting knife and its head is cut off with a guillotine. Then it is sliced open with a slicing knife, scraped clean with a scraping knife, and finally it is washed and thrown in the hold. There, the salter stacks the fish, throwing a shovel-full of salt over it with a special little shovel. These rare tools, when they are found, still show the marks of heavy toil. Cod-fishing is done from 'dories', those little rowing or sailing boats with a trapeze-shaped cross-section, which have stood the test of heavy weather. Of the fishing-dory equipment the collector will be interested in the dry or liquid dory compass, the big baskets for the fishing lines, the hooks in all shapes and sizes. (A very good collection could be built up just from fishing hooks: anything from the bone hooks of Eskimos and South Sea Islanders to the intricate hooks of Swedish and German make.) There are furthermore the grapnels to get cut lines back from the bottom, and the galvanized metal boxes containing ship's biscuits and drinking water. To take the catch on board the mother ship the crew remaining on board use a barbed hook.

On board the tunny-fishing vessels we find big swivel-hooks, which, inserted in a beard of maize, make very effective baits for the voracious tunny, which are fished with drag-nets at six to seven knots, under sail.

The whaler's equipment, often portrayed in paintings, is poorly represented in the museums of Europe. The last whale-hunters were indisputably Americans. All the specialized gear that they used consists in essence of a few elements. First, there were the marvellous, long, light rowing boats with slim lines, which flew across the

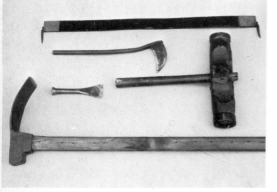

Caulking and carpenter's tools. *From top to bottom:* draw knife, rave hook for cleaning out old caulking, caulking iron, caulking mallet and carpenter's adze.

waves at each stroke of the oars. For us collectors, there will scarcely be anything in this boat except the harpoons and the spears. Like side-arms, the harpoon had its fashion. One must re-read *Moby Dick* to see what trouble the harpooner took with his weapons. The harpoon was greased, sharpened, housed in a thick leather scabbard, ready for use. The weight and balance of a harpoon was critical. The harpooners practised with their weapons like athletes with the javelin, and their accuracy of shot was stupefying. Once the harpoon had been landed in the animal, they would wait for it to sound, dragging its line, then for it to come up again, towing the boat at mad speeds. When the whale was out of breath, they would come up to it and put it to death with long spears, which hit the animal's vital interior parts. Other barbed harpoons might be thrust in to secure the body for towing. Once the animal was alongside the whaler, chained up so as not to drift away, the work of dissection began with the help of helved knives and cutting shovels of all types, while a special hook, rigged on to the strip of blubber which was being cut off, pulled the greasy length up on deck, where it was chopped into little squares and thrown into the melting cauldron, an enormous cast-iron cooking-pot set up on a brick oven on deck. Across the world, numerous examples of these enormous boilers still exist, indestructible reminders of an adventurous past and very representative of the toilsome task of whalers.

As to the equipment peculiar to the slave-trading vessels, it is what one might expect: miserable implements of punishment and penance, arm- and leg-irons, whips and cats-of-nine-tails. What port can boast of not having practised the trade? Every now and then a piece of this sinister ironmongery turns up, the supply of which was ensured by a number of specialized blacksmiths.

At this same period there also appeared on the seas the first steamers, equipped with a whole new set of gear, which goes on growing, perfecting itself, and becoming more specialized. For the collector only the bridge of these ships will be interesting,

Emergency drinking-water cask of No. 1 lifeboat of the Portuguese passenger vessel *Angola*. It is of elegant proportions and made of fine wood.

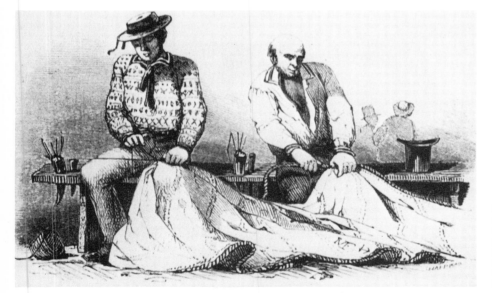

Dexterity, patience and love of good workmanship was needed in the sailmaker's work. This illustration shows the sailmaker and an assistant sailor stitching and roping a sail. On the bench, stowed in holes, we see a few of the simple tools used: hooks, needle horns, sailmaker's palms and fids made of iron, boxwood, ivory or bone.

A round document-case from the beginning of the 17th century, in which important papers were stored on board.

for a number of very fine objects are gathered here in surprising density. As the saying has it: the bridge is the brain of the ship, and so one must expect to find here the duty officer, the helmsman, and at night or in fog the look-out, who is no longer at the bow, as on the sailing ships, but out in the wing of the bridge.

We do not intend to go into the history of bridges, from the flying bridge between the two paddle-boxes of paddle-steamers, on which the officer of the watch stood alone, to the modern bridges of the automation age, on which the three key services of the ship—navigation, engines and radio—are concentrated. We shall simply pay a visit to the bridge of a mail and passenger steamer of the thirties, when there was still some ornamented wood and copper about to delight the eye.

On the wings of the bridge we find the bearing discs, mounted at eye level, and the ring buoys marked with the vessel's name, with their self-igniting lights. Beautiful teak sliding doors shut the wheelhouse. Outside, mounted on an iron stirrup, the watch bell strikes the hours. Above the wheel-house and reached by companionways, we find the bearing compass on a wooden pillar covered by a tarpaulin. Likewise, there are the flag halyards, made fast to cleats or coiled in halyard tubs.

In the wheelhouse stands the helmsman on his grating, slightly raised (a heritage of the days of sail). The wheel is no more than a modest wooden circle with spokes, 1 metre in diameter at the most. It is kept rather on the large side to give it weight, which assists in steering. In fact, it only sets in motion two oil-driven pistons, which transmit their instructions to the rudder. This telemotor system requires very little effort by the helmsman. The modern gyro-hydraulic steering control with its small wheel, only 30 cm (1 ft.) in diameter, requires even less. The steering compass in its polished brass binnacle is right before the helmsman's eyes. The speaking tube, colloquially called 'blower', which communicates with the bearing compass, has a fine copper mouthpiece, as have the other blowers lined up in the forward part of the wheel-house. Small plates show with whom they communicate: 'Engines', 'Captain', 'Wireless' . . . . When not in use they are closed by a whistle at both ends. When someone blows in at one end, the whistle sounds at the other. Simple and efficient, blowers are still in use today. But the supreme symbol of triumphant machinery on the bridge is the engine room telegraph. Worked by a handle, it transmits orders like 'Slow astern', 'Full speed ahead', or 'Stop!' to the engine room, where the same dial faces the engineer, who confirms the order by moving the handle of his telegraph to the corresponding position, which in turn is indicated by the corresponding pointer on the bridge telegraph, thus showing that the order has been understood and is being executed.

Against a bulkhead we find a set of flag lockers, a binnacle clock for the helmsman, panels with warning indicators for position lights, large plans of the different levels of the ship with little lamps that wink when the temperature somewhere rises high enough to require investigation. There are no seats on the bridge, everyone does his job standing up.

Aft of the bridge is the chart-room. A black or opaque curtain acts as the door, so that the officer of the watch is not dazzled. In this sanctuary we find essentially the same furniture and navigation equipment that we saw in the chart-house of our sailing ship, with the notable addition of an early model of radio direction finder.

Before leaving this steam-ship, we must take a look at the tableware, which is ostentatious, as it should be on a passenger ship. Have we needed centuries of nautical civilization to attain such luxury at sea? Seemingly not, if we are to judge by what was discovered in the wrecks of galleons and notable vessels like the *Vasa*: quality tableware in silver and pewter, ewers, goblets, decanters, drinking vessels in all shapes and materials. They were the tableware of princes, evoking on board ship the atmosphere of lordly manors. They bear no nautical decoration but the arms of the great

Teak fire-buckets with copper hoops lined up in a space-saving way between the balustres of the poop rail. Handsome yet functional, they have rope handles with fancy knots at the ends, fashioned by a skilful sailor.

personnages who made the voyage. But as centuries passed, the sea and its connections gained increased influence on decorative features, and clouds or tritons, sirens, Neptunes, shells and ship began to appear on silver tableware. The maritime decoration of China Trade Porcelain, which is discussed in Chapter VIII, is well known for its influence on table porcelain, gold and silver. At the same time, warships and merchant-ships adopted strictly personalized table services. The silver of warships is decorated with simple motifs: interlaced oakleaves, flat and raised rims in twisted coil patterns, medallions which enhance the solemnity of the naval anchor, sometimes etched on the handles of knives, forks and spoons, sometimes moulded into the handles of soup-tureens, salad-bowls and punch-bowls.

The silverware of shipping companies like Cunard, P. & O. or French Line is decorated with the emblem or flag of the company. This is found on everything from the smallest coffee spoon to the voluminous champagne bucket. The china is normally simple and sober: blue or gold rims and in the centre of the plate, saucer or dish the emblem or flag of the company. Items marked with the name of an individual ship are rarer, since only the big, famous liners could afford such extravagance.

When shipping companies go bankrupt or are dissolved, all this tableware is sold, of course, as is out-of-date tableware of the Navy. Such pieces are always nice to have in a collection, even if they only have a symbolic value. We have seen remarkable collections of ash-trays marked with shipping companies' initials, and some collectors even have their hearts set on ships' linen: table linen, woollen blankets and sheets.

But these luxury items must not make us forget the crew's more modest implements, often of a more nautical and more original character. The humble materials—iron, wood, earthenware—have not generally stood up to the ravages of the elements, whether at the bottom of the sea or in some badly sheltered storage-place ashore. We are thinking mainly of mess cans, mugs and those small wooden vats with rope handles in which the sailors used to transport wine and solid food for the eight-man 'mess'. There is always some etched mark on them, a naval registration or service number. The regulation sameness of the mug, which was used for everything from wine and beer to rum and coffee, was sometimes brightened up by a scratched-in

Ship's silver table-ware, French national navy. 19th century.

Neptune—a figurehead of a
19th-century American ship.

design picked out in colour, and the name of a topman, stoker or gunner. Any of these practical everyday implements which survived many years of loyal service at sea and were finally taken ashore by their owners, were subsequently subjected to yet another spell of domestic use, which explains why they are now so rare. Some, though, have been preserved and handed down as family souvenirs, and these occasionally turn up at sales.

Ship's ornamentation

We shall not deal here with the magic and propitiatory aspects of the decoration of ancient boats and ships but concentrate solely on the rather more secular ornamentation of more recent types of vessels. What is ornamentation? Is it an added element, or is it in the ship itself? Contemporary aesthetic principles, developed in the Scandinavian countries, are based very largely on the hydrodynamic shape of the ship. Wooden construction imposes curves, sweeping outlines, which are not deliberately decorative but are necessary for strength. A little clinker-built yacht's tender or a rowing 'eight' are in themselves thoroughbred shapes. A well curved stem, the backward slope of a poop, the curve of a stern vault, the sheer of a clipper deck, the tumble-home of a main-frame are all elements which the eye does not fail to appreciate, even if they are made of coarse materials and painted black. The sails and the rigging, when seen from a distance, are also of great aesthetic appeal. Any small part of the ship may be decorative in addition to being functional: a wooden cathead at the bow, a topmast cap, a pin rail, a block, a fairlead, a deadeye . . . .

The deck fittings of yachts are certainly amongst the most decorative items, even the more modern ones in stainless steel or light alloy. The older bronze fittings have, in addition, a romantic feel about them. Theirs is the two-fold charm which all objects connected with the sea have in common: they please the eye and kindle the imagination. No-one escapes this spell. Even an old wooden block, its sheaves worn down to the very centre, or a staysail hank eaten away with rust will please a collector of modest means. But since we are here concerned with ships' ornamentation in the strictest sense of the word, let us keep looking at from the point of view of the collector who can reasonably install a piece of a ship's ornamentation in his living room. Not a piece of timber off a wreck, but a detachable piece of decoration.[1]

When, some years ago, the Swedish ship *Vasa* was hauled from her mud coffin and a list was made of her carved ornaments, no less than 700 separate decorative items were found. Launched in 1628, she was decorated in the style of her time, which was an excess of baroque ornamentation, also found at that time in France, England and Holland. After centuries of sobriety, ships seemed to take a pride in hiding their outlines beneath an inextricable jungle of gilded, interlacing patterns. Till then, only the aftercastle, bulwarks and forecastle had known decorations painted in the conventional sea colours: fleurs-de-lys on sky-blue backgrounds, coats of arms, or chequers in contrasting colours. It has been alleged that this was an adaptation of the ancient Norman and Viking tradition of decorating the sides of their ships with round or pointed shields.

The Renaissance movement, reacting against so much geometric severity, led the way into the fantasies of the 17th century. Soon wood carvers discovered the inviting surfaces of the huge aftercastles, the galleries, the vaults, the beak-heads, all of which lent itself admirably to massive decoration. It makes one wonder whether the very high, wide sterns, which seriously impeded the ship's manoeuvrability under sail, would not have been abandoned much sooner if they had not served as a support for the flights of imagination of a cohort of wood-carvers who covered them with coils and festoons, scrolls, diadems and palm-leaves, caryatids, tritons, sirens, trumpeting angles and grimacing faces? Until half-way through the 18th century warships, especially French and English ones, looked more like wedding cakes than fighting vessels.

Above all it was the extremes of the ship, which the wood-carvers overloaded.

A sacred piece of equipment:
the fresh-water cask. This is a very
handsome example off the ship
Africa with copper hoops, bronze
lock and rings by which it was
lashed to the poop deck.

[1]There are many ways in which ships' fittings can be put to new and unexpected uses in domestic surroundings. In the home of the writer Herman Melville at Arrowhead, for example, rowlocks have been let into the wall by the fireplace to take the fire-irons.

The stern of these large vessels was roughly trapeze-shaped, i.e. wider at the base, and had two or three galleries of glazed windows. On either side of the stern were the quarter-galleries, sometimes two-storied, which housed the officers' latrines. It is obvious that such vast virgin surfaces could not have left the wood-carvers indifferent, and drafts of decorations flourished in large numbers, arriving to lumber up admiralty offices, as the archives testify. For the wood-carver and his team the ornamentation of a ship represented several years of continuous work, which partly explains why artists of Pierre Puget's talent became interested in ship ornamentation. The drafts show to what degree the wood-carvers were indifferent to the ship as a floating vessel with obvious limitations. To them, the hull was just an excuse. Some of the ornaments were incredibly cumbersome, and some were so fragile that it was a miracle if they stood up to the onslaught of the sea. But that is how it was: in the shipyards the master-carpenter often had to yield to the irrevocable decisions of the artists.

It was not until the 19th century that a certain concept of 'integrated' ship's ornamentation emerged, in which the decorative elements embrace the ship's natural lines and even draw their inspiration from them. The broadside of the ship, which gets the gunfire, remained relatively bare, although in the 17th century certain ships, such as the 100-gun ship *Prince* (1670) and the *Sovereign of the Seas* (1637) had their sides, at the level of the upper gun-ports, decorated with wreaths or friezes.

In the 18th and 19th centuries fighting ships were usually painted black with white or yellow stripes to set off the gun-ports, the inside of the port covers being painted red, which made a fine pattern when these were open. Two or three rows of open stern galleries continued to be popular and could, in fact, still be found on the iron-clads of 1914.

In France during the Revolution and in England towards 1796, the admiralties were given instructions to economize, and the ornamentation of ships was very much reduced. The stern of warships was reduced to its structural elements, with some degree of sawn outline and polychroming, while the bow was graced by a figurehead or just a simple moulding at the cutwater.

Figureheads

The prow of the Viking ships and the beak of the galleys are certainly the distant ancestors of the figurehead, which, after disappearing for six centuries, reappeared in the 15th and 16th centuries at the bow of ships. The figurehead underwent various changes between then and the beginning of the 20th century, largely to adapt itself to the changing shape of ships' stems. About 1610 the cutwater of ships projected almost horizontally, and it was natural to put standing figures or equestrian statues on it. On the beakhead of the *Prince Royal* (1613), for example, a gentleman on horseback met the waves. However, this straight beak had the drawback of plunging into the seas like a ladle and thus slowing the ship down. Towards the end of the 17th century the cutwater started to bend upwards and the figurehead was flattened against the top of it. Upright, with slightly arched back and head thrown back, the person or symbolic animal always appeared slightly stiff. The lion was the favourite motif on English and Dutch ships up to the end of the 18th century, when more elaborate groups supporting coats of arms appeared. These escutcheons and medallions were found again on the iron ships, where the inverted stem no longer permitted the incorporation of a human figure. Forgotten for fifty years, the tradition is returning today, for a number of Scandinavian cargo ships decorate the top of their stems with a sort of winged escutcheon.

It is the second half of the 19th century, when the clippers make their appearance, which is, for us at least, the golden age of figureheads. As we look at one after another we are never quite sure whether what we are looking at are works of art or simple objects of curiosity, which have attained popularity. The clipper's sloping stem lent itself admirably to sculptural decorations. In the United States, the spread eagle was often used as figurehead of warships, while merchant ships looked for a subject which illustrated as closely as possible the name of the ship. So it came that the *Lightning* had her bows decorated with a young woman in flight holding in her outstretched hand a threatening flash of lightning. More prosaically, the worthy gentlemen in old-fashioned top-coats were supposed to represent the owners of the ships. There were also plenty of romantic girls offering their ample bosoms to the caress of the spray, one arm graciously stretched towards the horizon and the opposite leg seemingly poised for a leap, suggesting the pitching movement of the vessel. Some Scandinavian figureheads were painted white all over, all their grace being expressed in the body's movement and the drape of the long robes. On the smallest merchant vessels the wood-carvers made up for a certain lack of proficiency by a naive, intense sensitivity, which does not fail to appeal. These popular carvings were far removed from the art of a Pierre Puget, or of a William Savage (carver of the *Victory*, 1765), or of a Gerard Christmas (carver of the *Sovereign of the Seas*, following the drawings of Van Dyck).

While a certain formal beauty was the aim of these great artists, the 19th-century wood-carvers, often anonymous, display a touching anxiety to fit in with the spirit of the ship and the company, i.e. name and type of vessel, nature of voyages. Since these wood-carvers were less well-known personalities, it was possible for the ship-owner and captain to intervene with their own ideas while work on a figurehead was in progress.

In the naval dockyards, on the other hand, the wood-carver used to receive precise instructions, the fruits of the Admiralty's deliberations, to which a document testifies addressed to William Savage by the British Admiralty at the time that the *Victory's* figurehead was being carved:[1]

'A new large figure . . . with the bust of His Majesty, the head adorned with laurels, and the body and shoulders worked in rich armour . . . , under the breast is a rich shield partly supporting the bust and surrounded with four cherubs' heads and wings representing the four winds smiling, gently blowing our successes over the four quarters of the globe. On the starboard side . . . a large drapery figure representing Britannia properly crowned, sitting on a rich triumphant arch, and in one hand holding a spear enriched and the Union Flag hanging down from it, and with the other hand supporting the bust of His Majesty, with one foot trampling down Envy, Discord and Faction represented by a fiend or a hag: at the same side above and behind Britannia is a large flying figure representing Peace crowning the figure of Britannia with laurels and holding a branch of palms denoting peace and the happy consequences result ng from victory. At the back of the arch is the British lion, trampling on very rich trophies of war, cut clear and open and the arch on this side supported by two large figures representing Europe and America properly dressed and agreeable to the countries; and at the lower part . . . is cut a young genius holding . . . a bunch of flowers . . .'

The identification of figureheads is often difficult, especially when dealing with merchant ships. We have nothing to go by, no models, yard drawings, artists' preliminary sketches, nor even wood-carvers' specifications, and what is more, the figure is sometimes not even representative of the ship, if the ship has meanwhile changed her name. This happened to a number of American sailing ships which were re-named with the names of the owner's gracious young daughters but, nevertheless, retained at the bow the clean-shaven and severe face of some stockholder of the preceding company. Changing the name of a ship was a redoubtable practice and not loaded with superstitions, but changing figureheads might have left the owner without captain or crew, for no-one would have dared go against the ancient custom.

In fact, a whole web of beliefs and superstitions was spun round the figurehead. While for the ship-owner it symbolized wealth and prosperity, the sailors did not escape from its magic influence, either. Damage and accidents to the figurehead were interpreted as very bad omens. Joseph Conrad, in his book *A Smile of Fortune* writes: ' . . . the figurehead was looked upon in a very personal way by the captain and was associated in his mind with the luck of his ship and his own fortune.' Obviously the mysterious powers of figureheads must have been very tangible, for a number of them, which fell into the hands of natives in the Pacific, were promptly worshipped as totems.

The fact that ships were shipwrecked or dismantled complicates the identification of figureheads further. A number of ships' figureheads have been washed up by the sea, especially on the dangerous reefs of Scilly. These have been collected at Tresco Abbey Museum and are by no means all identified.

[1] Quoted from 'Figureheads' by Peter Norton, National Maritime Museum.

Figurehead of the steam frigate
Lancaster. It is the work of John Haley
Bellamy of Kittery Point, Maine, and
dates from appr. 1880. It was one of the
last sculptures of this type. The distance
between the wing-tips of this eagle is no
less than 18 ft. John Bellamy was for
many years attached to the Navy Yard
at Portsmouth, New Hampshire, which is
the oldest American shipyard (1757).

Figurehead of the American clipper *Belle of Oregon*. It is in the great tradition of the famous carvers of figureheads in the second half of the 19th century, like J. Bellamy and A. Sampson, who are known in particular for their carving of the figurehead for the clipper *Belle of Bath*. Works by these tough and hardy men, who knew nothing whatsoever about Europe but embodied the spirit of the American pioneers, formed the backbone of the original yankee art born in the 19th century.

Even less than a hundred years ago, in the stock-yards and ship-yards, one would come across odd figureheads standing around amongst the piles of planks. Because of their association with particular ships they could not be used for any others. None the less, they were kept, because of some superstitious respect, till the day when, completely ravaged by the weather, their paint peeled off and their facial expressions faded, one no longer risked bringing the least of bad luck on anyone by using them as firewood. In defence of the iconoclasts let us say that 100 years ago nautical antiques were a vague idea, and a figurehead, the natural complement of a ship, had never had any value except at the prow of a ship. As long as it was in position it had the care and respect lavished on it that it demanded, but once ashore this dead human figure, no longer diving into the waves, no longer surrounded by flying spray, had no reason to receive from the shipyard the loving attention it had received on board. Anyone who knows what patience and expense the restoration of figureheads requires could not be surprised at the fact that nothing was done to save these monoliths once they had been reduced by weathering to the state of broken-down lumps of timber.

The passion for maritime objects is a recent thing. A piece of wreckage which today is worth a fortune was yesterday only worth the effort of throwing it on the fire.[1]

Figureheads remain the moving symbols of the Great Age of Sail. A number of sailing yachts of today are trying to bring the ancient custom back to life. But, alas, the art of the wood-carvers of those days is totally lost and so are the naive beliefs of the wooden navy which inspired the artists. If there is an art in which sincerity is of primary importance, it is, no doubt, popular art, and that, very likely, explains the fabulous prices one now has to pay for these beautiful, multi-coloured figures, who evoke for us the days of the great sailing ships and the embrace of the wide open sea.

[1]This has not happened in all countries, though. The United States, whose naval history is relatively recent, have taken great trouble to preserve their maritime heritage, in particular when it comes to vessels which are still afloat.

VII
Arts and crafts on board ship

The pictures we have chosen to illustrate this chapter would suffice in themselves to fill the few pages reserved for the subject of art and crafts on board ship, and it is not in order to provide reading matter at all costs that we are adding a few words but in order to give the collector some broad guide-lines to this extensive selection. En route, we shall endeavour to distinguish between the authentic and the inauthentic, between fact and fiction.

The general public has romantic ideas about the life of a sailor. Some twenty years ago a charming lady, who had come to view a cargo ship about to set sail, was surprised by all the activity going on on deck. The last pieces of cargo were being loaded, the hatches were closed and the tarpaulins that covered the holds were battened down. Steam was puffing out of the winches, while the blocks creaked as the derricks were lowered.

The lady, who was enthralled by all this feverish activity, asked us point-blank: 'But what will there be left to do for the rest of the voyage?' And, indeed, twenty-five days at sea lay before us, which this delightful creature imagined as being filled with sailors' yarns, sea shanties and reveries, while we were leaning on the ship's rail in ceaseless contemplation of the never ending sea. We smiled and, while the gangway was being taken up, the mooring lines cast off and the tugs were moving us out from the quayside, the everyday routine of life on board was taking shape, a routine which was to leave each member of the crew only a limited number of hours per day between keeping watch, sleeping, laundering, washing himself and eating; a limited number of hours, which he used as he saw fit but did not use to gaze out to sea.

From one end of the ship to another everybody busied himself with odd jobs in his spare time. Some made the soles and uppers of rope sandals, others cut and sewed caps and trousers in heavy canvas, yet others made waterproofs. Strong trunks were built in which to take back home groceries of which we had long been deprived. Aft on the poop-deck a single-seater canoe was taking shape in an improvised boatyard. Shark-lines were made, fishing nets for the sea-birds and cages for the exotic wild birds, which we hoped to bring back from Brazil. Hissing sounds came from the forge, as an old iron bar was fashioned into a harpoon for porpoises. Some old salts from the days of sail were busy making a model, while some amateur mechanics had set their hearts on getting their fob watches going again or repairing an alarm clock, which had given up the ghost. People also made what was lacking for their comfort: shelves, sea-chests, ventilators to slide into the port holes in the doldrums in order to catch the least little breeze stirred up by the movement of the ship. Tattered signal flags came to life again with the help of a few pieces of bunting from the bosun's chest. Jobs for the ship, jobs for himself, everyone was happily occupied in his spare time, and no-one could tolerate total inactivity. Every book and magazine was read or thumbed through at least twenty times. Our efforts on board were, no doubt, very mundane compared with the works of art produced by the men on the old sailing ships, but they showed that the old tradition of the sea had not been lost and that a sailor cannot remain idle for even a few moments.

Those of us who go sailing for pleasure know this well. Boats demand time and attention, which we lavish on them willingly. The sea is a good provider of jobs that need doing, with its corrosive salt, its perpetual movement, which wears things out; its sun, which cracks the paint and varnish; its humidity, which rusts iron and rots wood; its wind, which wears the sails and breaks the ropes. Without all that, what interest would there be in going to sea?

The sailor on the big sailing ships was used to all these necessary chores. It was his everyday life, a case of making the most of it. The maintenance of the ship was something at which he did not baulk, far from it; he went about his work with loving devotion, examining blocks with the eye of a clockmaker inspecting a chronometer, stitching sails with the patience and dedication of a seamstress, painting and repainting the hull and superstructure like an artist. The sailor in the days of sail had an undeniable advantage over the seaman of today: he was a man of sail, in love with tradition, steeped in religious belief, superstitions and folklore. His very language was idiosyncratic, peculiar to him and his life on board ship. He made all sorts of useless but traditional objects, which were a means of proving to himself that he was as good as and even better than the next man. He brought a touch of individuality to the most mundane objects and produced veritable works of art. To work to the best of his ability was his only reward, and he felt in this justified and at peace with himself.

But we could go on forever singing the praises of an attitude which has produced so many masterpieces of popular art without getting any nearer the objects which are of interest for our collection. In order to find some guide-lines amongst the incongruous medley, we think it best to categorize the objects and give some explanations where necessary.

Models

We shall add nothing here to what was said in the first chapter about models made by sailors: full models, half-models, dioramas and ships in bottles. They are all part of the old tradition of model-making, and some of them, especially those made by prisoners, are really outstanding works of art.

Engraving and sculpture

Shaping pieces of wood with a knife is a custom surprisingly widespread throughout the world. There cannot be a lad who has not, at some time, cut down the branch of a tree with a cheap pen-knife in order to make a walking stick, nor a wall that has not been disfigured by graphiti. This sort of primitive reaction is at the root of the art of sculpture. Sailors were simple, spontaneous people and could not resist the urge to use their good, solid clasp-knives on any odd piece of wood they found lying around. Apart from models, sailors liked to carve the lids of their sea-chests, tobaccoboxes in the shape of boats, butter moulds for the home, tool handles, tillers, cleats, and useful objects like traverse boards, perpetual calendars, mast trucks, playing pieces for chess, drafts, dominoes and lotto, the very handles of their knives and heads of their walking sticks.

Scrimshaw

Scrimshaw, an untranslateable word of Anglo-Saxon origin, the root of which is still obscure, comprises in its widest sense all the arts and crafts practiced by the men on board whalers, but more specifically it is understood to describe objects made of ivory from the teeth of walrus and sperm-whales. These objects probably first appeared at the time when whale-hunting took to the high seas, which was towards the beginning of the 17th century.[1] Until that time the whale and sperm-whale used

[1] Teeth of sperm-whale have been found in the dwellings of prehistoric man, coming probably from sperm-whales stranded on the sea-shore. Although these finds are not widespread, they have nevertheless given rise to speculation among some ethnologists on the symbolism surrounding whale teeth. A phallic symbol, they also appear to have been the weapons of conquered man and were preserved as trophies. Should one attribute the same deep, dark origin to the interest which the whalers took in the teeth of the sperm-whales?

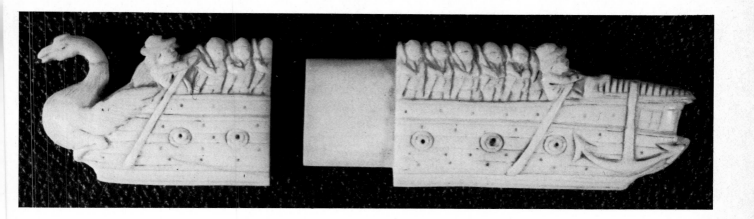

to be hunted not far from land in the Bay of Biscay, on the coasts of Norway and North America (Nantucket and New Bedford). Gradually, the migratory whales became inhabitants of the high seas, and in order to hunt them, ocean-going ships had to be equipped. The voyages were long, sometimes three years, for the ships only returned home when all the barrels in the holds were full. The days dragged depressingly, and as whalers have never been renowned for their smartness, unlike the clippers, the crew thought of better things to do between hunts than dabbling with paint and potash.

Scrimshaw became a veritable passion, and time and time again ship owners were forced to take measures to surpress it, because the men neglected their jobs over it. From cabin boy to captain everyone was busy decorating his piece of ivory. Even the topman took his tools up into the crow's nest with him and jeopardised all chances of a catch by failing to keep a look-out.

The raw material for such industry was hacked with chisels from the whale's jaws. The ivory tooth has a rough surface, which first has to be planed and polished. This was first done with a knife and finished with shagreen (skate or shark skin). Then, with a needle normally used for stitching sails, the men engraved the soft, smooth surface with infinite patience, following faithfully the outline of the design.

The most skilful and the most creative drew their design in pencil and went over it with a needle. The less skilful or less inspired drew their themes from illustrations in magazines and books, in particular human faces, which, once copied, always looked somewhat clumsy because of the proportions dictated by the size of the tooth.

Ivory needle-case depicting a galley. Sailor's work, 18th century.

Pie-crimper made from a sperm-whale tooth. The wheel is used to decorate the edges of the pastry, the point to pierce the pastry in the course of cooking. Work of an American whaler.

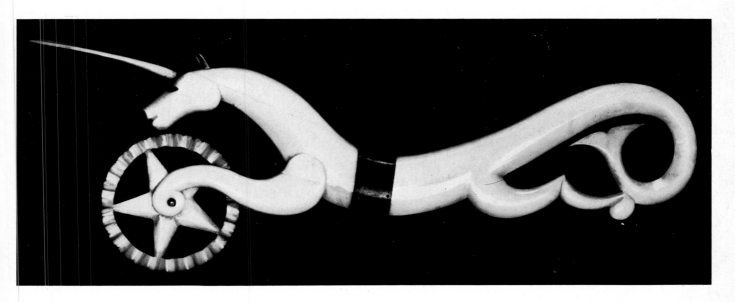

The themes are almost always the same: whaling scenes depicting various misadventures that beset the harpooners and the boatmen during the hunt, scenes of everyday routine, sentimental episodes in the life of a sailor: the departure, the return, the reunion with his fiancée, all encircled by names, dates, laurel leaves, floral decorations, hearts and national flags.

A good many of these sailors were, of course, pious Christians nurtured on the psalms and chapters of the gospels from childhood and revived each week in their faith by the reading of the scriptures, which puritanical captains delivered to them. Not unexpectedly, there is no shortage of biblical themes engraved on whale teeth. They were hardly likely to forget the story of Jonah, who, according to the bible, was the first man to come into close contact with the animal they were hunting.

The themes are interesting even in the absence of dates or titles, but in any case the types of boats which are depicted (one can rely on the sailors for accuracy of detail) seem to suggest that the origins of scrimshaw go back no further than the 17th century.

In the 19th century, when the whalers had to work frantically to compete with kerosene from Pennsylvania, which was beginning to threaten the candle industry, the pressure was no longer conducive to idleness, and the art of scrimshaw seems to have declined. Old, retired sailors and professional engravers then undertook to decorate sperm-whale teeth for collectors, this time with a wide variety of themes and precision tools. The result reflects this change to a large extent. The subject matter became stereotyped, without originality or flair. There is no improvisation, no hesitation, no subtle nuances of greys and shadows. Where each wave used to be a moment of graphic emotion, the whole scene is now composed of contrived little mechanical movements.

In parts of the world where sperm-whaling survives today, artisans still engrave whale teeth for tourists. Time being at a premium, the convenient tool is the dentist's drill. It makes one wonder whether this gives the whales a terrible headache!

In addition to engraved teeth, the whalers fashioned in ivory all sorts of other more or less useful objects, of which the museum in Nantucket, amongst others,

Writing case, work of an English whaler.

190

possesses an admirable collection. There are clothes pegs, bobbins, thimbles, needle cases, yarn reels and winding stools, tobacco jars, door handles, hooks, chests, baskets, bird cages, paper knives, yard sticks, rulers, compasses, seals and counters, knife handles, handles for cutlery and tools.

A number of small seals depicting profiles of whales and sperm-whales was made for the captain, who decorated the log-book with them: a solid profile for an animal which had been caught, an outline profile for one which had been hunted unsuccessfully, a rear half with the tail up in the air for one which had been sighted but which had sounded and disappeared.

Another favourite amongst the whaling fraternity were corset stiffeners, or busks, shaped like thin paperknives and engraved with naive verses. The majority of corset stiffeners, of course, were made from plain, undecorated baleen taken from the right whale. Other objects made from the thin, horny plates of whalebone, or baleen, were tobacco jars and miscellaneous boxes.

Although less frequently, walrus teeth were also engraved by the whalers. But walrus were encountered by them only occasionally, except when lack of whales obliged them to hunt any animal with blubber to fill the barrels.

Occasionally, a far inferior material, namely bone from the jaw of the sperm-whale was engraved, but the quality of the engravings usually compensates for the poor quality of the material.

We must not leave the whalers without mentioning a trophy which the men liked to bring back from their voyages, if they had the luck to find one: the horn of the narwhal, or sea-unicorn.

The narwhal's 'horn' is actually one of two top canine teeth of the male animal, the other tooth remaining atrophied. It can reach a length of 2.50 metres. Contrary to common belief, the narwhal is a peaceable animal which lives in herds in the polar seas. Occasionally, a narwhal which had lost its way would meet with a whaler and was immediately harpooned, as one can imagine. Today purely decorative, the 'horn' of the narwhal was in the Middle Ages used for testing whether food and drink were poisoned. The strange similarity between the horn of the narwahl and that of the

Scene from the everyday life of a whaler: the whale being towed to the mother-ship Engraving on a sperm-whale tooth by an American sailor.

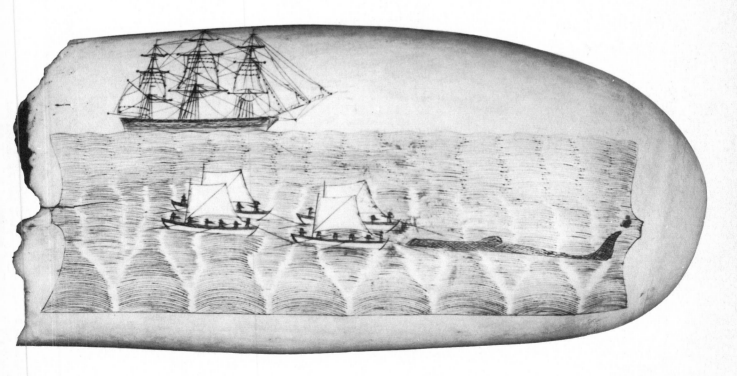

legendary unicorn led to the narwhal being named sea-unicorn, or unicorn fish.

According to Aristotle and Pliny, the unicorn is a horse with a purple head and a horn which is white at the base, black in the middle and red at the tip. In the Middle Ages it was the symbol of virginity and supreme power. Only a virgin could approach the animal and capture it without danger.

Works by deep-sea sailors

Less fortunate than their whaling colleagues when it came to the availability of suitable materials, ordinary deep-sea sailors had to make do with what happened to come their way. First of all there was material to be gleaned from captured birds and fish. Albatrosses were hunted for several reasons. Primarily, because a lot of sailors had old scores to settle with them. Any seaman who had ever seen one of his friends fall into the sea and have his skull split open by blows from an albatross's beak before anyone could put a boat into the water to save him, felt a mortal hatred for those kings of the high seas, some of them with a wing span of four metres. It is not surprising, therefore, that the sailors hunted them mercilessly. The birds provided, apart from a dreadful pâté (to which one had to add at least three quarters of pork fat) a beak 20 to 25 cm in length, which made a superb walking-stick handle. Occasionally an entire head was used for this purpose. The birds' webbed feet, once the bones and flesh had been removed, made unusual tobaccon pouches, and the thin yet strong wing bones provided unbreakable pipe-cleaners and sometimes supports for models.

Sharks fished with a drag-net provided unpalatable steaks, which were as tough as leather, but the jaw was also useful and above all the spine, which, stripped of its ribs and threaded on a steel rod, made a marvellous walking-stick. With a handle made from the beak of an albatross it was called a 'captain's cane'. Other standard heads of walking-sticks were in the shape of animal heads, closed fists, knots, Turk's heads, etc.

Of the materials available on board the sailors only used wood and rope. Wood was carved and shaped into a multitude of things, as we have already seen, including small items of furniture: writing desks, stools, shelves. With the rope, too, they could

Two busks made of baleen and a 'pan bone', all engraved with a needle in the best of whaling traditions.

Two pairs of engraved sperm-whale teeth. The fact that they form pairs makes them particularly valuable, as they are usually found singly.

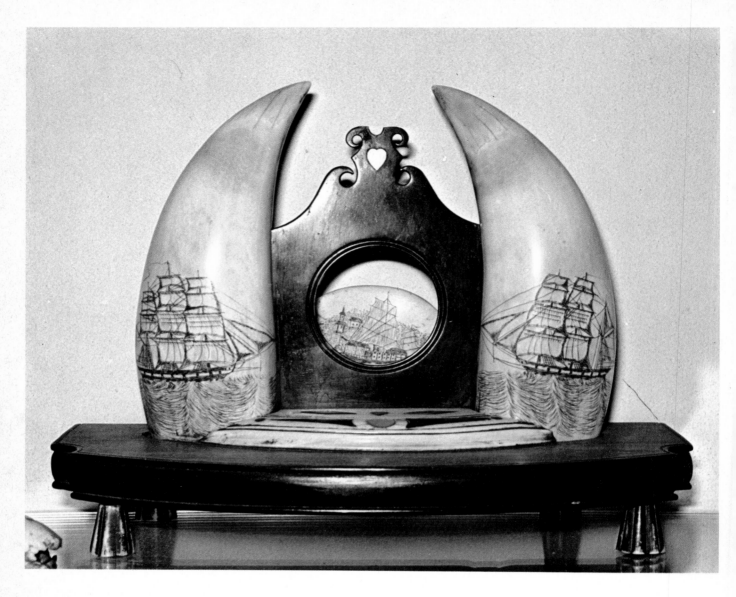

Clock-stand made of two
engraved sperm-whale teeth. Work
of an American sailor.

'A dead whale or a stove
boat'. One of the everyday scenes
of life on the high seas. Work of
an American sailor.

Ships in a port, scrimshaw by
an American sailor. Although the
port cannot be identified, the
design is very clearly of Eastern
inspiration and evokes a port of
call in India or Indonesia.

"A DEAD WHALE
OR A STOVE BOAT"

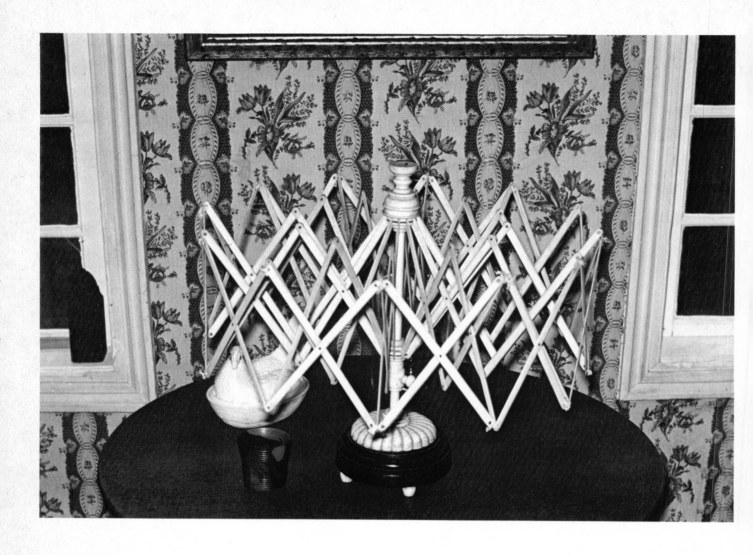

Yarn winding reel, also called 'swift', made from bone and ivory. Mid 19th-century work of an American whaler. This apparatus, which was found in most American country households in those days, was usually made of wood. The general shape and complexity of the instrument presumably presented a challenge to the sailors to copy it in ivory. Alongside the pie-crimper it was one of the most popular scrimshaws.

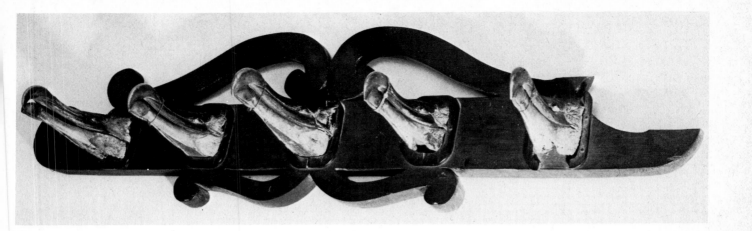

Coat-hanger made by a sailor from five very handsome Albatross's beaks.

make a thousand things. Apart from beautifying and improving things on deck (bell-ropes, bucket handles, servings and plaitings to the ends of the running rigging, plaits of rope round spars), the rope was used to fashion handles for sea-chests and also those extraordinary mats for the captain's cabin which we have mentioned in the previous chapter. The sailors called this 'fancy work'. They were good at plaiting and knitting and produced anything from bags, table-mats, curtains and rope embroidery to ties for themselves.

Another type of work done was delightful embroidery of coloured wools and silks on canvas. A number of officers produced this work, as much in the merchant service as in the navy, and even nowadays we have known captains and chief-stewards who used needle and thread with nimble fingers and had a keen sense of colour. Bead embroidery was also popular and was used in making purses, bags and heart-shaped pin-cushions for fiancées back home.

Still other men applied their talents to marquetry work with coloured straw on whitewood boxes. However, these straw boxes were only occasionally made by sailors on board ship. More frequently they used to buy them in the ports.

A knack taken over by sailors from people who practised it ashore was that of filling bottles with coloured soil much like those brought back as souvenirs from the Isle of Wight. The origins of this particluar practise were obviously to be found in Chile and on board the sailing ships engaged in the nitrate trade. Depending on the port, the soil was green, red, yellow, blue, white or grey. It was, therefore, only a matter of preserving samples from the cargoes of various voyages to have five or six colours, which could be combined in a bottle of successive layers. Those who were in a greater hurry could buy these decorative bottles from Chilean dockers, who willingly exchanged them for European merchandise.

In concluding this attempt at an inventory of the arts and crafts of the sailor we must not omit the complicated tattoo work which was undoubtedly practised more in the navy than in the merchant service. The more complicated and colourful tattoos were done in the ports by specialists. Tattoos done on board were simpler and the method used rather more primitive, resembling that used by convicts in jails. Certain sailors made a speciality of this art and devoted their leisure moments to decorating the epiderm of their fellow crew members.

We have mentioned above the use to which sailors put the pieces of wood which they found here and there on the decks or on the quays. Occasionally they made small items of furniture, and people have often thought that this amounted to much more than what it really was, namely a few boards nailed together. It was also thought that professional cabinet makers, possibly the ship's carpenter, had a hand in it. Thence evolved the myth of 'port furniture', furniture made by sailors in exotic types of wood in the course of their interminable crossings in sailing ships and sold on return.

It is only a myth, but since it has been handed down, we shall make a point of giving some details about these interesting items of furniture. A piece of 'port furniture' is a piece of furniture made in a port of non-indigenous types of wood, mostly exotic. There were five or six popular species: mahogany, lemon-tree wood, ebony, Brazilian rose-wood, lignum vitae and American walnut. We are talking here of solid woods and not just of veneers as used in Parisian cabinet-making. Amongst these items of furniture one finds all the standard pieces: two-tier side-boards with two, three or four doors, large cupboards, corner cabinets, chests-of-drawers, writing desks for ship-owners surmounted by a glass-fronted cabinet or small store-cupboard, tables and benches.

Port furniture owes its existence simply to the liking which cabinet-makers had for these top quality woods, which were straight-grained and free from knots and worm-holes. It shows evidence of the use of professional tools, which sets it apart from the amateur handiwork made on board with rough implements. Besides, it incorporates aspects of contemporary style with which only a professional cabinet-maker could have been familiar, especially when it came to foreign styles, which a sailor could merely have glimpsed in a port of call. At Saint-Malo, for example, one feels the influence of Dutch and Portuguese furniture in general shape and design and in design details which come obviously from the West Indies: pineapples, pomegranates, bananas . . . . Others show the influence of the navy: anchors, grapnels, ropes, etc. A great deal of experience would be required to copy such objects without making glaring mistakes.

Port furniture was primarily intended to grace the house of the wealthy middle-class and has, of course, nothing in common with the austere ship's furniture (at least not the few pieces which have survived). The consistent quality of the solid wood used was bound to attract the provincial bourgois, who were enamoured of what was durable and solid, providing that the general appearance was pleasant and presentable and likely to make a good impression on their guests. Besides, both ship-owners and the wealthy middle-class living in the ports, whose business was in some way connected with the sea, had a taste for the exotic, which they found in the unusual sheen and iridescence of woods like amboyna, cedar wood, macassar or lignum vitae. Perhaps it gave them a feeling of affinity with the source of their fortune, of which they were understandably proud.

For a long time it was believed that this port furniture was made on board ships, but actually nothing supports this theory but the exotic origin of the material and the evidence of colonial influence in the style.

Sailor's ear-rings worn by fishermen and deep-sea sailors. They were still sold by port jewellers at the beginning of the century. Underneath a purse in the shape of a wooden shoe with a secret opening mechanism. Work of a 19th-century sailor.

Lady's handbag with a silver
clasp. The bag is made of beaded
canvas on the theme of Robinson
Crusoe on his island. Work of a
sailor.

Heart-shaped pin-cushion
decorated with the Union Jack and an
embroidered inscription 'Remember
me'. This heart, destined to be pierced
by pins, was a favourite theme of
sailors in the navy in the 19th
century.

VIII

Inspiration from the sea

Artists have been inspired by the sea in a thousand different ways. We have already met models, paintings, technical and romantic literature, and all the artistic and useful objects made by seafaring people on board ships. From the high seas we turn inland, where men of imagination, artists inspired by voyages and adventures at sea, have created a profusion of things, which are in one way or another connected with the sea. Through the medium of their technical skill they convey to us, as if by magic, the emotion they feel when confronted by a natural element which both charms and terrifies them.

Sailors themselves rarely sing the praises of the sea. They love it with a wild passion, endure it and hate it all at once. Theirs is a strangely conflicting attitude of fierce defiance and moving tenderness. They are men of action, and everyday life absorbs them. They are completely taken up with the chores involved in looking after the ship and the trials of the voyage, but for all that they are still sensitive to the realism of images which artists recreate. How would an artist fare if he had to manoeuvre a four-masted ship in a storm? Similarly, how would a sailor fare if he had to lead the cloistered life of a painter or writer?

The inspired artist or poet is a visionary, his emotions are nourished by tales, by visions, by hearsay rather than by real live experiences. Another man's experiences become his own. Spokesman for the inarticulate, he gives sound to what is inaudible and shape to what is unformed, by means of recognisable allusions and symbols. It is in this way that the sea reappears transfigured, losing nothing of its force and realism, throughout the whole kaleidoscope of useful or decorative objects or curios, in which the sailor recognizes his way of life, charmed and amused by this new vision of his world.

Pottery

In the forefront of decorative marine art come ceramics (from the Greek *keramos* = pottery). The art of firing clay into solid vessels (hence: earthenware) was widely practised by the Greeks and Romans, the latter initiated by the Etruscans. The earliest portrayal of ships—black on a reddish background—is found on those large Greek vases which provide valuable clues to marine archaeologists. These are very rare, of course, and practically unobtainable for the ordinary collector. He will have to turn his interest to rather more recent pieces of decorative earthenware and china.

The making of decorated china, which appeared in Europe in the 8th century, is an old Eastern art imported by the Arabs first to Sicily, then to Spain and to Majorca (which gave its name to majolica). But it is in Italy, at Faenza (hence the French word *faience*) and Venice that china was to come to the fore in the 9th century. There are

Umbrella-handle in the shape of a cabin-boy. Engraved ivory, 19th century.

200

three types of china: varnished pottery, yellow or reddish in appearance, covered with transparent varnish, from which a number of inexpensive pots and pans are still made; everyday china, more delicate, of yellowish material and generally glazed with an opaque white underglaze, occasionally relieved by a design; porcelain, which is white and translucent and appeared in England about 1750, when a special variety of kaolin was discovered in Cornwall. Called 'English bone china', it largely superseded everyday china. The decline of everyday European china had actually begun in the early 17th century, when porcelain was imported from China.

Nevertheless, in spite of its fragility and its rather humbler origins, everyday china lends itself more readily to an original and varied design, for the low temperature of firing allows the use of a wide range of glazes.

We do not intend to give a list of the various factories which produced china with nautical designs. They were made in inland establishments and harbour factories alike. The mark, as for example the anchor for Chelsea ware, the crown-and-anchor for Derby and the trident for Caughley, means nothing in this connection. The nautical motif is to be found as much on the china of Liverpool as on that of Nevers or Moustier or on the famous Spanish porcelain of Pasajes. Everyone, of course, knows the blue tiles from Delft. In all these, the designs are largely stereotyped, made to please the general public. This is, for the most part, not the case with the so-called China Trade porcelain.

China had already a centuries-old tradition of earthenware when the Europeans arrived there. The Jesuits contributed to furthering this art, above all by bringing from Europe glazes unknown to the Chinese, which the latter managed to turn to surprising advantage. Whereas traditional Chinese porcelain was blue and white (its attraction stemming as much from the delicate, translucent material as from the grace of its design), porcelain now became polychrome with the famous series of 'famille rose' and 'famille verte'. This very high-quality porcelain was not exported, except at the risk of severe penalties, but was reserved for the Chinese gentry. Only the rejects were sold to Europe, and even then the quality was far superior to that of European porcelain at that time. It was, therefore, natural to think of ordering in China services with European designs. The East India Company and the Chinese

Popular porcelain and china with a maritime theme. Seaside souvenirs, 19th century.

Lids of early 19th-
century English snuff-boxes.
Enamalled copper.

manufacturers got together to foster this lucrative commercial enterprise, hence the 'China Trade' services.

European styles replaced the conventional styles of the Chinese services. The cup-handle, for example, was unknown in China, as were a number of accessories. The style itself evolved through the ages, but for the most part the standard services were finished in blue and white, for which there was the greatest demand in Europe. Coloured ware only accounted for 10 to 15 per cent.

A 'China Trade' table service consisted of large and small soup terrines and the round plates on which they stood, round and oval dishes· flat plates and soup plates, mustard pots, butter dishes and coolers.

The tea, coffee and chocolate services consisted of cups, saucers, teapots, tea-caddies, sugar-bowls and milk-jugs.

A number of toilet-sets were also imported, consisting of a jug and basin, shaving bowl, a water fountain with a tap, a soap dish and . . . a number of chamber pots.

In the vast majority of cases, these early items carried floral designs that had no connection with the sea or the navy. It is interesting to note that, in spite of very detailed design drawings sent to the Chinese manufacturers, a Chinese interpretation was imposed on the European design, while at the same time the European designs had a definite influence on traditional Chinese pottery. It is in the middle of the 18th century that the European-style nautical design appears, both in the centre of the dish and plate and on the rim. In default of a definite order, the Chinese artisans endeavoured to please the buyers by depicting European ships off Kwangchow in the Canton River, flying the appropriate flag, English or Dutch or even imaginary flags not at all recognisable.

The designers also drew their themes from pictures found in books: naval battles, genre pictures, the sailor's departure and return, views of foreign ports—London or Amsterdam—, but it is at the essentially Chinese scenes that they excelled: fishing scenes, seascapes, portraits of junks moored or sailing.

'China Trade' services made to individual requirements are particularly interesting. There are, for example, the ship's services of certain Dutch captains, and above all of American captains, who seemed particularly keen on having the ship they commanded depicted on china. In the great collections in the United States one can see services decorated with ships' portraits in the style of those done in oils or water colours in the large ports, for example by the Roux family, and it makes one wonder whether works by famous ships' portraitists were perhaps made available to Chinese designers for copying.

The nautical themes of the designs had, no doubt, a strong influence on European artists, for a number of ceramic artists were inspired in their turn to decorate tobacco jars and punch-bowls with ship motifs. Small multi-coloured figures of sailors in relief also appeared, and decorated china lids were fitted to sweetmeat boxes and snuff boxes.

In England, at the end of the 18th century and at the beginning of the 19th century, Staffordshire patchboxes were extremely popular, their nautical designs commemorating naval victories and other important events at sea. A number of pieces of ceramic jewellery were also made with naval symbols such as anchors and tridents.

Towards 1830, white transparent porcelain was put to a very strange use. By applying the process of 'lithophany', a process of hollowing out a design to different

'Lithophany' with and without lighting. The scene represents guns ashore firing at ships. 19th century.

Traditional Dieppe ivory.
Needle-case, 18th century.

depths, which was invented in France by Bourgoin, scenes were depicted in bas-relief on vases and lamp-shades. The scene, not much in evidence externally in direct light, becomes interesting only when lit up from behind. The varying degree of opacity of the porcelain produces a subtly shaded picture of striking effect. A number of naval scenes have been depicted by this process, but unfortunately these pieces, due to their fragility, are now very rare.

Enamelling was done not only on china but also on metal. The most accomplished designs are found on snuff-boxes and on silver jewellery.

Glass and crystal

The process of 'lithophany' can be applied, of course, to opaque glass, smoked or frosted with acid. But in the forefront of decorated nautical objects of glass stands cut or engraved crystal. Crystal lends itself admirably to the representation of designs by means of incision, especially those featuring a great many lines such as the rigging of a sailing ship or the waves of the sea.

Such designs are found on commemorative cups, presentation cups and goblets made for the occasion of a ship's launching, for example or to honour nautical exploits.

Less interesting are glasses for everyday use on board, which were engraved with the emblem of the shipping line.

Objects made of a paste of melted glass were very much in favour between the wars. They bear the mark of their age: lofty subject matter, exotic reminiscences, themes favoured by the clientele of luxury liners, who were also interested in the mirrors embossed with nautical designs like knots and ropework, anchors and crossed oars.

As for spun glass, it has produced as many masterpieces as it has monstrosities, and occasionally one sees hardly any difference between the galleons covered with little pink or blue threads and the curious giraffes with disproportionately large feet which one can buy at fun fairs.

A special place among maritime souvenirs made of blown glass is held by the so-called 'ships' rolling-pins'. The purpose of these long spindles of light-weight glass, which were in plentiful supply in the 19th century, is doubtful. Vaguely resembling rolling-pins, they were blown from white or tinted opaque glass, mostly in shades of sky-blue or navy-blue. Decorated with a stencil in one or many colours, they bear pictures of sailing ships or steamers and/or a couple, i.e. a sailor and his young lady, hand in hand at the moment of farewell. A doggerel verse accompanies the scene.

Souvenir of Dieppe, made of bone, mother-of-pearl and silver. 19th century.

Tobacco-jar in crystal and
nickel-plated metal, with port-hole
closure. A fine piece of Parisian
craftmanship of 1930.

Ceremonial and commemorative
glass. Engraving of a nautical scene.
Masterpiece of German glass-cutting,
18th century.

Tobacco-box signed Bourbon, decorated with nautical scenes. Brass, late 18th century.

Liverpool produced quantities of these rolling-pins. Sailors used to offer them to their intended, their wife or to a girl-friend they had made in a port of call, as a token of mutual love and faithfulness. Many of them, pierced at one end and filled with coarse salt, were hung in the kitchens or living-rooms of cottages, for salt, so it is said, wards off the dangers of the sea.

Most of these rolling-pins were some forty centimeters long, some as long as a metre. Some authorities on nautical traditions still maintain they were used as bottles in which messages were entrusted to the sea, but there can be no question of this, because they are much too fragile.

Ivory, mother-of-pearl and bone

Ivory is, no doubt, one of the earliest high-quality materials to have been engraved by man. Whether it comes from mammoths or sea animals, one finds remains of it, engraved with symbols and animal profiles, in pre-historic excavations. The material itself was largely used in marquetry-work in Egyptian, Greek and Roman furniture. Byzantium and the Arabs worked it in bulk around the 7th·century. But it

Small armoured toy-ship in enamelled sheet-metal. Late 19th century.

is towards the 12th century in China and Japan and in the 14th century in France, Italy and Flanders that this fine substance began to be used in the manufacture of objects which were to become classic. It was at Dieppe that many of the big ships arrived from Africa, laden with elephants' tusks from Guinea or Gabon. The Dieppe ivory carvers soon departed from making purely religious objects and turned to more nautical subjects. They even introduced ivory into navigation instruments such as sun-dials. Well-known were the Dieppe ivory figurines generally produced in pairs, which represented a fisherman and his wife. Dieppe ivory carvers also produced a whole battery of useful objects such as sewing boxes, needle boxes, thimbles in the shape of objects on board and in the form of ships.

Abundantly exploited, nautical themes are to be found also at the heads of walking-sticks and on umbrella handles. Instruments of navigation such as cross-staves, Gunter's rules and mounts for hour glasses did not escape the ivory carvers' enthusiasm either. The very skilled even made ships with all their rigging and gear, of which a number can be found in museums, protected from the light by cark covers. Later, ivory was used for the arcs of octants and sextants.

Mother-of-pearl also provided a wonderful substance which was, by its very nature, maritime. It was used to inlay in wood or metal, and from the 15th century

Tobacco-box in the shape of a sailor's cap. Embossed sheet-metal and brass. 19th century.

Pair of fire-dogs with sailors' busts. Cast iron, 19th century.

onwards for the manufacture of engraved goblets. The conche-shaped shells of certain molluscs lent themselves admirably to being turned into stylized ships, for example votive ships with rigging of twisted silver thread, sometimes even intertwined with gold thread. The rather thicker, calcerous shells with a lining of mother-of-pearl were often engraved by skilful artists in a way which made them appear like litho-phanies. The technique used was similar to that used by sailors when carving bas-reliefs from the shells of emu eggs.

Bone was occasionally used as a substitute for ivory for inexpensive items like those 19th century pen-holders, in the handle of which a small magnifying glass was let in on top of a harbour scene.

Metal

Metal, whether silver or sheet iron, has been used for a great number of objects inspired by the sea.

Snuff-boxes and tobacco-boxes of all shapes and sizes were made of sheet gold or silver with nautical designs engraved or embossed in the lid. At a time when pipes were made of clay and were, therefore, fragile, sailors used to protect them in special cases made of wood or metal. They used copper and occasionally even silver.

Tin plate, not particularly prepossessing, was from the beginning of the 19th century onwards used in the manufacture of tins for preserved foodstuffs. The finest tins with naval themes on them are undoubtedly the popular tea-caddies coated with golden yellow varnish and decorated with nautical transfers. But we must not forget the humble sardine tins and other sea-food tins, which are valued by some collectors for the nautical designs imprinted on them.

Painted sheet-metal was used not only in the manufacture of toy boats and figures but also in advertising, for ships and other nautical objects which were considered to have 'pulling power' on the public.

A number of objects were moulded from solid metal, i.e. cast iron or white metal. The most typical marine objects in this category are probably fire-dogs, walking-stick and umbrella-stands, money-boxes and those curious little Victorian sailors, some twenty to thirty centimetres high, which were used as door-stops.

White metal, an inexpensive material and delicate enough to take the impression of a mould, was used extensively to make souvenir ink-wells, light-houses, heads of typical old fishermen and other popular figures such as lifeboat-men throwing life-buoys into the tempestuous waves. Enthusiasts of 'kitsch' are ardent collectors of these. Gilded, inlaid and silver-plated cast iron as well as rolled sheet iron were also used in the manufacture of those incredible trophies presented to the winners of regattas. Some of these fine monstrosities, occasionally mounted on castors, must surely have been inspired by the Germanic ex-votos of the Middle Ages.

Money-box with whale motif in painted cast-iron. Inscribed on the base 'U.S.A. Pat. July 15, 1890'. Instead of projecting Jonah into the whale, a small catch situated on the left and released with a finger throws the coin placed on Jonah's head into the whale's open mouth. Money-boxes with a negro-head motif and based on the same principle were equally popular.

Automaton clock from the period
of **Charles X. Bronze**, size 60 × 45 cm.
The wooden plinth is decorated
with maritime attributes. The frigate,
set in motion by a clockwork, imitates
the motion of a ship in a heavy swell.
The glass dome has been removed in
the picture.

Decorative mechanical objects

Amongst the finest clocks with a maritime decor are the pendulum clocks made
under the reign of Louis XIV, which celebrate the success of France's trade at sea.
Symbolic figures, sailors and natives of the colonies stand alongside barrels, bales of
cotton and containers with sugar or tobacco amid a confusion of ship's cable, anchors,
grapnels and sculls, all highlighted with touches of patina and gold paint. This type
was popular until the end of the 19th century, when, under Louis XV, popular taste
turned to automatons. The ornamentation of a typical specimen would feature a
clockwork-activated three-master under shortened sail pitching and rolling in a sea
of painted silk before a background of a harbour scene with houses, jetties and a
lighthouse, all in gilded metal. The realism is gripping, and after prolonged contemplation the onlooker is in real danger of feeling sea-sick. Elsewhere on the clock and
the pedestal typical items of ship's gear are depicted. The wooden pedestals of the
Charles X clocks, which are under glass, are decorated with inlay work depicting
figures from marine mythology interspersed with shells.

French lighthouse-clock in white
metal and brass. Second Empire.

209

Lid of straw box, 19th century.

Less overwhelming but more amusing are the clocks in the shape of lighthouses. The time is not indicated by hands in the ordinary way but by a graduated paper cylinder revolving inside the lantern. Occasionally, on the hour, half-hour and quarter-hour chimes ring out, or one hears a pneumatic fog-horn, while the lighthouse-keeper appears on the parapet of the lantern with his spy-glass.

Fob watches of vast dimensions with steel case and dial of decorated enamel evoke the golden age of steam, the rise of steel ship-building and the ever increasing importance of time-tables. Indeed, in the centre of the dial a steamship sits enthroned, emitting clouds of black smoke and cleaving the sea with its proud stem.

Souvenirs from the sea-side

Turning now to bric-a-brac, let us take a look at souvenirs from the seaside. These are, nowadays, getting rarer and rarer or else uglier and uglier to the great delight of collectors of horrible kitsch.

All kinds of pottery items decorated with ships and boats, engraved skeletons of cuttle-fish, wooden plaques painted with sun-sets at sea are classic examples, as are cheap watches, barometers and thermometers mounted on anchors or ships' wheels. The glass-balls used as net floats by fishermen, with a little boat painted on them, as well as shells roughly 'decorated' with the help of a rubber stamp fall into the same category. Yet there are a number of objects which do not deserve to be sneered at, among them shell mosaics and bouquets, coloured sand bottles and straw boxes.

210

Interior of straw box. Two lids close
the two compartments of this sewing box.

The boxes decorated with shells and mother-of-pearl are, of course, of varying
quality and appeal depending on the variety of molluscs in the area and the inspiration
(often the tradition) of the local artisans. Certain of these small works of art present
very original compositions of people and ships, but the real quality of the picture
depends on the choice and tints of the shells. Long before collages and similar works
of modern art found their way into museums, compartmentalized shell pictures under
glass, like the one illustrated on page 215, represented the humble artistic expression
of coastal people. They are not always maritime scenes but more usually allegories,
palaces, castles, harbour scenes or merely geometric designs which are suited to the
cardboard or wood divisions.

The 'compartmental' character which is typical of these shell mosaics is also
found in the straw boxes. Only occasionally made by sailors, these boxes, intended
as work-boxes, are mostly the work of people living on the coast. The larger ones are
normally 30 × 20 × 15 cm, the smaller ones the size of a hand, and they are decorated
inside and out with pictures made up of lengths of coloured straw. Only the underside
is bare wood. As in sea-chests, the inside of the lid is decorated with the picture of a
ship, not in isolation but usually in a landscape with houses and numerous flags
flying at the end of long poles on the roof-tops. Other popular topics are the stepping
of a mast, careening and various sail manoeuvres, all interspersed and surrounded
by stars, flowers, butterflies. Judging from the types of ships most commonly depicted
it seems that the art came up towards the end of the 18th century and died out at the
end of the 19th century. The boxes are very fragile and difficult to restore once
damaged. What is needed is time and a wide assortment of coloured straw.

Among the typical curios let us also mention those small bottles in the shape of
an inverted tulip topped by a glass ball, which are skilfully filled with sands of various

211

colours to depict the local landscape. They are mainly found on the Isle of Wight. On the base of the bottle a round label certifies the authenticity of the souvenir: 'Isle of Wight, curiosity arranged with sands from the coloured cliffs of Alum Bay'. They were manufactured in their thousands, both simple and more elaborate models.

The unclassifiable and the unexpected

The sea has inspired land-based artisans to make so many weird and so many magnificent things that the few indications we have given may well appear inadequate. Looking round antique-dealers shops and collections of maritime antiques we contantly come across new and unexpected items, which have some nautical connection, as for example labels of rum and whisky bottles, cigar-bands with pictures of ships on them, match-boxes, tobacco and cigarette packets depicting some object with nautical connections. Some are easy to classify, others are not. In which category would one put that cradle from the Casa Marina d'Aranjuez made from timber of the hull of a First Empire sailing ship? History does not tell us whether the young Spaniard rocked in it later became Admiral of the Spanish Armada.

Straw work-box of English origin. The picture made of lengths of coloured straw shows a ship having its mast stepped.

212

So we conclude our work, in which we have occasionally touched the realms of fantasy but given precise details wherever possible. The expert may be surprised at the omissions, the specialist collector may only wish to refer to the themes which are of interest to him, while the amateur may well experience a sort of vertigo when confronted with the infinite variety of things inspired by the sea—either useful or simply enjoyable and satisfying.

It has been our aim to examine this vast selection of things as through the eyes of a sailor, trying to recapture the significance of each object so that the collector might not just be attracted by its rarity or unusual nature but might be able, in his mind, to replace it in its organic context: understanding how, when and where it originated and for what purpose it was used.

While we have endeavoured in this tour through museums and collections to give as comprehensive a survey as possible, it is very likely that a number of items have escaped our attention, that details are incomplete and that there is room for improvement. Any information our readers may be able to send us will always be gratefully received.

From left to right: ink-well in solid bronze in the shape of a sailor's head. Third Republic. The beret lifts up to uncover the ink-well. A writing outfit in white metal with ink-wells and pen holder, depicting the helmsman of a torpedo boat. *C.* 1890. The pen-holder in bone contains a miniature view of Marseilles harbour which can be viewed through a tiny magnifying glass. On the right an earthenware tobacco jar in the shape of a fisherman's head.

213

Bouquet of shells. Each flower petal
is made up of a marine mollusc shell
mounted on a copper wire. Work from
the Isle de Re, 19th century, in the
tradition of bridal bouquets.

'Compartmental' shell mosaic under glass. The divisions are cardboard. Work from the seaside, late 19th century.

The travelling writing-desk used to be an inseparable companion of travellers on long sea voyages. This one is a very fine example of 19th-century English ebony-work. The three souvenir bottles from the Isle of Wight, filled with sands from Alum Bay near the Needles illustrate this type of souvenir which was very popular at the beginning of the century. In the foreground two English 'rolling pins' of coloured blown glass, of which Bristol had an almost exclusive monopoly in the 19th century. Rolling pins were a token of fidelity and a kind of talisman which was to remind a girl of her fiancé or husband sailing on the high seas. They were decorated with portraits of ships and touchingly sentimental little doggerel rhymes:

Oh weigh the anchor, hoist the sails
Launch out upon the ruthless deep
Resolved however veers the gales
The destined port in mind to keep
Through all the dangers of the way
Deliver us good Lord we pray.
                    or:
From rocks and sands and barren lands
Kind fortune keep me free
And from great guns and women tongues
Good Lord, deliver me.

Bibliography

Chapter I

Donald Hubbard. *Ships in Bottles*. David & Charles, Newton Abbot.
Orazio Curti. *Modèles réduits*. E.M.O.M., Paris.
H. P. Spratt. *Marine Engineering*. Science Museum, London.
Jac Remise & Jean Fondin. *L'age d'or des jouets*. Edita.
Björn Landström. *The Ship*. Allen & Unwin.
Marco Pagani. *Le Modélisme naval*. Ed. de Vecchi, Paris.
Neptunia. Quarterly review of the Association des Amis du Musée de la Marine.
Henry Huddleston Rogers Collection of Ship Models. U.S. Naval Inst.

Chapter II

H. R. Calvert. *Scientific Trade Cards*. Science Museum, London.
John Wilmerding. *A History of American Marine Painting*. Peabody Museum, Salem.
Philip F. Purrington. *Four Years a Whaling*. Illustr. Charles S. Raleigh. The Whaling
    Museum, New Bedford.
Oliver Warner. *An Introduction to British Marine Painting*. Conway Maritime Press,
    London.
Harry T. Peters. *Currier & Ives, Printmakers to the American People*. Doubleday
    Doran & Co. N.Y.

Chapter III

M. Foncin, M. de la Roncière, M. Destombes. *Catalogue des cartes nautiques sur
    vélin*. Bibliothèque nationale, Paris.
Bibliotheca nautica. Catalogues 1926–1933. Maggs Bros., London.

Chapter IV

S. Guye & H. Michel. *Mesure du temps et de l'espace*. Bibliothèque des arts, Paris.
David W. Waters. *The Art of Navigation in England in Elizabethan and Early Stuart
    Times*. Hollis & Carter, London.
The Mariner's Astrolabe, Royal Scottish Museum, Edinburgh.
F. A. B. Ward. *Time Measurement*. Science Museum, London.
F. Marquet. *Histoire générale de la navigation du XVe au XXe siècle*.
R. T. Gould. *The Marine Chronometer*. Holland Press, London.
H. Michel. *Scientific Instruments in Art & History*. Barrie & Jenkins, London.
E. G. R. Taylor & M. W. Richey. *The Geometrical Seaman*. Hollis & Carter, London.
C. H. Cotter. *A History of Nautical Astronomy*. Hollis & Carter, London.
M. Daumas. *Les instruments scientifiques aux XVIIe et XVIIIe siècles*. P.U.F., Paris.
V. Marguet. *Histoire de la longitude à la mer au XVIIIe siècle* en France.

Chapter V

Armes à feu françaises, modèles réglementaires. Collection Jean Boudriot, Petitot.
    Paris.
W. E. May & P. G. W. Annis. *Swords for Sea Service*. National Maritime Museum,
    London.
W. E. May & A. N. Kennard. *Naval Swords and Firearms*. National Maritime
    Museum, London.
Bottet. *Monographie de l'arme blanche et de l'arme à feu portative*.
Peter Padfield. *Guns at Sea*. Hugh Evelyn, London.

Chapter VI

Basil W. Bathe. *Seven Centuries of Sea Travel*. Barrie & Jenkins, London.
M. Y. Brewington. *Ship Carvers of North America*.
Peter Norton. *Figureheads*. National Maritime Museum, London.
Gervis Frere-Cook. *The Decorative Art of the Mariner*. Cassell, London.
Alfred E. Weightman. *Heraldry in the Royal Navy*. Conway Maritime Press.
Pauline Pinckney. *American Figureheads and their Carvers*.

Chapter VII

A. Hayet. *Us et coutumes à bord des longs-courriers*. Denoël, Paris.
Dictions, tirades et chansons des anciens de la voile. Denoël, Paris.
N. Flayderman. *Scrimshaws & Scrimshanders, Whales and Whalemen*. N.Y.

Chapter VIII

R. Picard, J. P. Kerneis, Y. Bruneau. *Les Companies des Indes*. Arthaud, Paris.
J. Goldsmith Philips. *China Trade Porcelain*. Cambridge & Harvard University Press.
J. Mc. C. Mudge. *Chinese Export Porcelain for the American Trade*. Delaware University Press.

General

Brandt Aymar. *A Pictorial Treasury of the Marine Museums of the World*. Crown Publishers Inc., N.Y.
Trois millenaires d'art et de marine. Catalogue of an exhibition at the Petit Palais, Paris, under the direction of J. Ducros.
L'art dans la marine. Art et artisanat des gens de mer. Pont-Royal, Paris.
Catalogues et monographies des collections. Published by the French Maritime Museums.
The American Neptune. Peabody Museum, Salem, Mass.

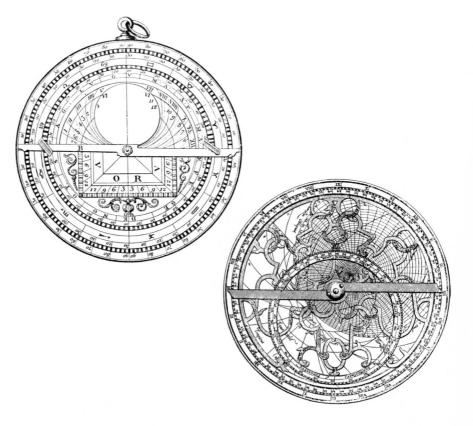

The sea and the navy in the museums of the world

Argentina   ● Buenos Aires: Museo naval de la nación
Australia   ● Victoria: Institute of Applied Sciences

Belguim   ● Antwerp: National Scheepvaartmuseum

Canada   ● Vancouver: The Maritime Museum
    ● St. John, New Brunswick: The New Brunswick Museum

Denmark   ● Copenhagen: Orlogsmuseet
    ● Elsinore: Handels-og Søfartsmuseet

Finland   ● Mariehamn: Ålands Sjöfartsmuseum

France   ● Paris: Musée de la Marine (Palais de Chaillot). Conservatoire national
        des Arts et Métiers
    ● Dieppe: Musée du Château
    ● Dunkerque: Musée place De Gaulle
    ● Le Havre: Musée du Vieux Havre
    ● Honfleur: Musée du Vieux Honfleur
    ● Granville: Musée du Vieux Granville
    ● Saint-Malo: Musée du Château. (it also houses the Musée de la pêche.)
    ● Saint-Servan: Tour Solidor. Musée du long cours cap-hornier.
    ● Concarneau: Musée de la pêche
    ● Nantes: Musée des Salorges
    ● La Rochelle: Museum Lafaille (oceanography)
    ● Rochefort: Musée de la Marine
    ● Bordeaux: Musée de la Marine (Palais de la Bourse)
    ● Biarritz: Musée de la Mer
    ● Marseille: Musée de la Marine (Palaise de la Bourse)
    ● Toulon: Musée de la Marine
    ● Saint-Tropez: Musée naval (à la Citadelle)
    ● Nice: Musée Masséna

Germany   ● Brake/Unterweser: Schiffahrts-Museum
    ● Bremen: Focke Museum
    ● Bremerhaven: Deutsches Schiffahrtsmuseum
    ● Hamburg: Altonear Museum
    ● Munich: Deutsches Museum
    ● Nuremburg: Germanisches Museum

Great Britain   ● Beaulieu, Hampshire: Buckler's Hard Maritime Museum
    ● Scilly Isles: Valhalla Maritime Museum
    ● Greenwich: National Maritime Museum
    ● Liverpool: City of Liverpool Museum
    ● Hull: Maritime Museum
    ● London: Science Museum
    ● Sunderland, Durham: Sunderland Museum
    ● Portsmouth, Hants: The Victory Museum
    ● Edinburgh: Royal Scottish Museum
    ● Glasgow: Glasgow Art Gallery and Museum

Holland   ● Amsterdam: Nederlandsch Historisch Scheepvaart Museum, Rijksmuseum
    ● Rotterdam: Maritime Museum Prins Hendrik

Iceland   ● Reykjavik: National Museum

Israel   ● Haifa: The National Maritime Museum

Italy	● Genoa: Museo navale
	● Trieste: Museo del mare
	● Milan: Museo delle scienze
	● Venice: Museo storico navale
Japan	● Tokyo: Transport Museum
Monaco	● Monaco: Musée océanographique
Norway	● Bergen: Bergens Sjöfartsmuseum
	● Oslo: Kon Tiki Museum, Norsk Sjöfartsmuseum
	● Sandefjord: Sjöfartsmuseum. Christensen's hvalfangstmuseum
Portugal	● Lisbon: Museu de Marinha
Spain	● Madrid: Museo naval
	● Barcelona: Museo maritimo
Sweden	● Goteborg: Sjöfartsmuseet
	● Karlskrona: Marinmuseum
	● Stockholm: Statens Sjöhistoriska Museum. Wasavarvet

United States

● San Francisco: The Maritime Museum
● San Pedro, California: Cabrillo Beach Marine Museum
● Washington D.C.: Smithsonian Institution. Truxton Decatur Naval
     U.S. Navy Memorial Museum
● Bath, Maine: Marine Museum
● Searsport, Maine: Penobscot Marine Museum
● Annapolis, Maryland: U.S. Naval Academy Museum
● Navy Point, Maryland: Chesapeake Bay Maritime Museum
● Boston, Massachusetts: Museum of Sciences. Museum of Fine Arts
● New York: Museum of the City of New York. Seamen's Church Institute
● Cohaset Village, Massachusetts: Cohaset Maritime Museum
● Nantucket, Massachusetts: The Whaling Museum. Nantucket Historical
    Association
● New Bedford, Massachusetts: The Whaling Museum. Old Dartmouth
    Historical Society
● Mystic Seaport, Conn: Marine Historical Association
● Salem, Massachusetts: The Peabody Museum
● Cold Spring Harbor, LI.: The Whaling Museum
● Sag Harbor: Suffolk County Whaling Museum
● Philadelphia, Pen.: Maritime Museum
● Newport News, Virginia: The Mariner's Museum
● Portsmouth, Virginia: Portsmoth Naval Shipyard Museum

U.S.S.R.	● Leningrad: Naval Museum
Yugoslavia	● Dubrovnik: Maritime Museum of the Academy of Yugoslavian Arts and Sciences

Acknowledgements

We are grateful to the following people for their invaluable help and encouragement:

P. G. Bernard, J. Boudroit, J. P. Busson, Cdt. L. M. Bayle, M. P. Chaintreuil,
J. H. Chambon, J. Chamenal, M. Chastagnol, M. A. Ciolkowska, M. Cerbasson.
M. Cordelier, Dr. Cras, Ph. Dauchez, H. de Finfe, De Ves, J. Ducres, S. Galanis,
J. Grout, M. Gruénais, M. Johnson, D. Lailler, J. C. Lambert, C. Lasserre,
Colonel Martel. Dr. J. Meyer, P. Orange, J. Polak, H. C. Randier, J. Remise,
M. de La Roncière, O. Roux-Devillas, Dr. J. Soulaire, G. Suc, Colonel Wemaere.

Sources of Illustrations

Author's collection
National Maritime Museum, Greenwich
Musée de long-cours, St. Servan
The National Maritime Museum, Haifa
Ph. Dauchez collection
Musée de la Pêche, St. Malo
Musée du Vieux Honfleur
Jac Remise collection
O. Roux Devillas collection
J. H. Chambon collection
Science Museum, London
Musée de la Marine, Paris
Maritime Museum, Hull
P. G. Bernard collection
J. C. Lambert collection
Nationaal Scheepvaartsmuseum Antwerp
G. Suc collection
H. C. Randier collection
Kendall Whaling Museum
Marie Ange Ciolkowska collection
Seamen's Bank for Savings, New York
The Mariner's Museum, Newport News
Grenet collection
Société du Géographie, Paris (Ancienne Collection du Prince Rolland Bonaparte)
Yacht Club de France collection
J. Polak collection

Young deck-boy in the French Navy. Decorative motif on a stick-rack. Painted cast-iron, appr. 30 cm high.

Nicholson Whaling collection, Providence
Capt. Byrne collection
Cristofer collection
Museum of the City of New York
G. Prin collection
Cdt. Vivielle collection
Sylvie Galanis collection
Conservatoire des arts et métiers, Paris
Gruénais collection
Musée de l'armée
Johnson collection
F. Duffort collection
Boudriot collection
Søfartsmuseet, Elsonore
Cutty Sark
Librairie le Yacht, Paris
Altonaer Museum, Hamburg
Marine Historical Association, Mystic Seaport, Conn.
Statens Sjöhistoriska Museum, Stockholm
Jack Grout collection
M. Chastagnol collection
The Whaling Museum, New Bedford
Private American collections
Dr. J. Soulaire collection
Corbasson collection
Dr. Steinmeyer collection
Service Historique de la Marine, Paris
Musée des Salorges, Nantes
Museu de Marinha, Lisbon

The rest were taken by museums, Creative Publishing and the author.